Chinese Poetry and Prophecy

Asian Religions & Cultures

Edited by

Carl Bielefeldt

Bernard Faure

Great Clarity
Fabrizio Pregadio
2005

Chinese Magical Medicine
Michel Strickmann
Edited by Bernard Faure
2002

Living Images: Japanese Buddhist Icons in Context
Edited by Robert H. Sharf and Elizabeth Horton Sharf
2001

Michel Strickmann

EDITED BY BERNARD FAURE

Chinese

Poetry and Prophecy

The Written Oracle
in East Asia

Stanford University Press
Stanford, California 2005

Stanford University Press
Stanford, California

Printed in the United States of America
on acid-free, archival-quality paper

Library of Congress Cataloging-in-Publication Data

Strickmann, Michel.
    Chinese poetry and prophecy : the written oracle in East Asia / Michel
Strickmann.
        p. cm. – (ARC: Asian religions and cultures)
    Includes bibliographical references and index.
    ISBN 0-8047-4334-7 (cloth : alk. paper) – ISBN 0-8047-4335-5 (pbk. : alk. paper)
    1. Divination–China.   2. Oracles.   I. Title.   II. Series: Asian religions & cultures.
    BF1773.2.C5S865 2005
    133.3'248'0951–dc22

                                                                                2004023933

Typeset by TechBooks in 10/14.5 Sabon and Gill Sans

Original printing 2005

Last figure below indicates year of this printing:

13   12   11   10   09   08   07   06   05

To the memory of Wolfram Eberhard

CONTENTS

ILLUSTRATIONS

FIGURES

The casual foreigner visiting Japanese Buddhist temples or Shintō shrines will have noticed how some visitor, seeking a consultation, shakes an oblong box containing divination sticks bearing numbers, until one of them falls out. That person then takes it to a booth and exchanges it (for a small fee) for the corresponding oracle—a slip of paper called *omikuji* ("divine fortune"), which is usually inscribed with a Chinese verse and a "judgment" ("great good luck," "good luck," "bad luck," "great bad luck," and so on). When the oracle is negative, the client can get rid of it (thus warding off the bad luck) by tying it to a branch of a sacred tree or to some auspicious figure. This practice can be traced back to an ancient form of Chinese divination.

For most people, the mention of Chinese divination immediately calls to mind the *Book of Changes* (*Yi jing*, or *I-ching* in the Wade-Giles transcription adopted by Strickmann). Many other similar oracular texts existed, however, some of which were authored by Taoists, and others by Buddhists. Although their oracles were often placed under the patronage of a particular deity, their pragmatic content was usually in line with conventional morality, and did not follow sectarian fault lines. They constitute a vast literary corpus, halfway between oral and written cultures.

Here is an example, marked "Great Good Luck":

> The pagoda, built of the seven precious things,
> Rests on the summit of the high peak;
> All men look up to it with awe,
> Let there be no neglectful glances.

And another, marked "Bad Luck":

> The household path has not reached prosperity,
> But is exposed to danger and disaster.
> Dark clouds obscure the moon-cassia-tree.
> Let the fair one burn a stick of incense.

[Aston 1908: 117]

Finally, a translation of an entire oracle:

> Number Nine: Bad luck
> Omikuji of the Inari main Shrine
> The Omen of Speaking First.

Since this is an omen that depicts adverse conditions in all matters, it should be used reverently and discreetly. At any rate, failures will ensue from the lower classes. There will be trouble among descendants. Be exceedingly cautious.

Directions (of the compass)	Northwest is good
Sickness	Will recover
The Person Awaited	Will come, but with losses return
Lost Articles	Will come forth
House Building, Changing Residence	Good
Starting on a Journey	Good
Marriage Proposals	At first troublesome, afterwards exceedingly good
Business	Great losses; nevertheless, if pushed hard good will result
Matters of Contest	Bad

[Buchanan 1939: 189]

Michel Strickmann's untimely death in 1994 prevented him from seeing through to the completion of the publication of several manuscripts. The present work, the first draft of which was written in 1990, is one of them. Coming after *Mantras et mandarins* (Gallimard, 1996) and *Chinese Magical Medicine* (Stanford University Press, 2002), it offers a guide to a neglected genre of Chinese religious literature, and its influence goes well beyond China. It also deals with the issue of oral and written media in Chinese culture. This kind of literature provided Strickmann with an excellent means for examining fundamental methodological questions. Indeed, temple oracles represent a living example of oral tradition and lend themselves to fieldwork observation. Written in classical Chinese, they are intimately related to the written tradition. They also illustrate the continuity between "elite" and "popular" cultures, as well as between the medieval and the modern periods, and between East Asia and the rest of Eurasia. In other words, they require a combination of philological, historical, anthropological, and comparative methodologies. The comparative approach is indeed one of the most fascinating aspects of this work, which shows, for example, the penetration of Hellenistic elements into Chinese mantic systems.

Had he lived longer, Strickmann would, in all likelihood, have continued to improve both his arguments and the work's organization. In the process of editing the manuscript, I was tempted to modify a few sections for greater coherence. Since this is a posthumous work, however, I have decided to keep changes to a minimum.

I would like to place this work briefly in the context of Strickmann's oeuvre and of contemporary scholarship. My account draws on his "Thèse présentée en vue de l'habilitation à diriger des recherches," entitled "Histoire des syncrétismes religieux taoïstes et bouddhistes en Chine et au Japon," Université de Paris X, 1991, under the supervision of Professor Léon Vandermeersch.

Strickmann began his studies on East Asia in Leiden (The Netherlands), where he studied Chinese language and literature under the direction of Professor A. F. P. Hulsewé, medieval Chinese history and Buddhism under Professor E. Zürcher, modern and classical Japanese with Professor F. Vos, and Tibetan language and the history of Indo-Tibetan Buddhism under Professor D. S. Ruegg. He graduated in June 1968 with a diploma in East Asian Studies. He then decided to pursue the study of Daoism in Paris under the direction of Professor Kaltenmark at the Fifth Section of the École Pratique des Hautes Études, as well as Sino-Tibetan studies with Professor Rolf A. Stein at the École Pratiques des Hautes Études and the Collège de France. This is when he became interested in mythology and ritual.

In 1970 he decided to focus his dissertation on medieval Daoism after discovering a collection of fourth-century texts in the Daoist Canon, which were based on revelations made to a thirty-six-year-old man, Yang Xi, by a cohort of goddesses and gods descended from the Shangqing Heaven. This collection of songs and poems was later found and edited by the great Daoist erudite Tao Hongjing (456–536) under the title *Zhengao* ("Declarations of the Perfect Ones"). This text is notoriously difficult, written in a literary style that often verges on extravagance, and, apart from Chen Guofu's reliance on it as one of the primary sources for his work on the origins and development of the Daoist Canon (1941), it had not been the object of any serious study.

Strickmann set out to reconstitute the social milieu of the first adepts of the Shangqing School. He soon realized that he had set his hands on a real ethnographic treasure. These fourth-century texts were so rich in detail on the everyday life of a circle of Daoist practitioners that there was nothing quite like it—at least not until ethnographic researches of the twentieth century. Strickmann was thus able to complement the work of Kristofer Schipper and Japanese scholars by reconstituting the social background from which these texts emerged. He was also able to reattach them to the aristocratic milieux of the kingdom of Wu, located in the Nanjing region. These milieux consisted of aristocrats who had lost their hereditary functions with the arrival of the court, when the latter took refuge in the South after the fall of the imperial capital at the hands of non-Chinese invaders. The religion of the newcomers was the Daoism of the Celestial Masters.

Stymied in their official careers by the influx of the Northern nobility, the Southern aristocrats turned their talents and ambitions to the elaboration of a new form of Daoism. For this, they used their own expertise regarding the exegesis of the *Book of Changes* and the *Book of Rites*, as well as al-chemical and occult practices. They accepted the Daoism of the newcomers, but gradually modified it. The fusion of these various traditions into a new synthesis was achieved within the framework of a revelation.

In order to consider the *Zhengao* in this sociohistorical context, Strick-mann was led to consider Daoism in its totality, including its scriptures. Indeed, the poetic genius and literary talent of Yang Xi (330-?), the young man who recorded his visions, was to pave the way to a long scriptural tradition, the effects of which were still being felt at the end of the Chinese Middle Ages. Strickmann's researches in this tradition led to his Ph.D. dis-sertation (Thèse de doctorat de troisième cycle), defended at the University of Paris VII in 1979, under the direction of Professors Marc Kaltenmark and Léon Vandermeersch. The following year he received the Diploma of the Fifth Section of the École Pratique des Hautes Études, under the direction of Professor Schipper. The "report" was written by Professors Vandermeersch and Hartmut Rotermund. A revised and expanded version of his dissertation was published in the Mémoires de l'Institut des Hautes Études Chinoises in 1981, under the title *Le taoïsme du Mao Chan, Chronique d'une Révélation*.

Apart from his French dissertation, Strickmann published several articles in English on medieval Daoism, including "The Mao Shan Revelations: Taoism and the Aristocracy," published in the sinological journal *T'oung Pao* in 1977, and "On the Alchemy of T'ao Hung-ching," in *Facets of Taoism*, a volume coedited by Holmes Welch and Anna Seidel in 1979. He also examined the renewal of Daoism under the Song, which he called "the Daoist renaissance of the twelfth century," in "The Longest Taoist Scripture," published in *History of Religions* (1978). Lastly, he attempted to show the cultural continuity from the twelfth century till today, in "History, Anthropology and Chinese Religion," published in the *Harvard Journal of Asiatic Studies* (1980), as well as the extension and penetration of Daoist ideas in popular Chinese culture and in non-Han culture, in "The Tao Among the Yao," in the Festschrift volume for the Japanese scholar Sakai Tadao (1982).

In September of 1972, Strickmann was invited to an international colloqium in Japan, where he remained over the next five years. During that time, he benefited from the hospitality of members of the Hōbōgirin Institute—Hubert Durt, the late Anna Seidel (another much-missed scholar of Daoism), Antonino Forte, and Robert Duquenne. Like many other scholars (including myself), he was able to use the Hōbōgirin library—a veritable treasure trove of primary and secondary source material. Soon, however, his own library came to rival that of the Hōbōgirin; the walls of his house on Mt Yoshida, at the back of Kyoto University, overflowed with books.

The ideal nature of the location of this house, which soon became known as the "Ānanda Panda Institute," perfectly situated in the midst of Buddhist temples, Shintō shrines, and ancient cemeteries, need hardly be emphasized. Just across the street was Shinnyodō, an old Tendai temple. Down the street were other important temples belonging to the Zen and Pure Land Schools. The prestigious Research Institute in Humanistic Studies (Jinbun kagaku kenkyūjō) of Kyōto University was a short walking distance away, as well as the "Philosopher's Path" (*tetsugaku no michi*). This neighborhood contributed significantly to the new direction Strickmann's research soon took. The defining moment was perhaps a certain morning, when he was awakened by the sound of a ritual performed literally on his doorstep, in a shrine connected to Shinnyodō. This ritual was dedicated to the fox-spirit Dakiniten.

The name of this deity took him back to the two Asian traditions he had studied in Europe: that of the Tantric ḍākinī, observed in Tibetan rituals, and that of the fox-spirits of medieval China.

This discovery of Japanese Tantrism was for Strickmann a kind of epiphany, revealing to him both the spread and impact of this religious phenomenon. The almost total lack of Western works on the topic, and the strongly sectarian nature of Japanese works, written from the standpoint of Shingon and Tendai esotericism, led him to focus, above all, on Tantric practice. He was fortunate to find, in the person of a young Shinnyodō monk named Okumura Keijun, a precious informant who, over the course of five years, initiated him into the rituals of the Tendai sect. The ritual most often performed at Shinnyodō was the *homa* (Japanese *goma*) or oblation ritual. It was performed twice a month on behalf of Ganzan Daishi (tenth century), the founder of the Shinnyodō lineage, and the putative ancestor of the *omikuji* (Eanzan Daishi) (which were to become the object of study of the present book), and once a month on behalf of Dakiniten. This homa ritual also played an important role in Shugendō, the school of mountain ascetics, in which Strickmann also found certain practices of medieval Daoism. While preserving the Indian nature of its origins, it also presented notable differences, in particular the act of burning wooden tablets inscribed with the names of the faithful. The incineration of a written memorial addressed to the god is a fundamental characteristic of Chinese popular religion and of Daoism. The study consecrated by Strickmann to this type of ritual was published as an article in Frits Staal's monumental work on the Fire ritual, *Agni*; and as a chapter of Strickmann's work on Chinese Tantrism, *Mantras et mandarins*. These essays, by showing the genetic relationships between a certain number of Tantric rituals found from one end of Asia to the other, led Strickmann to redefine Tantrism, detaching it from the pejorative connotations that had accompanied it since the first writings of Étienne Burnouf in the mid-nineteenth century.

Unlike most of his predecessors, Strickmann endeavored to consider the domain of Tantric studies under its dual aspect—synchronic and diachronic. In India, its place of origin, Tantrism survived most notably (in its Shaivite, rather than Buddhist, form) at the two ends of the subcontinent: Tamil Nadu in the Southeast and Kashmir in the Northwest. Outside of India, Tantric influence is found all the way from Mongolia to Bali, from Nepal to Japan. These multiple variants have unfortunately led the various subfields of Tantric studies to develop in isolation from each other. This is particularly true in Japan, where sectarian scholars, intent on proving the specific "purity" of their brand of Shingon or Tendai esotericism (*mikkyō*), have downplayed the common elements.

In reaction against this tendency, Strickmann set out to study Tantric rituals and beliefs in their broader historical and cultural contexts. In order to overcome ethnic, linguistic, and sectarian barriers, he attempted in particular to formulate a definition of Tantrism that took into account such common ritual elements as mantras, mudrās, and visualization practices, as well as cultic paraphernalia such as the scepter (*vajra*) and the vajra-bell. However, what struck him as particularly significant was the ritual grammar of Tantrism, a syntax based on the laws of Indian hospitality: after purifying himself, the officiant would invite the deity and its retinue into the ritual area, and make offerings to them. What characterizes Tantric ritual, though, is the fact that the officiant goes on to unite with the deity. Empowered by this fusion, he is then able to attain his goal. Having done so, he comes out of this fusion and eventually sees off the deity. This ritual schema is what, for Strickmann, constitutes "Tantrism." It is in complete opposition with that of Daoist ritual, which takes place around an incense-burner (rather than a homa hearth), and includes the delivery of a written document—in the style of Chinese bureaucracy. Nevertheless, Daoist Ritual also involves identification of one's body with the body of a diety.

Both models seem to have influenced East Asian religions. In China and Japan, many rituals combine the two aspects. If Tantric Buddhism disappears from the Chinese stage as a distinct social entity around the twelfth century, it survives in what Strickmann calls "Tantric Taoism." Indeed, a substantial part of Daoist rituals and iconography, and consequently of Chinese popular culture, derives from Tantrism. It is from such a viewpoint that Strickmann, in 1979, embarked on the publication of the *Études tantriques et taoïstes* in honor of Professor Rolf Stein, the first scholar to have brought together the study of Tantrism and Daoism in China and Tibet. Three volumes (out of four originally planned) of these Tantric and Daoist studies were published in the series *Mélanges chinois et bouddhiques*, edited by Hubert Durt.

In 1978, Strickmann was invited to teach at Berkeley as an Assistant Professor, and in a record time was promoted to the rank of Associate Professor with tenure. During the next decade, his innovative teaching influenced a generation of students, some of whom (Judith Boltz, Terry Kleeman, Steve

Bokenkamp, Donald Harper, Edward Davis) went on to become leading scholars of Daoism and Chinese religion in their own right. Toward the end of that period, his scholarship was stimulated by a series of seminars he held at the Fifth Section of the École Pratique des Hautes Études, where he had been invited by K. Schipper, the first time in 1987, and again in 1990. Upon returning to the United States, he was invited to spend one year at the Woodrow Wilson Center of the Smithsonian in Washington, D.C. In 1991, he relinquished his position at Berkeley, and, at the invitation of the French sinologist André Lévy, accepted a position in Chinese Religions at the University of Bordeaux. The manuscript that resulted from this new approach, *Mantras et mandarins*, was submitted in 1991 to the French publisher Gallimard. It was eventually published in 1996, owing in large part to the hard work of Brigitte Steinmann, two years after Strickmann's death. An English translation is forthcoming from Princeton University Press.

During his teaching years at Berkeley, Strickmann, increasingly influenced by anthropology, and still trying to reach, beyond doctrinal controversies, the heart of everyday practice, had tackled another problem: that of the healing rituals in medieval China. Working on mostly unpublished materials, he aimed essentially at bringing to the fore the medieval ritual synthesis that was at the heart of the modern religious synthesis. From September 1983 to January 1985, he was invited as Fellow at the Wissenschaftskolleg in Berlin, and participated in 1984 in an international conference on "Classic Rituals in Asia and Ritual Theory." In this stimulating context, he was able to continue his research on ritual.

The result of this research was a manuscript, *Chinese Magical Medicine*, which he unfortunately was unable to complete, and which was posthumously published in 2002 by Stanford University Press. In it, he examined once again side by side the Tantric and Daoist traditions, revisiting the Shangqing texts with which he had begun his sinological career. However, rather than a modern vision of Chinese medicine (centered on acupuncture and other treatments), he described a demonology that developed against an eschatological and apocalyptic background. In the troubled times of early medieval China, the privileged method of ensuring salvation was through a kind of "homeopathic demonology," and in particular through the cult of powerful demons who had converted to the true (Daoist or Tantric) Law. Among the exorcistic techniques that constitute that "magical medicine,"

Strickmann documents, in particular, the use of carved seals and of induced possessions.

A third direction of Strickmann's research, one that found its fruition in the present book, was determined by the fact that his position in Berkeley's Department of Oriental Languages was labeled as "Chinese Language and Literature." In response to the needs of his students, he was led to emphasize the cultural history of China, the cultural transmission from India to China ("India in the Chinese Looking-Glass", 1982), and "syncretistic" traditions represented in the so-called apocryphal scriptures of Buddhism—that is, texts produced in China ("The *Consecration Sūtra*: A Buddhist Book of Spells," 1990). He was also able to integrate purely literary texts into a broader corpus (including, for example, medical texts or Daoist scriptures) and into a broader social context.

It was during his stay in Japan that Strickmann became interested in particular in divination systems, which he had observed there. The first draft of the present work was completed in 1990. It was originally intended to appear in French under the title "Poésie et prophétie en Chine," as a volume in the series *Mélanges Chinois et Bouddhiques*. Owing to the kindness of the series editor, Hubert Durt, this manuscript was eventually submitted to Stanford University Press as a companion volume to *Chinese Magical Medicine*.

I would like to thank all the friends and colleagues who have helped at various stages in the publication of this work. In particular, Hubert Durt for making the manuscript available to me, Brigitte Steinmann for providing me with documentation, Helen Tartar for accepting the manuscript at Stanford University Press, Irene Lin for typing it, Steve Bokenkamp and Donald Harper for reading it and offering precious suggestions, and Muriel Bell and all the others at Stanford University Press for seeing it through to completion. Lastly, I would like to thank Michel's parents, Leo and Marjorie, his brother Pete, and his sister Bonnie.

Bernard Faure
Stanford
June 2004

INTRODUCTION

"Elite or popular, popular or elite?" So runs the plainchant nowadays in the choirs of sinology. It dimly echoes antiphonies sung by an earlier generation of European historians. There is comedy in this hot pursuit of virile popular culture by the academic elite. Twenty years ago, American sinologists began to struggle into a tweed straitjacket of "Great" and "Little" traditions woven (and subsequently discarded) by anthropologists long before. In its Chinese refitting, whatever appealed to the taste of these academic mandarins—Confucianism, the bureaucratic State—was Great. The rest (Buddhism, Taoism, "folk religion," and "superstition" generally) was Little. Now a new wardrobe is being spun, and once-little traditions are in vogue. Yet slicing and segmenting are still of the essence, and sources must be accommodated to a narrow range of categories. Some American scholars have even produced rigid descending scales, from hyperelite to most utterly pop. On such Procrustes-machines for the splintering of Chinese culture and society, future generations of scholars are invited to martyrize their Chinese authors, texts, and audiences.

For these theoreticians, it is axiomatic that different social levels should be characterized by distinctive cultural traits. Despite their new jargon and brave show of statistics, this is only another variation on an old ditty. American academics used to identify Chinese authors as Confucian, Buddhist, or Taoist according to their phraseology, the texts they cited, the company they kept, or their political status. Religious affiliation was thought to have been a function of social class or official position; men were supposed to have been Confucian when in office, Taoist when unemployed. Every figure in the Chinese historical landscape had to have some sectarian affiliation, and was packaged and labeled accordingly.

Such blatant projections of the Protestant conscience and the American suburban scene are no longer fashionable in Chinese studies. Nevertheless, certain recent emphases in transatlantic sinology can perhaps best be understood in the light of current American "liberal" manias, for example, agonized self-consciousness regarding minority groups. The American academic obsession with theories of oral versus written traditions, too, takes on color when we remember its setting, a country with compulsory education which is now being exposed to fearsome statistics confirming its prevailing illiteracy. No wonder if American professors attempt to resolve, for Imperial China, the very "problems" that threaten to engulf them in their own lecture halls.

Elite or popular society, written or oral culture? In the oracle texts presented here, we have a vast body of literature that belongs to both worlds. Such printed texts are often subjected to intensive oral exposition, as the medical anthropologist Arthur Kleinman has shown. The dead letter and crabbed commentary come alive in the temple. And the written message itself often leads back into a vivid world of performance and entertainment. Some oracle sequences are shot through with allusions to characters and situations in historical tales, novels, and plays. They tacitly invite the person in quest of divine guidance to place himself or herself in the role of an historical or legendary exemplar and act accordingly. The solution to all one's problems is found in a well-known precedent. Even as such-a-one long ago got out of *his* scrape, so now may *you*.

Wolfram Eberhard, a complete sinologist, was the first to recognize this aspect of modern Chinese oracles. Never daunted by bibliographic boundaries, Eberhard realized that this universally accessible form of divination mediated between Heaven and man by recourse to a full range of Chinese cultural properties. Its substance reflected the rich culture shared—not splintered—by all Chinese.

I have long believed that Chinese regional differences were always more significant than class distinctions. Yet how did "normative" Chinese culture spread so far, to be shared by so many? I suspect that our oracles may have much to reveal about this process. They are ubiquitous, and some have even crossed linguistic frontiers to bring a divinely inspired vision of Chinese culture to outsiders.

Rather than the New World ideal of perfection through segregation, we might instead think of the old centers of cities like Rome and Naples. There, different classes live in the same place, hear the same songs and the same noises, smell the same smells—but do so at different altitudes, from the *basso* upwards through the *piano nobile* and on into the garrets. Vertical stages, yes, according to ancestry, income, and social status. But also, a shared culture and countless references in common. Is this Italian cityscape closer to traditional East Asian realities? It is in any case a more pleasing picture.

Anyone may consult a Chinese temple oracle and draw from it whatever he/she wishes. What are the clientele getting? Conjectural answers have varied according to the investigator's disciplinary affiliations. Medical anthropologists tend to view the consultation as a kind of home-grown psychotherapy, a talking-cure. (Their attention is chiefly focused on the interaction between the querent and the layman, stationed in the temple, who interprets the responses.) Explanations favored by social anthropologists, sociologists, and social historians usually center on power relationships, or on the imposition of ethical codes: this, of course, from the standpoint of the oracle-givers, the ruling class, or ecclesiastical authorities. From the perspective of the querent or consumer, the main function of such mantic systems is often said to be the justification of random behavior. Outside the Chinese sphere, similar materials have been used to advantage by an even wider range of authorities. Economic historians have drawn conclusions about social classes and institutions from the lists of fixed questions that some oracles imposed on their users. Remarkably similar European and Middle Eastern divination systems have been profitably studied by historians of science and technology, art historians, literary historians, specialists in church history, bibliographers, and authorities on folklore and children's games.

 I owe fealty to none of these disciplines, though I shamelessly, gratefully plunder them all. My own current fascination is with ritual, with patterned, theoretically repeatable behavior and its cultural epiphenomena. I believe that the study of history will be transformed as it increasingly comes to focus on such compulsory acts, their art, literature and technology, their place in society, their changes over time, and the elaborate intellectual machinery assembled to justify them. Consulting an oracle is a ritual, albeit a comparatively simple one. If we study this form of divination in the context of ritual, we may discover fresh perspectives to add to those already mentioned.

Consulting an oracle obviously involves posing a question and receiving an answer. This might seem to set divination apart from other forms of ritual, as a personal, individualized act. Yet question-and-answer sequences figure in many other ritual contexts. Riddling and recitation of enigmas formed part of Vedic ritual, and Rolf Stein has shown the importance of enigmas (*lde'u*) in the ritual culture of Tibet.[1] In a monastic context, the stylized postures and gestures of Tibetan monastic "debate" are familiar exoticisms, and similar ritual interrogations are still found in Japanese Tantric Buddhism, as well. In Lhasa during the Scapegoat Ceremony at the end of the second lunar month, a "debate" between a lama and the scapegoat was resolved by casting loaded dice: again, a matter of set questions-and-answers with a predetermined outcome. Among the Tamang, Tibetan people of Eastern Nepal, both liturgical and poetic enigmas appear in numerous ritual contexts, as Brigitte Steinmann has demonstrated.[2]

Like mock combat, questioning seems to be an important feature of many rituals. It may have been frozen in texts like the early Chinese "Heaven's Questions" (*T'ien-wen*), where the original ritual matrix has long since been lost, or in the many folktales that hinge upon a series of questions rightly answered or "riddles wisely expounded." There is always a right answer, but even wrong answers may usually be remedied by prescribed means. In some cases, superficially "wrong" answers may even be the right ones—so paradoxical is the initiate's knowledge, when set against worldly common sense. A perplexing question may evoke an even more enigmatic answer, and through wordplay, figures of speech, or even sheer homophony, the dialogue may be raised to another plane of understanding.

In contrast to such ritual word-jousts, mantric questioning might seem to be much more open-ended. But every one of the written oracles we will be discussing is limited. Some comprise only twenty-eight answers, others a hundred, but even the prodigious Taoist sequence that contains 365 responses is still finite. To what extent will regular users have known a particular sequence almost by heart? How stereotyped were these responses for those who sought them? We find many cases in which the simplest, most fatuous oracles are enhanced by the most complex numerical means of access.

Many oracle texts seem so utterly vapid or inane that we must assume that procedure, or ritual context, takes precedence over content and substance. This can be seen, I think, even when divination has been built into the structure of larger rituals. The two major Tantric examples are Consecration (*abhiṣeka*) and Oblation (*homa*). In both, dream-omens must be taken. Further, in Consecration, presages are drawn from sticks that the neophytes bite and then cast before them, while in Homa the officiant must scrutinize the flames and smoke. In theory, at least, these rituals could come grinding to a halt if the wrong signs turned up (as they often do, in literary accounts). But the prescriptive texts followed by all officiants not only list all the anticipated good and evil omens, but provide means for reversing unfavorable portents, as well.[3] As in all the other cases, the spectrum of responses is first severely limited by listing, then (in effect) made all but meaningless by ritual remedies. Such questioning is necessary, a bow to the will of the gods, but also somehow perfunctory: "ritual" in the weak sense of the term. The entire ritual sequence is compulsory—and asking questions about it in the middle may be an essential feature, a reaffirmation of divine complicity. The questions demand answers, but whether anything hangs on the response (or if any meaningful variation in response is permitted) is another matter. The question is asked, the answer is given, and the ritual goes on.

Sheer compulsion may help account for our oracles' astounding ubiquity. Not only are they everywhere in China and Japan. As soon as we raise our eyes from the Chinese sources, we begin to discover similar systems of two-step divination all across Eurasia and in Africa. Literate societies abound in books of printed or written oracular responses, generally in verse. In nonliterate cultures, the same sort of operations go forward without a tangible text, yet the various bodies of memorized answers are apparently no less stable (or variable) than their written counterparts. Most of these systems are "two-step" in that they begin with some randomizing procedure for selecting one of the numbered responses, which must then be pondered and interpreted. Access to the encoded treasuries of divine wisdom is granted through a variety of means: drawing or casting lots (or dice, or cards, or coins), making marks in the sand, spinning wheels or tops, or sometimes even direct drawing from among the written answers themselves: single-step divination.

Some of the numeromantic methods of selection are so technologically idiosyncratic that they reveal genetic links among widely scattered mantic systems. The most remarkable example is *al-raml*, Islamic geomancy (also known as *Ars notoria*, *Sandkunst*, or *Punktierkunst*). Found throughout Islam from around the ninth century on, by the twelfth century it had conquered Western Europe. In time this Islamic scribal magic, which greatly exercised the ingenuity of the learned, also exerted a powerful influence upon nonliterate societies in Africa and Madagascar. The tradition lives on in Islam and among European occultists too. It is this "geomantic" system of access that was used to unlock many of the oracles that we will be discussing.

Still, it is vital to remember (as T. C. Skeat has stressed) that the various means of access are essentially interchangeable, hence arbitrary. The triumphs of *al-raml* and its historians are impressive, but it should prove even more challenging to compare the oracles themselves. Effective cross-cultural approaches will have to be devised. One immediately thinks of analyzing that important subspecies of oracle which limits inquiries to a set list of questions. As T. C. Skeat and G. M. Browne have shown, such works are so structured, crafted with such premeditation, that once they have all been identified and compared, it should be possible to make meaningful statements about their affiliations.[4]

Study of mantic imagery, or thematics, is another attractive possibility. Birds, for example, make significant appearances in oracles everywhere, and not merely as poetic "symbols." Different species preside over certain mantic sequences, which are organized under the aegis of "Twelve Birds" or "Thirty-Six Birds" (Kings, Judges, Prophets, or Apostles can also serve in this capacity). This naturally recalls a rich ornithomantic background: auspices from the flight or the song of birds, birds as messengers between the gods and men, the secret language of the birds (and the uncanny phenomenon of "talking" birds), egg-divination, and the origin of writing (according to Chinese tradition)—in the observation of bird-tracks. Living birds are still used to pluck forth oracle texts today (cf. p. 147, n. 14 of Chapter 1). This avian presence is also connected with the primordial role of arrows in divination. Arrows were once universally important—economically and politically—and underlie many games as well as mantic procedures. Though they have been outstripped in most technological applications, they still hold their own in Tibetan divination. Apart from birds and their analogues, the study of oracular animal-imagery in general could prove fruitful. It might well begin with those Central Asian systems in which animals seem to have played a primary role, but many other oracles abound in portentous fauna, from ancient Greece to modern China.

Most of our Chinese examples are offered to the public in religious establishments of one sort or another, and so belong to the genre commonly known as temple oracles. Some of the same texts are also conveniently available in printed scriptures and almanacs, and each oracle normally stands under the patronage of a deity, whose words it represents. Obviously, religion plays a role in the origin and dissemination of these works. But which religion?

A small number of oracle texts were produced under explicitly Buddhist auspices. A few others were evidently created or diffused by Taoists. But very few indeed display, in their contents, any consistent ideological association with either of these two organized religions. Many oracles voice the conventional morality that formed part of ordinary Chinese official doctrine and education, but there are other sequences whose ethics, if any, must be deeply implicit or subliminal. Generally speaking, though found in temples, the oracles are not at all "religious" in tone. Nor are their divine patrons necessarily permanent fixtures. Some texts exhibit relative faithfulness to a single deity, but the same oracle may turn up with different patrons in different temples. Divine sponsorship may certainly illuminate some of the pathways of diffusion, but it is not an infallible guide. Most Chinese temples are owned not by a religion, but by the community. Temple affairs are in the hands of a committee of laymen, who invite ritual specialists in to officiate as needed. Function is foremost, "sectarianism" an afterthought. Our oracles are delivered in an entirely pragmatic world of ritual.

Mantic texts from medieval Central Asia suggest a similar state of affairs. Turks, Sogdians, Tibetans, and Chinese, all in their several tongues, had recourse to closely related, if not identical, oracle texts. The authorizing agencies were variously Buddhist, Taoist, Christian, and possibly Manichaean, and content was largely nondenominational. Some of these Central Asian oracles represent developments of Chinese models. But others ultimately derive, through India, from the Hellenistic world. At Tun-huang, Greek divination entered the realm of the *I-ching*, and all for the greater glory of a most diverse pantheon. The oracles furnish a clear example of ritual transcending any particular "religious" context: they are sponsored by all religions, but unique to none. Such facts of Asian life may contradict all our ideas about religion, and the "secular" nature of most oracle texts may seem grotesquely at odds with their "sacred" setting. But this tells us more about our own hackneyed categories than about oracles. Religion in traditional societies is no less (nor more) a matter of table, bed, or toilet than of temple. The alleged dichotomy of Sacred and Secular is a romantic academic invention; the Idea of the Holy is a modern German myth.

This study obviously falls far short of completeness. As Norman Douglas was fond of quoting, "As we know a little more, we know a little less." As I followed up references and found unsuspected connections, I began to realize that for satisfactory results one would have to establish the history and genealogy of every extant oracle or oracle family. Before that, each text would need to be closely studied in its own cultural setting. To accomplish this even for the Chinese specimens was beyond my powers. To mask this impotence, I have indulged in a cross-cultural mantic orgy.

The full task before us involves more than genealogy, textual history, and literary analysis. Even though divination is a genre of ritual and works (or so I believe), according to special, compulsive rules, its social function must also be investigated in every historical context that fosters it. So far, the explanation advanced by scholars of China seems partial and incomplete. Despite recent attempts at rapprochement, the matter and methods of anthropology and history remain distinct. The paradox of temple oracles is particularly instructive. They represent a "popular" phenomenon within a living oral tradition, and thus call for fieldwork and direct observation. Yet they also embody a written tradition, with a venerable, complex, and copious documentation in Classical Chinese. Neither pure history nor pure anthropology can adequately account for them, and though philology, too, may have a role to play, it is even more limited. Historians who forget that oracles are still alive will miss precisely that "oral" element which they now crave. But even those anthropologists of China who cogently defend studies grounded in the present tense are not necessarily working in the light of the best examples.

In the past several decades, the most extensive anthropological research on divination has been carried out by Africanists. I will take a single outstanding study: Alfred Adler and Andras Zempléni, *Le Bâton de l'aveugle; divination, maladie et pouvoir chez les Moundang du Tchad.*[5] First, the authors deal with divination proper: the Mundangs' *kindani* system and its technique, the relevant deities, and the diviners themselves. Their second section addresses the relations of divination with disease, and sets oracle-consultation in the context of traditional medicine. The third part of the book discusses divination and power, and analyzes the role of oracles in the social hierarchy and the diviner's function in the rain-magic that is vital to political control.

The materials, methods and personnel of divination, its associations with healing, and its place in society generally (occult knowledge as a fulcrum of power) all these exactly correspond to the three classes of information which we should seek to draw from our oral and written Chinese sources. Adler and Zempléni have demonstrated the autonomy of oracles in the treatment of disease. Healing is the principal focus of divination, but the inquiry is normally carried out in the patient's absence. The oracles explain the illness and reveal directions for carrying out the possession rituals that serve as treatment. Among the Mundang, divination first generates a diagnosis, then produces specific ritual instructions. Adler and Zempléni speculate that the role of oracles in directing the "colleges of possessed women" who perform the cures is related to the ambiguous social status of such feminine institutions. Divine authority acquired by mantic means protects women officiants from potential censure and other negative consequences of their uncertain position in the hierarchy.[6] In illustrating the function of oracles as mediators between groups of differing status and authority, these anthropologists have shown divination to be a major force in social history.

On the face of it, one could hardly find a setting more remote from traditional China than among the Mundang of Chad. But the interest of *kindani* divination for the sinologist is enhanced by a quirk of cultural history. The Mundangs' oracle belongs to the vast family of mantic procedures derived from geomancy, and Adler and Zempléni devote one chapter to a systematic comparison of *kindani* and classical Islamic geomancy, *al-raml*. Of course this has nothing to do with the Chinese topology (*feng-shui*), which is often called "geomancy" in the West. Yet some scholars have suggested that *al-raml*, the most widespread and prestigious mantic method of the Middle Ages, was originally inspired by the *I-ching*. Whatever one may think of the genetic hypothesis, there are certainly remarkable structural parallels between the two systems.

In the end, even the unwritten African oracles testify to the extraordinary potency of writing. The scribal tradition of Islam (a "Religion of the Book"), with its superior magic, generated a profusion of related mantic systems among nonliterate Africans. The written oracle is obviously not hindered by cultural and linguistic frontiers, and can even create oral tradition. And if written oracles work these wonders across such vast distances, imagine how much more powerful they must be within the confines of Chinese society, where writing is sacred even among the illiterate (ingested, it is a panacea).

Our Chinese oracles have been borne upon most of the materials that have carried Chinese script. Ancient texts were written on bamboo strips—like tally-sticks or lots—which were then bound into bundles to form a consecutive text. With the invention of paper, paper became their medium, though in the fifth century, the first Chinese Buddhist oracle was meant to be written on strips of silk. We do not know when they began to be printed, but a thirteenth-century Buddhist incunable survives. Apart from the *Book of Changes*, was any Chinese oracle ever graven in stone (like their distant Greek analogues in Asia Minor)? Printed paper is their chosen vehicle throughout East Asia today.

Clearly, writing was vital to the genesis of this form of divination. Such oracles developed at a time when ultimate spiritual and political authority had come to be identified with the written word. Whether embodied in the venerable *Book of Changes* (which opens the canon of Confucian scriptures) or in flimsy printed divination-slips at a friendly neighborhood temple, the written oracle is intrinsic to Chinese culture. Léon Vandermeersch has even suggested that the parallel style which dominates all Classical Chinese literature may derive from ancient mantic texts.[7] In medieval China we can trace the subsequent progress of script as, like a possessed medium, it transforms itself into a god. This study of written oracles is presented as a tentative chapter in the greater history of the apotheosis of writing and the cult of the book.

That I have been able to get even this far in mantic studies is due to the prior work and current help of others. This book's dedication to the memory of Wolfram Eberhard is entirely fitting. Eberhard's studies of temple oracles are fundamental, and represent only a small portion of his pioneering research in every area of Chinese social and cultural history. Eberhard was also a valued friend during long years of struggle in what was then the Department of Oriental Languages at Berkeley.

I gladly thank the many friends who have helped me complete this study: Ann Arnold and Ian Jackson, Elaine Tennant and Frederic Amory, Susan Naquin, Elling Eide, Nathan Sivin, Stephen F. Teiser, Daniel Overmyer, and Laura Stevens. My gratitude is particularly due to seven friends, my students: Anna Shtutina, Sarah Frazer, Constance Cook, Edward (Ned) Davis, Bruce Williams, Keith Knapp, and Peter Nickerson. For information and advice I am grateful to Piet van der Loon, Glen Dubridge, Werner Banck, Marc Kalinowski, Carole Morgan, Judith M. Boltz, Donald J. Harper, Martin

Schwartz, Kenneth Eastman, and Allison Kennedy. In Paris, I could never have survived without François and Itsuko (Mieko) Macé, Donald and Jacqueline Holzman, André and Céline Padoux, Sandy and Pauline Koffler, Marc and Hélène Kakinowski, Lucien Biton and Régine Pietra, Patrice Fava, Christine Mollier, Kristofer and Wendela Schipper, Kuo Li-ying, Danielle Eliasberg, and Yolaine Escande. Survival would not have been worthwhile without Brigitte Steinmann. The constant support of my parents, too, has been essential.

I acknowledge with pleasure the assistance of Gesine Bottomley and Dörte Meyer-Gaudig, librarians at the Wissenschaftskolleg (Institute for Advanced Study, Berlin); Zdenek V. David and Amber Olson at the Woodrow Wilson International Center for Scholars, Smithsonian Institution; Eugenie Bruck of the Center for Japanese Studies, University of California, Berkeley; and Hubert Durt at the Hōbōgirin Institute (École Française d'Extrême-Orient) in Kyoto. My title is a homage to Nora K. Chadwick, *Poetry and Prophecy* (Cambridge, 1942). The study of traditional China can only gain by setting our documents in a broader social and literary context, as exemplified by H. M. and N. K. Chadwick's great work, *The Growth of Literature* (Cambridge, 1932–40).

Washington, November 24, 1990.

RITUAL AND RANDOMIZATION

The Chinese are an ancient people

Before us is a hard campaign.

MANAS (Kirghiz epic)

Among its immediate neighbors, China has long enjoyed fame as the homeland of divination. Chinese mantic systems are legion and are found in the most diverse settings, from elaborate and formal temple altars to boisterous marketplace stands. In one form or another, fate-calculation appears in nearly every context, from the most solemn to the most mundane. This obsession with destiny (or what the future holds in store) is one of the most deeply rooted features of Chinese life. The art and science of fate has spread far beyond temple confines and the stalls of mantic professionals into the deepest matrix of Chinese culture: cuisine. What other culture could have welded its two chief concerns, eating and fate-reading, into the institution of the fortune cookie?[1]

The central nature of divination in Chinese culture has been recognized by those neighboring societies most indebted to the Chinese example. A twelfth-century chronicle, the *sBa-bzhed*, repeatedly describes Tibetan envoys being sent to China in the eighth and ninth centuries to acquire mantic techniques or consult Chinese diviners.[2] In the quadripartite schema of world monarchy propounded in an influential fourteenth-century Tibetan source, the ruler of India is King of Religion, Iran's ruler King of Riches, the monarch of the North is King of Armies, but the ruler of China, King of Divinatory

I

Sciences.[3] The awesome phenomenon of lasting Chinese empire was thought to rest upon a consummate mastery of mantic arts—a notion which we find reflected in the oral literatures of Central Asia. These depict the redoubtable Chinese troops as fearsome adversaries, and their Khan as a ruler who owed his sovereign powers to magic.[4]

At the heart of China's reputation in the field of occult inquiry lies the *I-ching*, the *Book of Changes*; beneath it, supportively, the mantic tortoise.[5] Still other systems flourished under the early Empire: divination, prognostication, hemerology, and medical diagnosis. Recent archeological discoveries have brought us closer to an appreciation of certain universally accepted methods and assumptions of fate-calculation that provided the underpinnings of daily life: beliefs and practices hitherto known chiefly from literary sources such as the *Lun-heng* and *Ch'ien-fu lun*.[6] Yet already by the Later Han period, the religious situation in China had altered considerably from the time when tortoise and milfoil had supposedly reigned supreme. By the first century C.E., Buddhism had begun to make its way in China, and in the course of the second century, Taoism came into being as an organized socioreligious system. By the fifth century, the basic amalgam of Buddho-Taoist ritual was already in process—an amalgam that has influenced Chinese culture down to our time. By the end of the Early Medieval period, then, the moral climate of China had changed for good. A new set of otherworldly instances and sanctions had come into being, to evaluate and prescribe life and conduct in this world. This development radically affected all aspects of communication with the spirit-world, including, naturally, those practices subsumed under the rubric of "divination."

Into the new ritual system were incorporated many, perhaps even most, of the preexisting components of Han cosmology. As the consciously sinocentric Taoist system developed, progressively endowing older elements of Chinese culture with new significance, we find the classic cosmology being reassembled within a new theogony. Thus, in medieval Taoist sources, we are able to trace a large measure of continuity with, for example, the Ma-wang-tui materials.[7] Taoist ritual texts abound in references to the classic mantic systems of China and hallowed cosmological principles. We find the trigrams and hexagrams in use as spatiotemporal signposts in ritual and as symbolic emblems of good or ill fortune in hymnody.[8] The asterisms, too, were portentous and central to Taoist cult. Yet curiously, early medieval Taoism strictly forbade its votaries to practice divination. Recourse to the mantic arts was lumped together with a host of common activities deemed undesirable by Taoists. These included offerings to deceased ancestors, blood sacrifice to local deities ("the gods of the profane," *su-shen*), and giving money to priests. Through allegiance to Taoism, the faithful had put themselves in the hands of a far higher power than the spirits invoked by diviners. Divination was superfluous or, worse still, a direct insult to the Tao.[9]

For all of Taoism's absorbing interest as a crystallization and internal reform of Chinese tradition, Buddhism represents a far more imposing phenomenon in the history of Asia. Some may bridle at the notion of listing Buddhism among China's gifts to East Asia, but I think there can be little question regarding the essential originality of the Buddhist rites and institutions which China transmitted to Korea, Japan, Tibet, and Vietnam. The compartmentalization of our studies has regrettably drawn a *cordon sanitaire* around Chinese Buddhism, enabling many self-declared specialists to operate largely independently of Chinese social and cultural history as a whole. Here we have a truly massive body of primary sources cordoned off from the field at large. A more mature historiography, and one more fully liberated from native categories, would never tolerate the neglect of this material on the grounds that it somehow represents an alien intrusion into the culture. The history of Chinese Buddhism of course comprised a good deal more than a millennium of translation activity. The vast majority of the 3,360 works contained in the hundred volumes of the Taishō Sino-Japanese Buddhist Canon were written, not in India, but in China and Japan.[10]

Small wonder, then, if many of the components of Chinese culture reached the encircling countries together with Buddhism—and may even have come there in Buddhist guise. The system of divination which we shall be considering belongs to this category. It testifies to the steady infiltration of the fabric of Chinese Buddhism by a massive, if diffuse, complex of Chinese ritual practice. As found outside China, it is, in fact, a Chinese oracle in Buddhist vestments, and we shall discover that the system's oldest recoverable Chinese torso is also Buddhistically draped.

Observers throughout China have long noted a divinatory procedure combining sticks and a printed oracle in verse. The system is striking in its ubiquity no less than its banality. It appears to have been found everywhere in China, in every colony of overseas Chinese, and in every country directly influenced by Chinese culture. There are two essential operations. First, a stick is obtained at random from a collection of numbered sticks—often one hundred—by shaking their container, which may be either open or closed; if closed, a hole at one extremity permits the egress of a single stick. The number on the stick is then matched with the corresponding printed sheet, or page of a booklet, which contains the querent's fortune. Different observers have documented a variety of situations in which these procedures take place as well as variations of detail. The most formal setting is a temple; the sticks are found on an altar, before an image of the deity who serves as the oracle's patron (and is presumably deemed to be its source). A. J. A. Elliot, for example, writing of Singapore in the fifties, tells us that Cantonese women there will go to the temple with paper money, incense sticks, and food offerings. After having presented her offerings, the supplicant has a choice of several bamboo vases of sticks. She will take up one of these which is specifically designated for the type of request she has in mind. She faces the image of the deity, and shakes the vase until one and only one stick falls out (should more than one emerge, she must start over). If she wishes, she may then seek the deity's further confirmation of the stick chosen, through recourse to the kidney-shaped divining blocks that lie on the altar. If they land with one flat side up, the other down, the god has validated the chosen stick. She will then take the stick to the temple attendant, who gives her the corresponding printed sheet of paper, and helps her interpret it.[11]

This is comparatively elaborate; the procedure may also be reduced to its bare essentials. It may be conducted independently of professional guidance, and even privately, for booklets exist in which all the numbered oracles of a single sequence are contained. They too stress the sacred and solemn character of the proceedings; whether or not material offerings are specified, reverence to the sponsoring deity is essential if a true response is to be obtained. In temple oracles as well as in the booklets, the mantic verses are often headed by evaluations of relative auspiciousness, "quality-tags," as it were; the oracular poems are frequently accompanied by additional explanatory matter, in prose and/or verse, sometimes credited to the patron deity itself, or to celebrated literary or historical figures.

By the nineteenth century, this characteristically Chinese system was known to the pioneer scholars of world folklore, and we find it described in a number of classic works by nonsinologists. The German ethnographer Adolf Bastian gave an account of its use among Cochin-Chinese sailors; it also figures in *La mythologie des plantes*, by Angelo de Gubernatis, and in the Rev. Hilderic Friend's *Flowers and Flower Lore*. Friend, who had lived in Canton and so seen the oracles in operation, had no hesitation in linking them with the rhabdomancy of the Magi as described by Lenormant. He saw in the divining sticks a source or reflection of the magic wand.[12]

Closer to our own time, the keen eye of the expressionist poet Henri Michaux calmly noted the mechanical, prefabricated aspect of the system (which he associated with the "innate craftsmanship" of the Chinese): "On fait rouler des petits bâtonnets dans une boîte, il y en a toujours un qui s'avance un peu plus que les autres, vous le retirez. Il porte un numéro. On cherche la feuille d'avenir correspondant à ce numéro, on lit . . . , et il ne reste plus qu'à y croire."[13] Indeed, the artisanal aspect here would appear to have supplanted the inspired descent, or ascent, of the spirit in the quest for hidden knowledge. Still, there are elements of potential interest, and the entire procedure may nevertheless prove to be in close alignment with the perceived configurations of the invisible world. The first gap to be closed by the intervention of the divine will concerns the choice of stick. Thereafter, the supplicant must confront and wrestle with the god's own words, in often cryptic poetic form. For all its foreshortening of the mantic horizon, there is still room in this scenario for the *mysterium tremendum*—at least if we can find in our hearts a measure of sympathy for the Chinese otherworld, which has long since taken on the guise of a vast bureaucracy, the original paperwork empire. It may be that the time is ripe for greater sympathy; perhaps our own spiritual culture will soon begin to tread the same path, in step with our increasingly regimented social life. It would in any case be rash to dismiss these Chinese oracles before we have scrutinized the poetry itself; may there still linger traces of mantic frenzy after all?

Numbered sticks need not be the only means of access to the verse sequence. The oracle in the *Kuan-ti ming-sheng chen-ching* (Ch'ao-chou 1858: 3.10a–b) informs the reader that should he be unable to go to the god's temple for a consultation, he may use the booklet at home, with ten coins. Varying numbers of coins are referred to in earlier sources, as well. Doolittle records another alternative. One of the six classes of professional fortune-tellers whom he observed in nineteenth-century Foochow "traverses the streets in pursuit of employment." In one hand he carries a bamboo-and-horn clapper, to announce his presence; in the other, a caged bird. His equipment also includes "sixty-four small sheets of paper, on each of which is sketched a figure of a god, or bird, or beast, or person; on each sheet is also written a short verse, usually four lines, each of seven characters. These sheets are

folded up in such a manner that the picture and the poetry shall be unseen."
When a client summons him, the diviner sets out the slips of paper, opens the
cage, and allows the bird to select one, or sometimes two, which will then
be expounded for the client's benefit. Birds as agents of the divine have, of
course, a long prior history. In Taiwan and Hong Kong, birds are still pluck-
ing forth destinies today. Note, too, that this nineteenth-century Foochow
sequence included a pictorial element.[14]

   If the oracle itself is fixed and bookish, inspiration and ingenuity may be
directed toward discovering new means of access. William P. Lebra tells us
that "Okinawan diviners... most commonly rely on books used in association with divining blocks or sticks and do not claim supernatural powers as
in the case of a shaman... One was found to be using the abacus in place
of the divining sticks or blocks, and some informants appeared to be rather
impressed with this novel method."[15]

CHINESE ORACLES
IN PARTIBUS

The system has spread far beyond China's borders. We find it in Tibet, among the many forms of Chinese divination of which the Tibetans expressed such keen appreciation. Though themselves not lacking in mantic inventiveness, they also made use of precisely the same method. The method has been described by David Macdonald, of Scottish and Sikkimese parentage, who spent his early years in the vicinity of Darjeeling and served from 1905 to 1925 as a British agent in Gyangtse, Central Tibet. His evidence is significant as showing the system's presence in central Tibetan culture, rather than simply on China's periphery, in Amdo or Khams. He describes the bamboo sticks as being used in conjunction with a booklet, and also notes that this form of divination (like Tibetan arrow-divination) is connected with Gesar. This legendary hero was seen as an incarnation of Vaiśravaṇa and explicitly equated, in Ch'ing times, with Kuan Ti.[1] René de Nebesky-Wojkowitz describes a Gesar arrow-divination (*Ge-sar mda' mo*) in which a large number of numbered arrows are shaken in a high vessel until one or more arrows emerge. Their numbers direct the inquirer to the corresponding passage of a divining book.[2] During the Ch'ing times, in the eighteenth and nineteenth centuries, the cult of Gesar/Kuan Ti swept Tibet and Mongolia. The Mongols, too, have this form of divination, under Kuan Ti's auspices, and their oracle booklets also include predictions of his imminent advent as hero and savior.³ We will find Kuan Ti as a prominent patron of this type of divination in China, as well.

The use of divinatory booklets (*mo-dpe*) in conjunction with a system of lots (either sticks or cards) or dice is common in Tibet. Several varieties have been described by Austine Waddell.⁴ Rolf Stein has published a manual of thirty-three slips. This appears to represent a somewhat different system, and Stein's close examination of the text is one of the few such studies in depth.⁵ Stein's remarkable analysis of a series of frequently recurring narrative vignettes in the Tibetan manuscripts from Tun-huang is also noteworthy, for these fragments of myths and legends were used in the formation of oracle texts as well as in the etiological justification of rituals; they thus illustrate the original Tibetan component of what was to become, in later Tibet and Mongolia, a highly Sino-Tibetan oracular idiom.⁶ The Tibetans have been amazingly inventive in devising and assimilating mantic systems, but it is strange that Robert B. Ekvall, in his description of numerous highly idiosyncratic methods in use until recently in Tibet, never mentions the seemingly ubiquitous consultation of an oracle book by means of lots or dice.⁷ At all events, Tibetan data are highly relevant to the study of all forms of divination in China, structurally as well as historically. Sinologists should be alerted to the bulk and the importance of these Tibetan materials.

Returning to the mantic system that concerns us here, there is also evidence for its currency in Korea. Maurice Courant lists two Korean sequences, nos. 2428 and 2429 of his *Bibliographie coréenne*. The system is discussed in *Chōsen no senboku to yogen*, a comprehensive account of Korean divination assembled by Japanese ethnographers and published in 1933. The examples recorded there emanate from the South Temple and East Temple of Seoul, respectively. Both are under the patronage of Kuan Ti, the God of War; an inscription at the South Temple stresses that deity's protective role in Korea, ever since the Japanese invasion and devastation of 1592. The East Temple was headquarters for a society of Kuan Ti devotees, who administered the temple; this organization promoted the civil virtues. Buddhists would come there, too, according to our source—but never Christians. In use at the East Temple was a Kuan Ti oracle in hundred stanzas. The same work gives response no. 8 from that sequence in full. We will presently find the identical sequence elsewhere in East Asia.⁸

The Japanese of the Tokugawa period, of course, also claimed Kuan Ti's exclusive protection for themselves, and the Nagasaki merchants were not laggard in importing the god's oracles from the continent. The account books for 1726 list an *Oracle of Monarch Kuan*. In a list of the books imported in 1847, we also find a Kuan Ti oracle.[9] Yet present-day Japan can boast of oracular sequences of many sorts, some claiming still greater antiquity. Examples of this type of divination are found everywhere throughout Japan, at Buddhist temples and Shintō shrines. Oracular sequences also circulate in printed booklet form. I have one example, comprising thirty-two quatrains of five-syllable Chinese verse, credited to the authorship of Ingen Daishi (Yin-yüan, 1592–1673). Ingen was the patriarch of the Ōbaku/Huang-p'o school of Ch'an—the last Chinese Buddhist lineage to be imported to Japan. He arrived in Nagasaki in 1654. The text is illustrated (as are many of the other Japanese oracles), one woodcut per each stanza of oracular verses; it opens with the general instructions for use, including an illustration of the divining sticks and their container. Each set of verses is accompanied by *furigana* transcriptions and an explanation in Japanese. I can provide no information on the extent of this sequence's diffusion in Japan. The copy in my possession is a 1925 reprint of an edition originally published in 1905, in Kyoto, entitled simply *Kichikyō kafuku sanjūni-ban mikuji*: "Thirty-Two Oracle-Slips for Good and Bad Fortune, Weal and Woe"[10] (Figures 1 to 7).

The single most popular sequence in Japan, at least from Tokugawa times to the present, must certainly be that passing under the high patronage of another *daishi*, Ganzan. This is the most commonly met-with of many posthumous titles of the great Tendai Buddhist patriarch, Ryōgen (912–85), also popularly known as The Horned Master (*tsuno daishi*—alluding to his demoniform manifestation) and the Master of the [Demon-dispelling] Beans (*mame daishi*); his formal posthumous title is Jie Daishi. Famous during his lifetime as a strong opponent of the uncouth and arrogant martial monks of Hieian, Ryōgen enjoyed a steadily growing posthumous cult as a protector against demonic forces. Talismans of his image as demon-king still guard many Japanese homes and shops. He was considered to have been an incarnation of Kannon (Kuan-yin) and like that bodhisattva was regularly called upon for succor. Eighteen icons of Ganzan Daishi (so called because he died on the third of the first month: *ganzan*) are enshrined at temples scattered through Kyoto, and form the foci of a miniature pilgrimage, which a severely diminished band of traditional devotees still attempt to cover (by car) on the third day of every month, sacred to Ganzan. He is supposed to have brought the oracle back from China, though he never went there in person.[11]

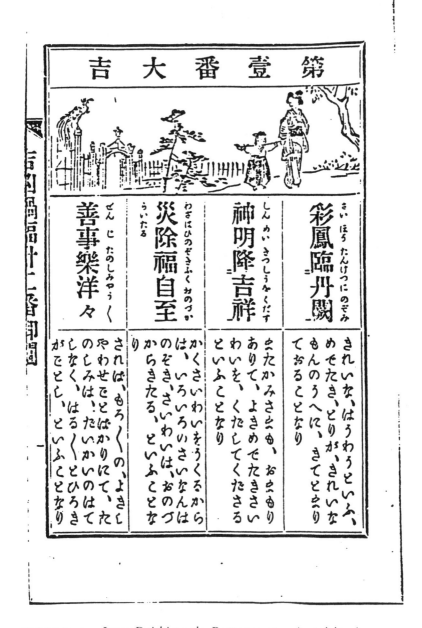

FIGURE 1.   Ingen Daishi oracle: Response no. 1 (auspicious).

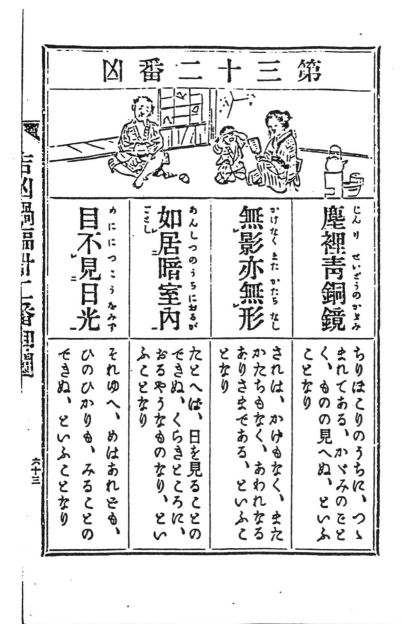

FIGURE 2.   Ingen Daishi oracle: Response no. 32 (inauspicious).

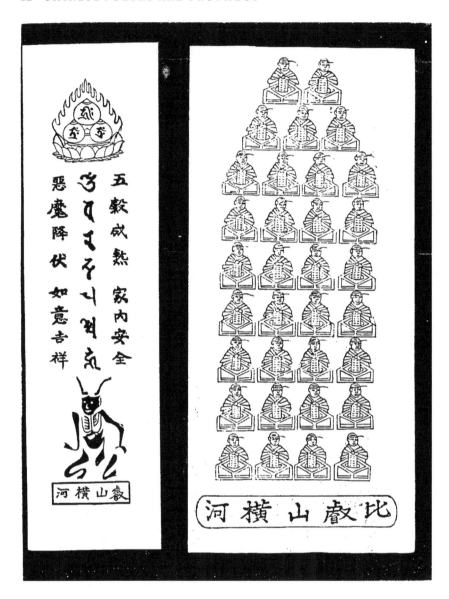

FIGURE 3.   Ganzan Daishi talismans from Mt. Hiei.

The oldest edition of this sequence in my possession, in booklet form, is entitled *Ganzan mikuji handan*, "Judgements of the Ganzan Oracle." Undated, it is probably from the early nineteenth century. Another set is from 1868, the very opening of the Meiji era; it terms itself a third edition (Figures 4, 5, 8–12). The edition currently on sale in Buddhist bookshops is a

慶應戊辰復三刻

增補
改正
元三大師御鬮諸鈔

皇都書林
平
阪
倉君
五書舍藏梓

○占法并吉凶判斷口決
○願文并奉送之支
○元三大師と眞像并御傳
○御籤箱十法之事
○御本地觀音御影眞言
○御鬮不取時之事

FIGURE 4.   Ganzan oracle, title page, third edition (1868).

FIGURE 5. Ganzan oracle, 1868: Portrait of Ganzan Daishi.

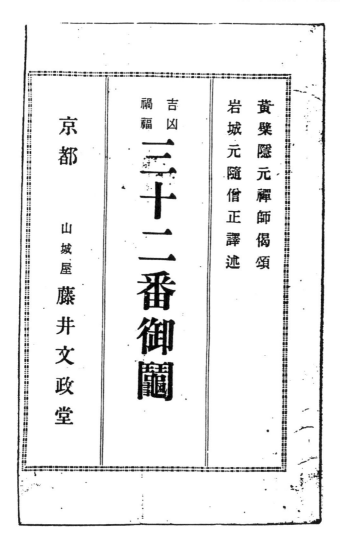

FIGURE 6. Ingen Daishi oracle, title page (Kyoto: Fujii bunseidō, 1905; rpt. 1925).

moveable-type resetting of this version, first produced in 1916 and since then several times reprinted (Kyoto: Kōbundō). Like its predecessors, it provides full instructions for use, including an illustration of the requisite container for the sticks (Figures 13–16). Yet though all these editions claim the authority of the great Tendai saint and demon-queller, we must note that the same oracular sequence also circulates under different auspices.

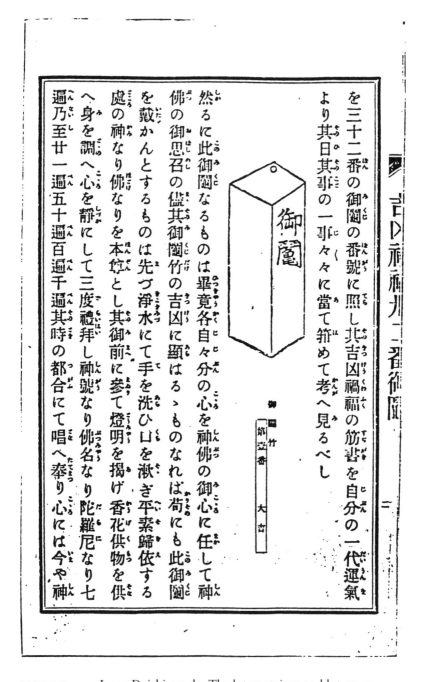

を三十二番の御鬮の番號に照し其吉凶禍福の筋書を自分の一代運氣より其日其事の一事々々に當て鬮めて考へ見るべし

然るに此御鬮なるものは畢竟各自々分の心を神佛の御心に任して神佛の御思召の儘其御鬮竹の吉凶に顯はるゝものなれば苟にも此御鬮を戯かんとするものは先づ淨水にて手を洗ひ口を漱ぎ平素歸依する處の神なり佛なりを本尊とし其御前に参て燈明を揚げ香花供物を供へ身を調へ心を静にして三度禮拜し神號なり佛名なり陀羅尼なり七遍乃至廿一遍五十遍百遍千遍其時の都合にて唱へ奉り心には今や神

御鬮
御鬮竹
第壹番
大吉

FIGURE 7. Ingen Daishi oracle: The lot container and lot no. 1.

FIGURE 8.   Ganzan Daishi in his horned manifestation; Ganzan oracle, 1868.

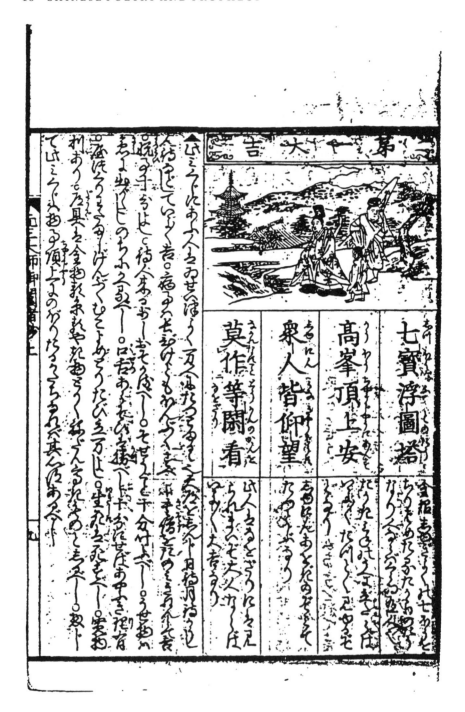

FIGURE 9.   Ganzan oracle, 1868: Response no. 1 (auspicious).

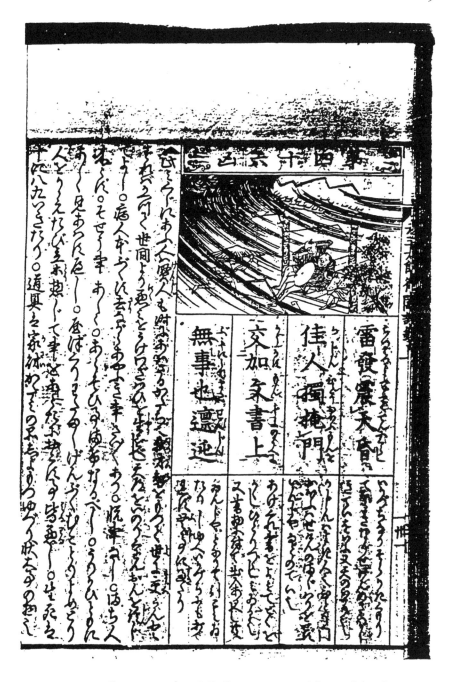

FIGURE 10. Ganzan oracle, 1868: Response no. 46 (inauspicious).

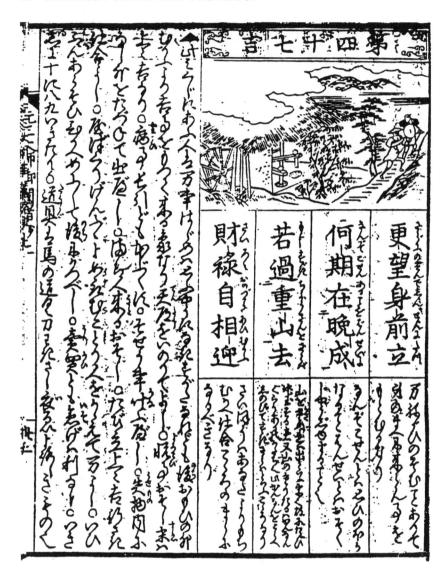

FIGURE 11. Ganzan oracle, 1868: Response no. 47 (auspicious).

Figures 17 and 18 are taken from the *Myōshū mikuji eshō*, the work of a Nichiren-lineage cleric; my "corrected and augmented" edition dates from 1889. After illustrating a prominent selection from the Nichiren pantheon, the booklet proceeds to set forth the very same oracle—*sans* Ganzan. Nichiren devotees apparently need only know that it is a *Nichiren* oracle, neither more nor less.[12]

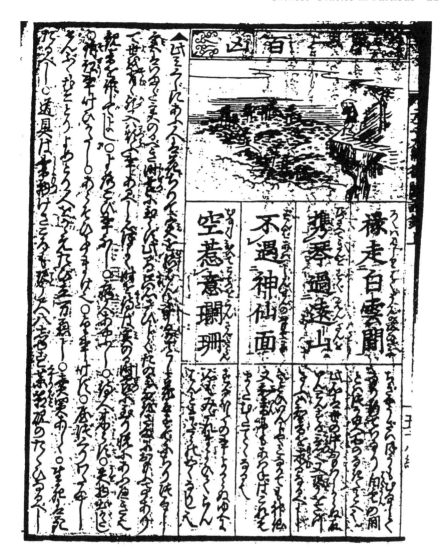

FIGURE 12.   Ganzan oracle, 1868: Response no. 100 (inauspicious).

Comparison of illustrations from the several versions shows that they are all quite different from one another. Even the 1905 resetting of the Meiji "third edition," though faithful to the earlier text, has a new series of illustrations. A specialist in popular printing and iconography would find profitable material here. Illustrated versions have proliferated in modern Japan, a fact that attests to the country's cultural conservatism. Comparable illustrated oracles circulated in Sung China. Similar woodcuts are used

(b)

(a)

FIGURE 13. Ganzan oracle, 1964: "The Horned Master" and the lot container.

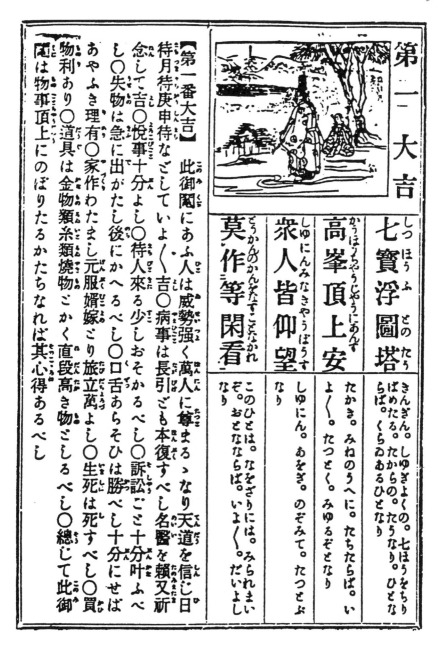

第一大吉

七寳浮圖塔

しっぽうふどの
たう

きんぎん。しゆぎよくの。七ほうをちり
ばめたる。たからの。たうなり。ひとな
らば。くらゐあるひとなり

高峯頂上安

かうほうちやうじやうにあんず

たかき。みねのうへに。たちたらば。い
よく。たつとく。みゆるぞとなり

衆人皆仰望

しゆにんみなきやうばうす

しゆにん。あをぎ。のぞみて。たつとよ
なり

莫作等閑看

そうかんのかんたなすこだになかれ

このひとは。なをざりには。みられまい
ぞ。おとなならば。いよく。だいよし
なり

【第一番大吉】此御䰗にあふ人は威勢強く萬人に尊まるゝなり天道を信じ日念して吉〇悦事十分よし〇待人來る少しおそかるべし〇訴訟ことは十分叶ふべし名醫を頼又祈待月待庚申待なごしていよく吉〇病事は長引ごも本復すべし

物利あり〇道具は金物類糸類燒物ごかく直段高き物ごしるべし〇總じて此御䰗は物事頂上にのぼりたるかたちなれば其心得あるべし

〇失物は急に出がたし後にかへろべし〇口舌あらそひは勝べし十分にせばあやふき理有〇家作わたましし元服婿嫁ごり旅立萬よし〇生死は死すべし〇買物

FIGURE 15. Ganzan oracle, 1964: Response nos. 46 (inauspicious) and 47 (auspicious).

(a)

(b)

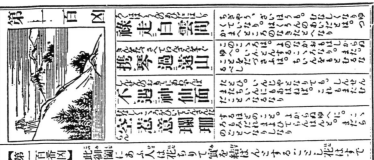

(b)

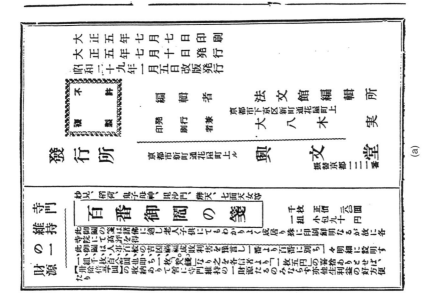

(a)

FIGURE 16. Ganzan oracle, 1964: Response no. 100 (inauspicious), and colophon.

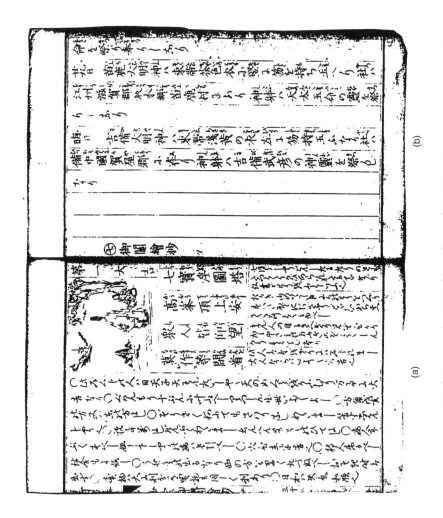

FIGURE 17. Nichiren oracle, *Myōshū mikuji eshō*, 1889: Response no. 1 (auspicious).

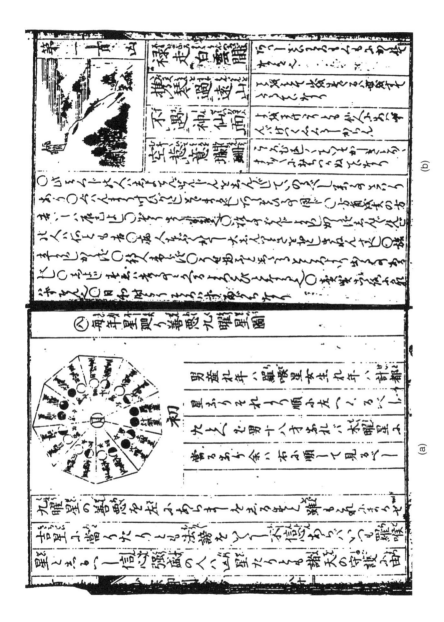

FIGURE 18. Nichiren oracle, 1889: Response no. 100 (inauspicious), and an astrological table.

(a)

(b)

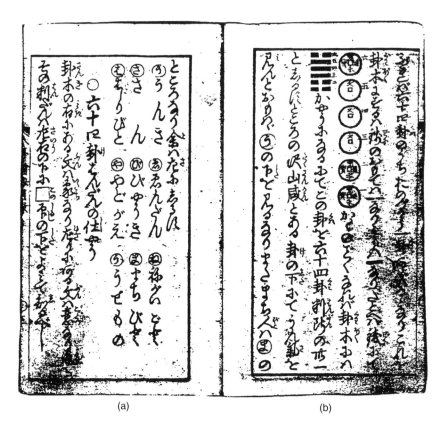

(a)   (b)

FIGURE 19.   *E'iri tsūzoku Ekigaku shoken*, "Little Mirror of Popular
I-ching Science, Illustrated." Instructions for using six coins to obtain a
hexagram.

in Japan to illustrate booklets containing other types of mantic sequences,
including popular adaptations of the *Book of Changes* (Figures 19 and 20;
undated nineteenth-century blockprint).

Another conspicuous feature of Japanese oracular usage is rejectability.
Hard by every temple or shrine that offers an oracle of this kind stands at least
one tree (sometimes suitably blighted) festooned with twisted paper—oracles
rejected as ill-omened. Some of the texts are really quite forbidding, and being
labeled "greatly inauspicious" (*daikyō*) can in no way increase their appeal.
The dazed recipient may therefore tie them to a tree, or wedge them into a
crack or cleft; and in theory, at least, he should take away someone else's
rejected oracle (*sute-mikuji*) from the ample supply displayed, since (they
say) what is bad for one person at a certain age may be suited to someone

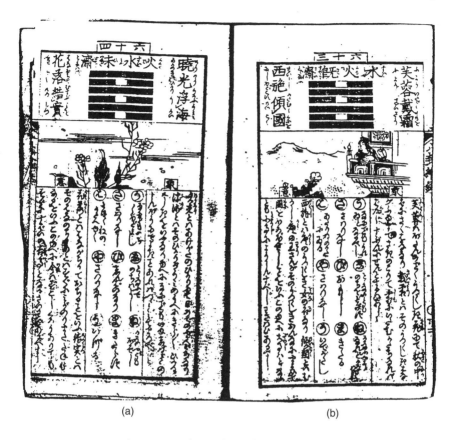

(a)   (b)

FIGURE 20. *Little Mirror of Popular I-ching Science*, Illustrated: Response nos. 63 and 64.

else at a different time of life. But my own observation suggests that not many twisted papers, fruit of that forbidden tree, are willingly taken—any more than one need eat the cookie containing a fortune one does not wish to ingest and thus assimilate.

In Lafcadio Hearn's account of his own consultation, his Japanese friend shakes forth three sticks in succession, of which two were auspicious—thus giving a broader base to fate.[13] Even this, as we shall find, has a foundation in medieval Chinese practice. Curiously enough it is possible to tell, from the evaluations of relative auspiciousness on each of the sticks which Hearn's friend read out (51, good fortune; 99, great good fortune; 64, evil), that this oracle, too, was the Ganzan Daishi sequence.

TERMINA TECHNICA

In the course of considering the relevant terminology, we can wend our way back to China. The usual Japanese term for these oracles is *kuji* 籤 (honorifically *mikuji* 御籤; or even, carrying awed good manners to excessive lengths, *omikuji* お御籤). In medieval times this was sometimes written with the homophonous characters 孔子; the pun inevitably recalls the Tibetans' veneration of Confucius as a conspicuous patron of divination, presumably because of his alleged infatuation with the *I-ching*.[1]

In Japan, the characters *chiu* 籤 and *ch'ien* 籤, both pronounced *kuji*, have been used interchangeably in this connexion. The former, visually connoting a struggle with a tortoise, is glossed as originally meaning "take," "grasp," "seize"—a divining stick, obviously. Here the tortoise of course functions as phonetic, yet there is little doubt of a crafty semantic intentionality, as well. In China, the word was being used to designate lotteries by the latter part of the thirteenth century, as we shall see.[2]

As for *ch'ien*, "numbered marker," "counter," "counting stick," there is no clear-cut division between phonetic value and radical signification; or, in other terms, the graph is a full emblem of the word itself. For it early stands for confirmatory sign, or prophecy, and is from the first interchangeable with *ch'an* 讖, prophetic or oracular writing or utterance. As early as the *Yü-p'ien* (fifth century C.E.) it is attested as designating "bamboo rods used in divination." The construction of this character cannot but remind us of another *signifiant* and its *signifié* that also often figure in an oracular context: 讖. We know that we are here on treacherous, "popular" ground when even our greatest philological oracle, Morohashi, gives "meaning unknown" for this character.[3] An anthropologist may be less perplexed than the redoubtable classicist; this is the term used to designate the kidney-shaped divining blocks.[4] As *ch'ien* may serve for *ch'an*, "prophecy," so may *kao* or *hao* 告 (Hokkien *pue*) stand in parallel relation to *kao*, the "declaration" of a god or spirit (cf. *Chen-kao*, "Declarations of the Perfected Ones," a collection of fourth-century C.E. Taoist visionary and oracular utterances; also, the later genre of "divine edicts" (*shen-kao*) in the Ming *Tao-tsang*). The oracles are most commonly termed *ling-ch'ien*, "transcendent" or "empowered" lots. A common strand in all this mantic skein signals the appeal to divine authority; ever-present, no doubt, in even the most secular-seeming of Chinese divinatory systems—those hallowed by "classic" status—this aspect was from the start both basic and explicit in the later system with which we have to deal. The bamboo radical, for its part, serves as a constant reminder of the material aspect of the oracular procedure.

Apart from all the general accounts of oracle-consultation in temples, a few extracts from sequences in use in twentieth-century mainland China have been published. In an attractively illustrated work on the various sorts of mantic and prophetic texts current in China, the philologist Ishiyama Fukuji, known for his excellent dictionary of Chinese, reproduced nine slips from a *Chung-shen ling-ch'ien* sequence. He also adduces, for purposes of comparison, three pages from different Japanese recensions of the Ganzan oracle, two of them illustrated.[5] The Chinese example is not illustrated, nor are its verses those of the Ganzan sequence. Is its Chung-shen the eponymous god of Nanking's Chung-shan, previously North Mountain, celebrated in early medieval song and story? Ishiyama regrettably gives no indication of provenance.[6]

The great folklorist Nagao Ryūzō amassed a collection which would have been a prime wonder of the traditional Chinese world, had it only survived the war. (Only volumes one, two, and six were published, out of a projected thirteen). Here Nagao has given us one set from a sequence in use in the thirties at the Kuan Ti temple in Peking. He provides a facsimile of the oracle's opening sheet, and a Japanese translation. He notes the temple's popularity, and also that it was an important repository of moral tracts, or "books on goodness" (*shan shu*), an observation worth remembering.[7]

Oracles of this sort were often, though by no means exclusively, connected with the prognosis of disease. For example, a set of a hundred numbered bamboo sticks was to be found before the image of Sun Ssu-mo in the Temple of the Eastern Peak in Peking, on an altar devoted to the great healers of classical tradition: Hua T'o, Pien Ch'üeh, Chang Chung-ching. The oracle was consulted on matters related to illness and on other affairs as well. Anne Swann Goodrich has translated or paraphrased after a fashion three responses from the sequence: nos. 83, 73, and 71.[8] They are chiefly noteworthy for the unrelieved mundanity of their preoccupations.

A more highly specialized form of oracular lots is still to be found in some temples of Taiwan, Hong Kong, and Southeast Asia: "pharmacological oracles" (*yao-ch'ien*). In these, poetry has entirely ceded to pharmacy; each printed paper slip in the numbered series contains a prescription rather than a quatrain. The querent seeks them in the same formal manner as the verse oracles, with incense, paper money, and other offerings and preliminary invocations and prayers. Subsequently, confirmation of the slip is obtained by means of the divining blocks. Yoshimoto Shōji collected examples of medicinal sequences from two temples in Taiwan, the Ch'ao-t'ien kung in Pei-kang and the Nan K'un-shen miao's Tai-t'ien fu, Tainan. Temples offering oracular pharmacology of this sort necessarily provide a choice of specialized sequences. At the Ch'ao-t'ien kung, Yoshimoto found a sequence of 120 answers "for adults" (*ta-jen k'o*), a 60-answer "pediatric" sequence (*hsiao-erh k'o*), and an ophthalmological sequence of 84 slips (*yen-k'o*). The Tai-t'ien fu likewise furnished three sequences; the most general one, 120 slips, is there entitled simply "pharmacological oracles" (*yao-ch'ien*). Also available were pharmacological oracles for children (*hsiao-erh yao-ch'ien*), 60 slips, and "pharmacological oracles: ophthalmology" (*yen-k'o yao-ch'ien*), 91 slips. Yoshimoto notes that the prescriptions make use of native Taiwanese medicinals, as well as a specialized local or regional terminology.[9]

In our own time, then, the practice can still be found wherever Chinese have settled. On the mainland, until recently such oracles were firmly ensconced at the metropolitan center of Chinese culture. They were also omnipresent on the periphery, whence they radiated wisdom and a mantic model beyond China's borders. Their diffusion took on a new dimension when they came to form part of Chinese language training for foreigners. In 1872, C. F. R. Allen translated two oracles from Foochow for Justus Doolittle's *Vocabulary and Hand-Book of the Chinese Language*.[10] Despite this early advantage, we have been slow to assimilate the lesson.

MODERN STUDIES, EDITIONS, AND TRANSLATIONS

A thorough search would doubtlessly turn up additional examples, but even this arbitrary and selective survey indicates the remarkable ubiquity of the system. It appears to be virtually coextensive with Chinese culture and its influence. Yet despite its omnipresence, it has only just begun to be studied. Too trivial to arrest the attention of the philologist or historian, yet, paradoxically, too literary to interest the anthropologist, the printed verse oracle appeared forever doomed to languish in that vast no man's land that harbors the bulk of Chinese traditional culture. Wolfram Eberhard characteristically rescued this forgotten genre. His 1965 article "Orakel und Theater in China" is a terse yet thorough account of the phenomenon, based on a broad survey of examples.[1] Eberhard remarked on the wide diffusion of certain oracles. He also noted the considerable variation in prosody exhibited by the genre as a whole, as well as the different lengths of various sequences. There were sequences of 24, 28, 32, 50, 60, 100, and 200 stanzas, and oracles with five-syllable verses, and others with seven syllables. He found that many seemingly unrelated sequences—even those differing markedly in extent and versification—proved on closer scrutiny to be cognate.

Beyond this valuable survey of this material, Eberhard recorded another discovery. Certain sequences regularly include mentions of persons and their deeds, either historical or legendary. Eberhard showed that these allusive phrases refer to plays, of the sort regularly given in the past throughout town and country China. The supplicant before the oracle was presumably well acquainted with this extensive stock of dramatized lore and legend; the oracular allusion will bring the story to her mind, illumine her own situation, and thereby make her choice of action clear. Eberhard concluded that the extensive corpus of plays, evidently known intimately to the ordinary Chinese, were viewed inter alia as guides to right conduct, and that the values expressed were generally shared and accepted.[2]

Elsewhere, in studying the question of fatalism in traditional China, Eberhard called attention to the special character of those oracle texts which immediately set the inquirer in a preexisting historical situation. Action by analogy, through historical example, seems a remarkable feature of so common a system of divination, and must say something about the essential unity of Chinese culture.[3] Despite the potential importance of these findings, there was no sequel to Eberhard's work on oracles until 1976. Then, however, the reverberation was a resounding one.

It was in 1976 that Werner Banck published *Das chinesische Tempel-orakel.*[4] This volume of 1131 pages contains the complete texts, in facsimile, of fifty-five oracle sequences. These represent only a small selection, Banck tells us, from the vast number of oracles that he has collected from Taiwan, Hong Kong, Macao, Singapore, and from Chinese communities in Korea, Southeast Asia, and the United States. In his introduction, Banck stresses the need for more research on this form of divination, which he sees as the last offshoot of the *I-ching* tradition. He remarks that oracular verses are frequently cited in literature, apparently from the Five Dynasties period on, and emphasizes the importance of the sequences for the study of social, literary, and religious history as well as for linguistic analysis.

Simply by providing so many sequences in full, Banck made an outstanding contribution to the study of traditional literature and divination. Most of the fifty-five oracles emanate from Taiwan (including one sequence from Quemoy and another from the Pescadores). Three come from Hong Kong, one from Macao, one from Penang, one from Thailand, and one from Marysville, California. They range in length from 18 to 100 stanzas, as given in Table 1.

The predominance of 60 and 100 stanzas was to be anticipated; some of the other sequences may be incomplete (those with 37 and 57 responses, for

TABLE I   Banck's oracular sequences.

No. of stanzas	No. of sequences	No. of stanzas	No. of sequences
18	1	50	3
24	1	56	1
28	8	57	1
30	2	60	12
32	6	64	3
36	2	81	1
37	1	90	1
48	1	100	11

example). The majority of the oracles are in seven-syllable verse, but sixteen are in lines of five syllables. Even a rapid perusal of the material suggests that oracular authors made very full use of what might appear, at first glance, a tightly constraining poetic form.

We cannot yet allow ourselves to delve deeply into this trove, since our center of gravity lies elsewhere, in the early Middle Ages. Still, we may demonstrate the value of Banck's collection by making use of it to round off, to some extent, our preliminary survey of resources. There is not as yet a comparable assemblage of Japanese material from Buddhist temples and Shintō shrines, though such a collection should certainly be made and published. We do have, as noted, at least two Japanese sequences in widely diffused booklet form. Our first question might now naturally concern their provenance, as well as their place in the pan-Asiatic corpus of oracular poetics. As we have seen, one is attributed to Ingen Daishi, a Chinese Ch'an patriarch from Fukien, transplanted to Japan in 1654. The other claims to have been imported by a tenth-century Japanese Tendai saint. Both, then, circulate under Buddhist auspices. Is this of significance with regard to their possible Chinese prototypes? Can the Ingen sequence be traced back to Fukien? And was the other, the Ganzan sequence, truly brought from the continent in the tenth century?

Banck's compendium supplies the relevant evidence. One of the Japanese sequences ushers forth an interesting problem involving the composition of the oracular genre. The sequence attributed to Ingen is, first of all, not nearly so widely diffused as the other in Japan. Second, it is attributed to a figure whose lineal Dharma descendants still carry on his traditions in Kyoto and

Nagasaki. The Ōbaku lineage that he implanted in early Tokugawa Japan was closely associated with the history of printing, notably with the first Japanese printing of a full Tripiṭaka. It was also a conspicuous agent for the transmission and diffusion of Chinese vernacular literature, as well as Buddhist scriptures and tracts. All this might confer a particular significance upon an oracle transmitted under Ōbaku lineage auspices, and the sequence in question is marked by its rather special form: it comprises only thirty-two sets of verses, quatrains in lines of five syllables.

Banck's collection contains no oracle identical with the Ingen booklets. But two of his sequences are sufficiently close to warrant comparison. Both can be promptly identified in the mass of fifty-five oracles, since they share the same length and prosody:

Every verse has some element—words or images—shared among at least two, usually three, of the versions. They are, without question, closely cognate, and further study should reveal whether they all refer back to some common prototype, or if one of the three in fact represents the original version. Our Japanese sequence, at all events, has proved to belong to an extended Fukienese family.

Nine years after bringing out his initial collection, Banck published a second volume. It includes a complete annotated translation of one sequence, no. 3 in the earlier book, said to be the most perplexing and allusive oracle of all. Banck provides this integral rendering of a characteristic, widely diffused sequence to give the reader some notion of both the complexities of interpretation and the literary quality of such mantic verses. The remainder of the volume is given over to analyses of structure and content, in tabular form, based on a total of 161 oracular sequences in 852 specimens. Banck maintains that these tables, constituting the essence of his book, allow us to discern the underlying structure of temple oracles and to evaluate some 45,000 individual oracular answers. Finally, he analyzes the questions that were put to such oracles—insofar as certain sequences include a list of relevant questions (72 different sequences, in 402 specimens). The book is a remarkable application of scientific method to an all too often overlooked facet of Chinese daily life.[5]

The oracle attributed to Ingen illustrates the likely genesis of many sequences that may have come into being as free variations on earlier models. The three examples given above almost suggest a set of linked verses; except that the extreme closeness of many of the lines, their fidelity to prototype, indicates a less than normally ingenious will to diversify. Rather than recherché elaborations, the alternatives appear to be deliberate and heavy-handed attempts at stamping each new oracle with a specious individuality.

The Ingen sequence allows easy comparison and spotting of cognate versions owing to its distinctive number of stanzas: thirty-two, composed of quatrains of five-syllable verses. Banck 19 exhibits the same format, but is otherwise unrelated. It is clear that the oracular verses as a group draw upon a stock, perhaps quite extensive, of common imagery, but the initial task is obviously the isolation of subfamilies. For this work, already well begun by Eberhard, the number of responses in a sequence and their prosody provide an obvious first breakdown of the material—but these criteria can sometimes prove misleading. Within the initial Banck corpus, for example, sequence no. 2 (100 stanzas) is intimately related to 45 (60 stanzas). Our other Japanese example, the Ganzan Daishi sequence, will illustrate potential anomalies even more clearly.

Perusal of the Banck archive soon turns up a Chinese example of this celebrated Japanese oracle, Banck 23. Discovery of this sequence on Chinese soil might at first glance seem to authenticate a Chinese origin. But Taiwan, of course, is not ordinary Chinese soil. It was under Japanese domination from 1895 till 1945, and Japanese efforts to meddle with local customs are well known. With regard to Banck 23, other circumstances seemingly combine to weaken the hypothesis of a purely Chinese transmission. Banck collected his sequence from the Miao-hsin ssu, Taipei, in March 1973. He notes that this temple was founded sometime in the 1930s, and that it is dedicated to Śākyamuni. A Buddhist foundation, then, bearing the name of one of the most renowned Zen temples of Kyoto (the Myōshin-ji); examination of the foundation's history will doubtlessly confirm the unsavory circumstances of its origin—and hence, perhaps, the derivative and alien nature of its oracle.

Yet as it happens, whatever the temple's background and its oracle's immediate provenance, suspicion is ultimately groundless. Another Formosan member of Banck's collection also proves to be the Ganzan oracle, in altered form. Banck 22, from the eighteenth-century Feng-shan ssu in Lu-kang, is the identical hundred-stanza sequence, but in quatrains of seven- rather than five-syllable verse. The five-word originals have been deftly expanded, as the example of stanza no. 1 will reveal. Banck's hundred-set sequence from the Ma-tsu temple in Macao also shows affinities in its first stanza, but not, apparently, in the remainder (Banck 47):

Ganzan booklets, Japan, and Banck 23 (Taipei)	Banck 22 (Lu-kang)	Banck 47 (Macao)
七寶浮圖塔 高峯頂上安 衆人皆仰望 莫作等閒看	七層寶塔瑞光環 直照高峰頂上安 遠遠衆人皆仰望 休將俗眼一般看	千尺浮居寶塔成 高峰頂上立停停 時人莫作尋常看 不是神仙難解登

Note the giveaway seven-jeweled (or, seven-storey jeweled) pagoda that rears up tellingly in the opening verse. Many other oracles start out as portentously. Some evoke the emerging sun (Banck 1, 8, 27), others the moon, spring (opening of the year), wealth, blessings, goodness, health, longevity, immortals—all generic good omens. Particularly striking are those that refer to the oracle itself. A few state the obvious: "You have sought the oracle, and obtained the first slip" (54), (35); "You have made divination and obtained the oracle's chief; all manner of things shall be well" (16). Most incisive of all: "This oracle has fallen to the ground and separates Yin and Yang" (97)—from a Kuan Ti temple. Only two other sequences in the Banck volume have openings as explicitly Buddhist as the pagoda-dominated Ganzan oracle: "Ten myriads of Buddha's Law, self-luminous and numinous" (24), from Taipei, and Penang's contribution: "When his sixteen-foot gold body appeared in the world" (48). Yet we must note that the pronounced Indianizing tone is not maintained in any of these sequences, including the Ganzan Daishi oracle—despite the will to Buddhist affiliation, which they all proclaim in their dramatic opening verses.

As both Eberhard and Banck have remarked, the early history of printed oracles in verse is linked with Buddhism. The most precocious surviving example of printed oracle slips is the hundred-set *T'ien-chu ling-ch'ien* sequence. Cheng Chen-t'o has published it in his *Chung-kuo ku-tai pan-hua ts'ung-k'an* (Shanghai: Ku-tien wen-hsüeh, 1958). Cheng dates it to the middle of the thirteenth century. I would suppose that the T'ien-chu of its title connects this oracle less with India than with the famous monasteries of that name, near Hangchow. *The Chronicle of the Buddhas and Patriarchs* (*Fo-tsu t'ung-chi*, completed 1269) lists three sequences of oracular verse already current in its time: the *Oracles of the Great Being* (Kuan-yin, Avalokiteśvara:), the *Hundred Oracles of T'ien-chu*, and the *Hundred Thirty Oracles of Yüan-t'ung in Yüeh*. "They are used to determine good or ill fortune; they respond like an echo. It is said that they were transmitted by an incarnation of the Great Being."

The T'ien-chu oracle is noteworthy not only for its antiquity and its Buddhist provenance. Each of its mantic stanzas is accompanied by a prose explanation, and above the poem and its gloss stands a picture—the vigorous image of some vaguely analogous situation in human affairs, to which the prose explanation sometimes alludes. A common feature of Sung, Yüan, and Ming printed books, such running illustrations are also found in Japan. It is all the more significant, then, that the T'ien-chu oracle proves to be identical with the Japanese Ganzan sequence—Japan's most popular oracle, featuring a varied series of illustrations, and propagated in a Buddhist context (like the T'ien-chu oracle, under the patronage of Kuan-yin, of whom Ganzan

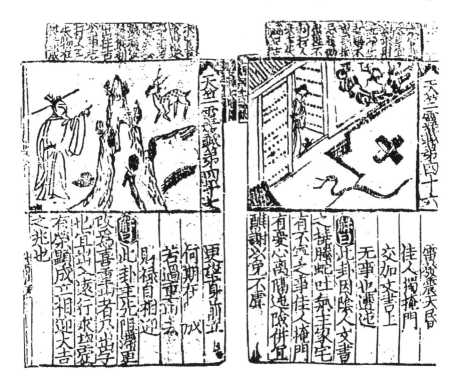

FIGURE 21. The T'ien-chu oracle: Response nos. 46 and 47 (cf. Figures 10, 16, and 17, above: The identical Ganzan Daishi oracle).

Daishi was supposed to have been an incarnation). Though it is improbable that the tenth-century Ganzan brought back this thirteenth-century oracle from a China he never visited, its antiquity cannot be disputed, nor the fact that its earliest attestation is in a Chinese Buddhist context.[6] Although there is nothing especially Buddhist in most of the poems, certain illustrations do reveal a monkish presence (Figures 21–23; the monk in action, Figure 22).

Banck's monumental work on verse oracles is a trove of well-ordered information, and will certainly guide all studies of the subject for years to come. Yet there is still ample room for research on individual oracles and oracular groups, or textual families. The present-day functions of such divination also deserve scrutiny, and have drawn the attention of various observers from diverse disciplines. A Taipei doctor, Jin Hsü, has contributed a psychological study of the practice, and does not hesitate to identify its "psychotherapeutic implications": "the giving of hope, the elimination of

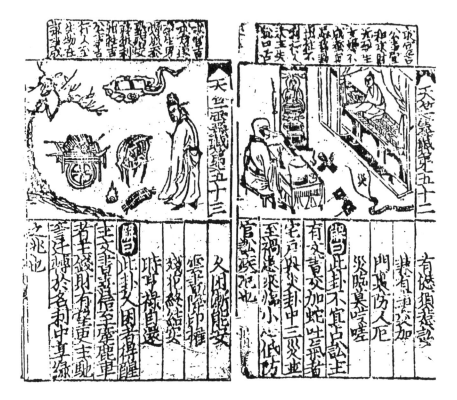

FIGURE 22. T'ien-chu oracle: Response nos. 52 and 53 (in 52, right, a monk performs a protective ritual).

anxiety, the strengthening of self-esteem, and the reinforcement of adaptive social behavior." Writing in an American volume on "ethnopsychiatry and alternative therapies," he does not surprise us when he finds the "placebo effect" to be an important factor. Hsü draws conclusions from his observations of mantic consultation, which he believes are applicable to "the theory and practice of modern psychotherapy in Taiwan." The Chinese expect authority figures to be authoritative. Temple oracles and their interpreters issue orders. Psychotherapists would be well advised to follow suit. Further, "the Chinese consider it rude to express emotions directly and openly and value subtle and symbolic ways of expression." The Western-trained therapist might profitably adapt himself to the Chinese symbolic world, exchanging one gnomic mode of mystification for another. Not for the first or last time, "research" on a Chinese phenomenon proves to be a ground plan for invasion.[7]

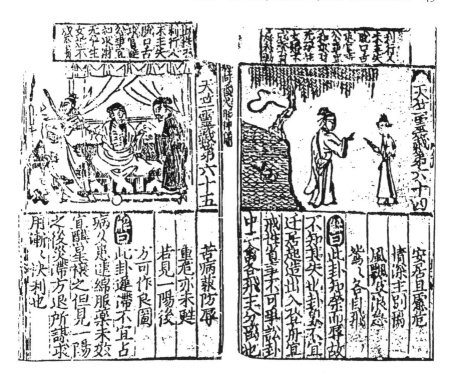

FIGURE 23.   T'ien-chou oracle: Response nos. 64 and 65 (in 65, left, an ailing man is examined by a physician).

Arthur Kleinman offers a more useful analysis of temple oracle consultation as fruitful interaction between the interpreter, stationed in the temple, and the client. He describes it as "probably the most widely resorted to form of talk therapy" in Taiwan. Kleinman provides information on the different methods of various interpreters, and gives several examples of client/intepreter dialogues. "The popular ideology holds, of course, that it is the written words, the characters on the *ch'ien* paper, that are effective. But as our examples disclose, it is the communication between *ch'ien* interpreter and client that is the chief psychosocial intervention and the main source of efficacy." Owing to the relatively informal character of client/interpreter exchanges, Kleinman finds that consultation of a temple oracle "is more like supportive psychotherapy than the other major indigenous treatment forms."[8] Whatever we may think of such analogies, there is good reason to ponder the dependence of the divine, immutable oracle on such fluid negotiations. Kleinman has demonstrated the present-day bonding of oral and written, and we would do well to remember these Taipei palavers as we try to plumb the oracular past.[9]

Such verse oracles are not restricted to a temple setting, though, and we can safely assume that some of those who consult them are prepared to read and apply them without outside help. As we have seen, written oracles also circulate in booklet form, and each poem is often accompanied by explanatory matter in prose. This is true of the most influential oracle in Hong Kong, also well represented among the Cantonese-speaking diaspora overseas. The oracle of Huang Ta-hsien, "Huang the Great Immortal," has been studied and translated by Carole Morgan. She focused on this single, widely diffused example as a straightforward means of illuminating the entire tangled genre.[10]

Morgan suggests a significant evolution between the older sequences and those created in modern times. In the earlier oracles, the interpretive commentaries grew directly out of the poems: the verses themselves were mantic. In a modern sequence like that of Huang the Great Immortal, "the quatrain loses its oracular power. It is often limited to the description of a landscape, of a feeling, of a meeting of friends, and so on, from which it would be impossible to draw an omen without the adjunction of another element."[11] The interpretations in the Huang Ta-hsien sequence, like many other modern oracles, depend on an historical vignette that serves as the allusive "title" for each stanza. "Le présage n'est plus dans le poème mais dans le titre."[12] The linkage between oracles and theater or storytelling, discovered by Wolfram Eberhard, was evidently forged sometime after the thirteenth century, and reflects the popular culture of more recent times.

Like many other mantic centers, the Hong Kong temple of Huang Ta-hsien is widely famed for its medical oracles—an entirely different collection, unconnected with the poetic/anecdotal responses, but accessible through the same set of hundred numbered sticks. In 1980 a clinic was opened within the temple compound, where the client in search of healing can go to get the divine prescription filled. Previously, the temple simply gave away herbal compounds based on the same oracular formulae. Morgan notes that the medical oracle comprised 500 slips, divided among five categories of 100 slips each. They are masculine ailments (*nan-k'o*), gynecology (*fu-k'o*), pediatrics (*yu-k'o*), ophthalmology (*yen-k'o*), and external ailments (*wai-k'o*). Apparently, none of these series is actually complete—quite apart from their failure to cover the full array of human ailments. Morgan cites the revealing example of a client with an earache who consulted the oracle, was given a slip from the ophthalmological series (the interpreter told her that ears, like eyes, were part of the head), protested, and after some negotiation was given a slip from the gynecological series in exchange. This she took to the adjacent clinic, and later pronounced herself content with the effect of the herbal compound she received.[13]

Morgan completes her study with a description of the "Diviner's Lane" that has grown up beside the temple. At the beginning of 1985, she found no fewer than 131 male and female diviners practicing their profession there—and this figure only includes those who are officially registered; there are others, as well. The government of Hong Kong place the 600 square meter area at the disposition of the Tung Wah Group of Hospitals, which oversees the facilities and receives monthly rents for the sixty-four cubicles (hallowed number!) occupied by the diviner. The demand for office space typically exceeds the supply. When the Tung Wah board receives applications for renewal of rental contracts, it first selects the most experienced and celebrated practitioners. The remainder are chosen, fittingly, by lot.[14]

Huang Ta-hsien and his oracle are also found in New York. An officially sponsored offshoot of the Hong Kong temple was established in New York's Chinatown in 1985. The mantic verses are featured there, and two interpreters are on hand to assist the clientele. The saint's cult and oracle are also on offer in a wretched Chinatown basement—an unauthorized manifestation, of which the official temple's director speaks with contempt.[15] Carole Morgan's study is the most complete so far on any Chinese temple oracle. It includes both contents and context, history and hagiography, and happily avoids excessive absorption in the merely textual or statistical, as well as the biases of specialized *partis pris*.

One other recent study must be mentioned. Julian Pas has investigated the temple oracles current in the city of Taichung. He begins by describing the visit of a large group of pilgrims from Taichung to the temple of the great goddess Ma-tsu, in Peikang. The divining sticks stand in a great marble cylinder, too heavy to lift: it is the sticks themselves that are shaken. From his sampling of oracles throughout Taiwan, Pas concluded that what he termed Ma-tsu's oracle (Banck I, no. 1; II, no. 90) is by far the most popular sequence. Second in frequency came what he called the Kuan Ti oracle (Banck I, no. 2; II, no. 124). Turning next to Taichung, Pas found the Ma-tsu oracle employed in three times as many temples as the Kuan Ti oracle, its closest competitor. The Kuan Ti sequence in turn proved to be more than three times as popular as any of the remaining nine oracles in use in Taichung. Of course, as Pas notes, the two preeminent sequences are not exclusively associated with Ma-tsu and Kuan Ti; they turn up in temples of all sorts. In his efforts to classify and correlate oracles and temple-types, Pas largely depended on the municipal registry of temples—possibly not the best source. It predicably furnished him with a classification of temples as Confucian, Taoist, or Buddhist.[16]

Since Wolfram Eberhard's pioneering article of 1965, research on Chinese temple oracle has gone forward along the lines of textual and literary history, anthropology, and "ethnomedical" study. My own concern is with social history and the comparative study of ritual. In order to compass work in this direction, it will be necessary to amplify our documentary base. Even Werner Banck's encyclopedic efforts have not exhausted the textual evidence, and I will now add two substantial bodies of material to the Banck's documentation. The first, a corpus of oracles from the Ming Dynasty's Taoist Canon (printed in 1445), will take us back to the early thirteenth century. The second, a Buddhist scripture, will carry the story still further back, to the middle of the fifth century.

NEW EVIDENCE: A CLUTCH
OF TAOIST ORACLES

It is customary to deplore the chaos of the Ming Taoist Canon (*Tao-tsang*), last of a long series of officially sponsored Taoist collections, and the only Tao-tsang to survive (alone among great dynasties, the Ch'ing, 1644–1912, compiled no Taoist Canon). Centuries of accretion have obscured the original classificatory schema of the earliest Taoist compendia, although the original categories persist in spite of huge literary expansion. It is true that anyone attempting to find the history of Taoism clearly mirrored in the Ming Canon's organization would be vexed indeed. Yet in addition to including many more dated and datable texts than Henri Maspero ever realized, the Tao-tsang does maintain a certain faithfulness to literary genre, if not to history. Scriptures are usually among scriptures, commentaries adjacent to commentaries, and books of rules largely lumped together—in or out of chronological sequence. Thus it is that we find, toward the end of this collection of nearly 1,500 separate works, seven texts coming one after the other, all of them collections of mantic verse. In the Harvard-Yenching Index's enumeration (HY), they are HY 1288 through 1294. In the enumeration of Kristofer Schipper's *Concordance* to Tao-tsang titles, they number 1298–1305. None include illustrations.[1]

Soon the Tao-tsang's tale of dark chaos and ancient night will be but a memory. Analysis and description are far advanced, under the direction of Kristofer Schipper, and a *Handbook of the Taoist Canon* is anticipated in the near future.[2] The Canon's hoard of mantic matter has been assigned to Marc Kalinowski, who will give a full account of these texts.[3] With this in mind, a superficial survey of the Taoist oracles should serve our purpose here.[4]

The first sequence, HY 1288, is the *Oracle of the Perfect Lords, the Four Sages* (*Ssu-sheng chen-chün ling-ch'ien*). It opens with a prefatory encomium, followed by brief instructions for its use. The oracle proper consists of forty-nine stanzas, each of twelve verses (three quatrains), in verse of seven syllables. The poems are numbered by star-names in series of seven: 魁魁魁 魁, and so on, up to seven; then 魁魁, and so on. Each set of verses bears an evaluation of auspiciousness plus a descriptive epithet in two or four characters. This is followed by a description of the stanza's practical application: to marriage, trade, moving house, lawsuits, and so on.

The Four Sages—T'ien-p'eng, T'ien-yu, I-sheng, and Chen-wu—enjoyed a flourishing cult during the Sung dynasty and afterwards. I-sheng and Chen-wu appeared early in the dynasty, to communicate advice and support to Sung emperors. The dynasty's premier anecdotalist, Hung Mai (1124–1203), often refers to their temples in his monumental *I-chien chih*, and their ferocious images still glower in liturgical paintings, as well.[5] The forty-nine responses of this Oracle of the Four Sages occupy just forty-nine folios in the modern reprint of the Tao-tsang.

The next sequence is the largest and most complex collection among all the Taoist examples. HY 1289, *Precious Oracles of the Transcendent Response of the Sublime Perfect One* (*Hsüan-chen ling-ying pao-ch'ien*), sprawls across three *chüan* or volumina, on a total of 109 1/2 folio pages. Its oracles are listed according to the twelve hours (two-hour periods) of the day, with thirty responses or stanzas to each hour (360 responses). These are topped off by a response for each of the five phases (*wu-hsing*), making a cosmic grand total of 365 responses. They are in quatrains of five-syllable verses, each typed by a four-word characterization and a tag for relative auspiciousness. Each is followed by an interpretation in prose.

All the evidence indicates that this oracle is associated with the cult of Wen-ch'ang, god of literary/official careerists, and the tradition of the *Ta-tung hsien-ching* (or *Immortals' Book of the Great Cavern*) which appeared in the western province of Szechuan during the Southern Sung. An informative preface describes the growing popularity of this genre of oracle at that time, and how it had come to supplant incubation or dream-contact with the god while sleeping in his temple.[6]

The third sequence offers us ninety-nine responses, quatrains of seven-syllable verse, each followed by a terse explanation (*chieh*). There is no separate grading by degree of auspiciousness, and the sequence extends through 22 1/4 folio pages. It is HY 1290, *Precious Oracles of the Transcendent Response of the Sage Mother, Primal Sovran, Guardian of the Alcove of the Nine Heavens, Most Kindly Fosteress of Life* (*Ta-tz'u hao-sheng chiu-t'ien wei-fang sheng-mu yüan-chün ling-ying pao-ch'ien*). The preface quotes HY 16, the *Precious Book of the Jade Pivot of the Nine Heavens* (*Chiu-t'ien yü-shu pao-ching*, thirteenth century) on the perils of offending one or another baleful star during sexual congress. The oracles are intended to counteract this and other comparable dangers. The influential Book of the Jade Pivot is mentioned again in the oracular text itself, and this life-saving, life-enhancing sequence is clearly in the current of that potent scripture, central to Taoism's so-called Southern School (*Nan-tsung*).[7]

Fourth comes HY 1291, *Oracles of the Perfect Lords of Transcendent Succour and Vast Benignity* (*Hung-en ling-chi chen-chün ling-ch'ien*). Its fifty-three quatrains of seven-syllable verse occupy a mere eight folios. Each is tagged for auspiciousness. Though the little booklet has neither preface nor commentary, its title links it with the cult of the Perfect Lords of Transcendent Succour, the deified tenth-century Brothers Hsü, who became respectively Supreme Monarch of the Golden Porte (Chin-ch'üeh shang-ti) and Supreme Monarch of the Jade Porte (Yü-ch'üeh shang-ti). Their cult was accorded official recognition in 1236. In the fifteenth century, a Peking temple was established in their honor, apparently by merchants from Foochow, where the cult originated.[8]

The fifth oracle issues from the same divine source. HY 1292, *Transcendent Oracles from the Hall of Infusing Life of the Perfect Lords of Transcendent Succour* (*Ling-chi chen-chün chu-sheng t'ang ling-ch'ien*), is a sequence of sixty-four responses, quatrains of seven-syllable verse, tagged by gradings of auspiciousness but without explanations, and is a slim ten folios. Was the Hall of Infusing Life a temple of the Hsü Brothers?

The sixth Taoist example is HY 1293, *Wish-Fulfilling Oracles that Uphold Heaven and Enhance the Sages* (*Fu-t'ien kuang-sheng ju-i ling-ch'ien*). It comprises 120 responses, quatrains of four-syllable verse. Each poem is followed by an interpretation (*chan*) and even an evaluation of auspiciousness; they fill 60 1/2 folio pages.[9]

With the seventh specimen, HY 1294, we encounter something special. It is a sequence of hundred responses, quatrains in verse of seven syllables, with no separate notations of auspiciousness [the title: *Oracles of the King of Chiang-tung, Guardian of the State and Auspicious Succour (Hu-kuo chia-chi Chiang-tung Wang ling-ch'ien)*]. Each set is followed by an explanation (*chieh*) and an Opinion of the Sage (*sheng-i*), extended through forty folios.

The key to this work's provenance is found in a brief text that immediately precedes it in the Canon, not separately numbered in the Harvard-Yenching Index but figuring as no. 1304 in Schipper's Concordance: *On the Transcendent Manifestation at the Temple of Sagely Succour in Kan-chou (Kan-chou Sheng-chi miao ling-chi li)*. In this Kiangsi temple, the King of Chiang-tung was the principal cult-figure—the divine hypostasis of a certain Shih Ku from the beginning of the Han. The text tells how one Fu Yeh from P'u-t'ien (Fukien) composed a sequence of 100 oracular poems (*chou-tz'u*) for use in the temple.[10] The immediately following oracle in the Tao-tsang also comprises a hundred responses, explicitly associated with the same cult, and thus is without doubt the sequence written by Fu Yeh. It is very rare to have the name of an oracle's author—or better, perhaps, its mortal scribe—since oracles all represent the works of a deity.[11] Fu Yeh is said to have accomplished his work sometime between 1225 and 1227, making this the earliest oracle of certain date and provenance of any we have so far examined. We shall presently consider other evidence for its critical importance in the history of the genre.

In 1607, a supplement to the Taoist Canon was printed. Among the works it added to the official corpus of Taoism was one more oracle: HY 1471, *Sage Appellation in One Hundred Characters of the Supreme Monarch of Heaven Sublime (Hsüan-t'ien shang-ti po-tzu sheng-hao)*. After a preface, this sequence runs to forty-nine responses, with ample commentary (55 1/2 folios). Each response consists of multiple sets of poems. First comes a quatrain in seven-syllable verse, evaluated for auspiciousness, and designated "Opinion of the Sage" (*sheng-i*). There follow, in each response, fully *seven* additional quatrains, each with a specialized application to some category of action or concern: projects, household, marriage, lost articles, official matters, travelers, prognosis for illness. Each response then concludes with an explanation in prose (*chieh*).

The title of the oracular sequence proper is given as "The Supreme Monarch of Heaven Sublime's Transcendent Oracles of Response" (*Hsüan-t'ien shang-ti kan-ying ling-ch'ien*). The preface contains an encomium of this deity, the Perfect Warrior (Chen-wu), attributed to the Sung emperor Jen-tsung (r. 1022–1063). The initial quatrain in each set of responses is virtually identical with the middle quatrain (that is, the second of three) in the Four Sages's oracle, first of the Tao-tsang cluster described above (HY 1288). From this and the identity of its divine patron, fourth of the quartet of Sages, it is clear that this oracle, too, presents itself as a pillar of national security. Its kernel, then, probably goes back to the Sung, whatever the date of the present recension.

The Taoist Canon thus offers us eight sequences of respectable antiquity, with which to trace the history of the genre and compare the oracles in use today. Even from this limited sampling, one gains a sense of the possibilities open to the enterprising poet/medium in the golden age of oracular verse. Each of the first seven oracles comprises a different number of responses; the first and eighth oracles both have forty-nine. We find totals of forty-nine, fifty-three, sixty-four, ninety-nine, one hundred, one hundred twenty, and three hundred sixty-five. Four sequences are constructed from quatrains of seven-syllable verse, and this remains the most common form today. One sequence is entirely composed of four-syllable verse (apparently an uncommon form nowadays), and another in quatrains of five-syllable verse. In addition to their evident genetic relationship, the first and eighth oracles are also in a sense allies in anomaly. The former deploys three quatrains of seven-syllable verse to make each set of responses. The latter strings out eight successive quatrains per response: a quatrain of oracle proper, followed by seven specialized but no less poetic and oracular applications to daily life. After such mantic effusion, it is not surprising that sequences one and eight should also have the smallest number of total responses (forty-nine).

The printing history of the Ming Taoist Canon suffices to establish that the first seven oracles were already in existence prior to 1445, and the eighth at least before 1607. These Taoist oracles trumpet forth their cultic associations. All represent the words of high deities, whose cults were very much on the move between the thirteenth and fifteenth centuries, and beyond. We may suppose, then, that the oracles were widely diffused. Turning to the texts reproduced in Werner Banck's first volume, we immediately note that the Taoist Canon's eighth oracle (in the 1607 supplement) is identical to the one currently employed at—of all places—Marysville, California, at the famous Bok Kai Temple (Banck I, no. 52). This means, too, that it is also the same as the second quatrain in the first Tao-tsang sequence, *the Oracle of the Four Sages*. Banck's slips from the Maryville temple bear only the oracular stanzas, not the commentaries and applications. But it is nearly word-for-word identical with the versions in the Taoist Canon, save for a certain degree of edulcoration. In response no. 49, for example, the rather derogatory "Yin-persons" has been replaced by "family members." Unlike the Taoist texts, the Marysville sequence includes a fiftieth quatrain. Designated as being for "the Dhyāna community" (*ch'an-men*: the Buddhist saṅgha), it was presumably for that reason either omitted from or never added to the Taoist recension.[12]

This point, minor though it may seem, evokes once more the question of Buddhist or Taoist origins for the oracles. More evidence will be needed before the question can even be properly framed. Meanwhile, there are spectacular findings when we compare the seventh Taoist sequence, *Oracles of the King of Chiang-tung* (HY 1294), with the materials assembled by Werner Banck.

The confident spirit with which this sequence sallies forth seems fully justified by subsequent events: "Loftily stepping solitary towards the clouds" (*wei-wei tu-pu hsiang yün-chien*). It is identical with oracle no. 2 in Banck's first volume, a sequence collected in 1974 at the K'ai-chi wu-miao in Tainan, a Kuan Ti Temple founded in 1669. It also clearly provided the basis for no. 45 in the same volume, from the Pescadores—a set of free variations, sixty responses in place of the original hundred. The first verse exemplifies the use made of the model: "Loftily high-soaring beyond the worthies' gate" (*wei-wei kao-sung ch'u hsien-kuan*). But this is only the beginning.

It soon becomes clear that the King of Chiang-tung's oracle has been even more widely disseminated. At the outset we mentioned sequences from Peking excerpted by Nagao Ryūzō (Kuan Ti Temple) and Anne Swann Goodrich (Temple of the Eastern Peak). Both prove to be the same oracle, as does the one that David Crockett Graham found being used in rural Szechuan.[13] The identical sequence serves the Eastern Temple in Seoul. It is also the oracle included in the popular, widely diffused Kuan Ti scripture, *the Kuan-ti ming-sheng chen-ching* (which includes directions for domestic consultations, 3.11a–18b). As anticipated, Banck's second volume gathers in a rich harvest. He has collected 123 different examples of this sequence from temples: one in Hong Kong, two in Kuala Lumpur, one hundred twenty in

Taiwan. He records eleven different editions in separate booklet form. They include an illustrated Japanese edition, *A Hundred Oracle-Slips for Instant Consultation* (*Sokkō hyakusen*), with a preface dated 1824, as well as a Mongolian translation published in 1808, *Explanations of Great Heaven's Divination-collection*. Banck also lists forty-four further appearances of the oracle, either as part of larger works (in ten different editions of the Kuan Ti scripture, for example, as well as in general mantic compendia) or as referred to in the writings of authors since the seventeenth century.[14]

This is obviously the Kuan Ti oracle *par excellence*, and enjoys all the prestige garnered by that deity, the God of War and protector of the nation under the Ch'ing. But it also reveals Kuan Ti's debt to his predecessors or earlier avatars, Chen-wu and Hsüan-t'ien shang-ti, whose cults he in time incorporated, thus drawing strength from a powerful current of imperial patronage that dates back to the very founding of the Sung. It is also significant that the materials preserved in the Taoist Canon enable us to identify the oracular prototype as coming into being in Kiangsi, by an author from nearby Fukien, in the first quarter of the thirteenth century. This is one more indication of the spiritual fecundity of the southeastern region from the Sung onwards. Sung developments in Fukien and Kiangsi exerted a decisive influence on subsequent religious life throughout China and beyond its borders—as clearly shown by this example, an oracle that might at first seem humble, but which in fact proves to be ennobled with a prime lineage and a vast progeny. [15]

Taoism and temple oracles were certainly linked by the early thirteenth century. The deities had spoken to Taoist initiates from the beginning; they had uttered words of encouragement and admonition, dictated poems, and brought down holy books filled with directives for ritual and rules for daily life. Among the rules, in the early medieval period, had been injunctions against fate-calculation and recourse to secular medicine. Yet the very taboos they propounded were often couched in the same terminology as secular almanacs and mantic systems: the sexagesimal cycle of time (which also designates space), the stars and planets, the five phases (*wu-hsing*) associated with them. After all, as Susan Naquin has said, Taoists are simply Chinese writ large. Thus when temple oracles came into fashion, the inspired customs of Taoists, for whom the heavens regularly opened, put them in a direct line to celestial intelligence.[16]

By the end of the eleventh century, there were already signs of Taoist mantic exuberance, using scriptural texts. Hsü Shou-hsin was the very model of a Taoist temple-menial: a withdrawn, taciturn sweeper who devoted himself single-mindedly to his humble tasks of cleansing. Yet somehow word got out that Hsü was gifted with extraordinary prowess in foretelling the future. His method was simplicity itself. To all questions he would respond with a four-syllable phrase from the *Book of Salvation* (*Ling-pao tu-jen ching*), which he had learnt by heart. He would provide this, it appears, in writing, and although (or because) the scripture-extract might be dark and difficult, it was always borne out by events. Like other Taoist holy fools before him, he had a great following during his lifetime and a considerable cult and hagiography after his death (in 1108). In the case of Hsü Shou-hsin, the oracular machinery was concentrated in a single person: a silent, Tao-struck mortal who had incorporated a sacred book.[17]

Twelfth-century bibliographies list, among Taoist works, an *Oracle-Slips of the Twelve Perfect Lords*, and it seems certain that this designates a Taoist sequence of the sort with which we are now familiar.[18] There is literary evidence that poetic oracles, obtained by drawing lots, were in use by the tenth century—though by no means necessarily in a specifically Taoist context.[19] The Taoist case can be provisionally wound up by mentioning two curious examples that seem to parallel, perhaps anticipate, the later oracles.

The Book of Spirit-Spells of the Abyss (*Tung-yüan shen-chou ching*) is one of the great scriptural monuments of medieval Taoism. It comprises twenty chapters (*chüan*); the first ten form the nucleus, and the earliest of them (and possibly all ten) date from the beginning of the fifth century. The remainder were added later, but all were presumably more or less in place by the tenth century, when the celebrated Szechuan Taoist author Tu Kuang-t'ing (ca. 850–933) codified the Abyssal (*tung-yüan*) corpus of scriptures and rituals.[20]

Chapter eighteen, then, may well be as late as the tenth century. It contains a set of sixty stanzas that foretell conditions, year by year, according to the progression of the sexagesimal cycle. Each stanza is composed of a number of five-syllable verses. Each of the first two years is described in eleven verses; years three through six, in seven verses; years seven through nine, in nine verses. The prophecy or universal almanac then pretty much settles into seven-verse stanzas, breaking out once more into nine (year no. 37), eleven (year no. 52), and nine again (year no. 59). A note of gloom prevails: conditions will on the whole be poor. The main focus is on agriculture and meteorology; different regions of China are named and contrasted. These dreary verses seem to have been inspired by the earlier, fifth-century chapters of the *Book of Spirit-Spells*, with their interminable predictions of ghastly demonic apparitions, epidemics, and other grim apocalyptic phenomena. I draw attention to this weatherwise sequence chiefly for its formal parallels with our temple oracles. Despite their irregular length, the stanzas are consecutively numbered, in rhyming verse, and distinctly prophetic. They also occur in a resolutely Taoist context.[21]

A last Taoist specimen is rather more puzzling. It issues from the heart of revelation: the earliest Chinese revelation about which we have solid historical facts. Most of the texts in the *Declarations of the Perfect Ones* (*Chen-kao*, HY 1060) date from 364 to 370; the great Taoist polymath T'ao Hung-ching (446–536) had assembled them in their present form and added a commentary by 499. The fourth-century texts were dictated to a visionary, Yang Hsi, by a bevy of Taoist deities: the perfect ones (*chen*) of the title. They include a good deal of high-spirited poetry.[22] The text I have in mind, though, is a good deal more gnomic and thorny than any of the work's other verses. It is a square block of language: twelve characters high and twelve broad, an impenetrable fortress of 144 characters, toward the end of the *Declarations'* eighth chapter (8.10b8–12a5).

The text is a prediction of troubles for the state, which no doubt explains its cryptographic form. Various impending astroanomalies will mean "distress for the ruler, sorrow for the Son of Heaven, and the Chief Minister's seat will be shaken." In commenting on these prefatory words, spoken by a spirit just before she dictated the prophecy, T'ao Hung-ching observed that the communication clearly referred to the fate of the then-reigning dynasty. He believed that the mantic poem had been dictated to Yang Hsi in a straightfoward, intelligible manner, but that Yang then scrambled it, for security reasons. Now, though, T'ao had disentangled what he claimed was the original structure, and it can be read as a lucid prophecy of the Chin dynasty's eventual collapse (a long drawn out process, formally concluded only in 420).

T'ao's reconstruction was obviously made by fishing out the rhyme words and piecing together the rest to match. He turned the hopeless word-mass into a reasonably suave poem of seven-syllable lines, of gloomy political portent. Already in the 360s, the perfect ones could see that there was a poor outlook for the Chin Dynasty. Using verse of seven syllables to reduce the 144 characters meant that four characters would be left over. T'ao has marshaled them at the end: *Chin shih tsai tzu* ("The House of Metal is at Hand"). This is a blatant reference to the Chin's successors, the reigning family of Liu (in which the graphic element "metal" is prominent) of the Sung dynasty (420–479). T'ao's reconstruction will either confirm our confidence in the prescience of the perfect ones, or awaken grave suspicions: of T'ao's poetic skills, or worse. He was, at all events, an ardent believer. The chief point for our study is that this ambivalent text is termed a *ch'an*, a portent-text or prophecy. The word is clearly allied to *ch'ien*, oracle or oracle slip.[23] Such dark mantic verses of political import are attested from the early years of the Chinese empire, and continued to flourish in the hands of official apologists as well as proscribed dissidents and pretenders. Here we find a "hot" text of this sort being sent down the ages in the bosom of a major Taoist document. Poetry and prophecy were integral to Taoism from early on.

NEW EVIDENCE: THE OLDEST BUDDHIST SEQUENCE

Until recently, the most ancient temple oracle known to have survived was the illustrated Buddhist *T'ien-chu ling-ch'ien* sequence, dated by Cheng Chen-t'o to the middle of the thirteenth century. The Taoists have now yielded up, in a fifteenth-century edition, a sequence dating from 1225 to 1227. These two early oracles prove to be of great importance in the later history of the genre. They are the prototypes of what may be the two most influential oracle families. Each continues to be prolifically represented in Taiwan and the greater Fukienese cultural area. Also, the T'ien-chu oracle is the source of the most widely diffused sequence in Buddhist Japan, the oracle of Ganzan Daishi. The Taoist oracle of the King of Chiang-tung has long been attributed to Kuan Ti himself, and so is second to none in breadth of diffusion. It is almost as if these two supereminent oracles divided the world between them, one appealing to a Buddhist public, the other to a clientele more appreciative of the civil and martial virtues embodied in later Taoism.

By the thirteenth century, printing was so widespread that it would have been natural to commit a new oracle to this medium, a medium that would vastly enlarge its dissemination. Printing was unquestionably a key factor in the Sung renaissance of religious life, at every level of society. Yet temple oracles existed before the Sung, and in handwritten form. There are tenth-century references, collected by Werner Banck, as well as several even older forms of divination which, though not attested in temple use, are very similar, probably even related, to our oracles.[1] None of these systems are Buddhist, or even particularly Taoist, so we are none the wiser concerning possible Buddhist prototypes of the strikingly illustrated T'ien-chu oracle, which appeared in print—clearly with a long tradition already behind it— around the year 1250. But Chinese Buddhist literature is vast and deep, and the Buddhist Canon contains a text that permits us to carry the tale back some 800 years before the T'ien-chu oracle was printed: into the depths of China's manuscript age.

The earliest example of a Buddhist oracle sequence can be dated to the middle of the fifth century. It forms the tenth chapter of the twelve-chapter *Book of Consecration (Kuan-ting ching,* T. 1331). Long supposed to be a translation of an Indian scripture made by the renowned Kuchean specialist in spells, Śrīmitra, in the first quarter of the fourth century, at Chienk'ang (modern Nanking), the *Book of Consecration* was in fact written and compiled in 457 by a Chinese monk, Hui-chien, working in the same region.[2] Spells are indeed the work's chief substance, and it is rightly classed by the Japanese compilers of the standard Sino-Japanese Buddhist Canon among the *dhāraṇī-sūtras,* proto-Tantric incantatory literature. Yet though it presents itself as a translation from Sanskrit and frequently draws on various Indian prototypes, it is a product of Chinese and not Indian Buddhism. It thus falls among the so-called apocryphal sūtras, a class of works long despised by specialists in Indian and Chinese Buddhism alike as being "false," "fabricated," "spurious," or "forged." "Dubious" (*i-ching*) is probably the kindest term in the arsenal of abuse directed by scholars and bibliographers against these scriptures. Yet despite their condemnation, it seems that such original Chinese Buddhist scriptures contain the charters for nearly all the Buddhist rituals and institutions that were to survive and spread throughout East Asia.[3]

In addition to circulating as a complete and bulky unit, each of the *Book of Consecration*'s twelve chapters was complete in itself: designed as an independent scripture which could be copied and disseminated independently. We find, for example, separate T'ang manuscript copies of the tenth chapter, which will concern us here, among the texts recovered from Tunhuang.[4] Its title is *Book of Consecration Expounded by the Buddha Concerning Brahmā's Spirit-Tablets (Fo-shuo kuan-ting Fan-t'ien shen-ts'e ching).* It opens in the Buddha's grand assembly, with its customary cast of thousands. Brahmā, a tame god from the Indian pantheon generally present on such occasions, comes forward with a special request. He tells the Buddha that all ninety-five "heretical" (that is, non-Buddhist) schools have their various arts for resolving doubts and arriving at decisions. Buddhists alone have no such useful techniques. It is for this reason that he, Brahmā, has composed a hundred stanzas to serve as "spirit-tablets" (*shen-ts'e*). He requests the Buddha's permission to present this new material to the community, and approval is readily granted. The Buddha terms Brahmā's production a canonical book, or scripture, of divination (*pu-ching*) and commends it to the four classes of disciples (monks, nuns, laymen, laywomen) as a means of resolving doubt and predicting good luck or misfortune.

There follow a hundred rhyming eight-line stanzas (really only 99 1/2, since the hundredth stanza is a quatrain, not an octave) of five-syllable verse. The book concludes with directions for their use. Each stanza is to be written on a separate slip of bamboo or strip of silk, and they are all to be carefully kept in a particolored silken pouch. Before consulting them, one should abstain from wine, meat, and the five sharp-flavored herbs, and should rinse one's mouth. The inquirer is then to select three slips from the pouch. He may in fact take as many as seven slips, until his hesitations regarding the subject of inquiry are quite resolved. Not more than seven persons are to consult the oracle at any one time, and should any of them later find that events do not turn out as predicted, they are not to speak of it (a nice touch!).[5]

The method propounded here differs from later temple oracles in being a direct, one-step process of selection. There are no numbered lots, one goes straight to the responses. What, then, is the true significance of this text? The framework—Brahmā's presentation and the Buddha's authorization—is on the face of it banal, the standard *mise-en-scène* of every Buddhist scripture. Such formulaic openings carry the content of the text they preface back to the time of the Buddha himself, to local conditions on the Buddha's familiar circuit of North India as viewed by later tradition. But our text is actually a revelation. Behind the studied, if superficial, Indianizing verisimilitude (a pseudohistorical fantasy rendered almost realistic by dint of ubiquity) we can readily discern the true otherwordly venue of the scripture's genesis. Brahmā is of course a god—but then, so is the Buddha, so are virtually all the members of his suite. That a *Chinese* author should here be setting in motion the time-honored mechanism of Buddhist revelation ought to put us at once on the alert. What is written on the spirit-tablets whose genesis is being thus awesomely evoked? We may wager that whatever it is, it comes from China, not India.[6]

Though the components of the sequence are not separately marked for degrees of auspiciousness, most are either clearly positive or negative in tone and implications. The dire and the favorable seem on the whole roughly equally balanced. Bland optimism appropriately echoes from the initial set:

> 1. If you have heard the Buddha's Book of Spells
>   The Hundred spectres all dissolve away.
>   Your home will be secure,
>   Local officials will not oppress you.
>   You will progress towards the Supreme Tao;
>   Brahmā will ever guard you.
>   In public office you will achieve high promotion
>   and from birth to birth attain a noble fame.

Enthusiasm could at times reach quite manic heights:

> 22. How glorious this felicity!
>   It will bring forth the phoenix!
>   For you the unicorn will be aroused,
>   And sagely kings come capering!
>   How rare! No peer in all the world!
>   The devas shower down flowers!
>   Just recompense for merit that is yours;
>   All undertakings will be happy and auspicious.

> 27. How great the strength of this person's felicity!
>   In all things he receives the god's protection.
>   All he desires shall be as he wishes,
>   Nothing not secure and safe.
>   Of a certainty, no dangers will impede him
>   And his fame will flow forth far and wide.
>   Spoken by the mouths of Śakra and Brahmā,
>   This means all happiness, without deception.

But Brahmā does not pull his punches when it comes to evildoers and the morally suspect. Imagine the man of troubled conscience who draws the following pronouncement:

> 3. In your previous life there was no felicity or kindness,
>   So you fell into sin.
>   You had no faith in the Three Treasures
>   And mocked and made light of the Hero of the World [the Buddha].

In your present existence you have therefore obtained suffering,
And so it will be until your life is done.
You have amassed sins equal to a mountain,
And the retribution for these acts will be truly endless.

In its probing of consciences, the oracle sometimes confronts the querent with the accusation direct:

33. The goods and chattels earlier entrusted to you
    You have never looked after properly.
    Why have you casually spoken deceitfully on this subject?
    In reality, you have lost more than a few piculs [of their value].
    Restore those goods and valuables;
    Then make scriptures as well as images,
    For if you continue to show a disrespectful attitude
    You will certainly fall straight into the snares of hell.

A number of the sets are cautionary, some attempting to dissuade the inquirer from a proposed dangerous course of action, and others issuing a more general warning to repent and reform:

5. It is likely this undertaking will not succeed;
   In the end, others will find it out.
   More than one person will suffer and die
   and the sorrow will last for months and years.
   It is all a device of devils' malefice
   and thus if you follow it, you will perish.
   If you can only focus your concern upon the Three Treasures
   You will have a chance to abandon these impurities.

Yet even the will to reform and to do the right thing is not enough, without conscientious persistence:

44. When one intends to worship the Three Treasures,
    Take refuge in Truth and forsake all malefice,
    If he is not entirely settled in his thoughts,
    The devilish maleficks all come in upon him.
    They assail him, doing all manner of untoward things,
    And disaster follows—there is no escape.
    Calamities and destruction come on day after day,
    And he is freighted with sins as many as Ganges sands.

Among the outwardly zealous, hypocrisy is an ever-present menace:

46. One claiming to have faith in the Tao and its Virtue,
    To exert spiritual zeal and hold himself in quietude,
    While in his heart maintaining untoward longings
    Will in his next life fall amidst hungry ghosts.

Despite the clear moral tone of most of the oracular observations, occasionally even a highly pessimistic set will stand out by reason of its seeming moral neutrality:

21. If you intend to dwell in this house
    It will be greatly disastrous—you cannot stop here.
    Your descendants all will fall away,
    Fires and catastrophes will rise upon all sides.
    In all things, evil will be manifest;
    Your cattle will all die of pestilence.
    Brahmā is telling you the truth:
    Only by moving can you find repose.

This seems a forceful vision of amoral *feng-shui*—or perhaps the negativity lies with the previous inhabitants, their residual evil still haunting the site. House and man might then simply be mismatched; all will go well elsewhere. Sometimes, though, a doomed and deadly abode will be just the right setting for one with little to commend him to oracular clemency:

31. You are an ill-omened person
    And so have been made to dwell in this place.
    In it are maleficent phantoms and demons
    Which are constantly coming and loitering.
    Your three *hun* and your seven *p'o*
    Are bound and fettered to a vacant mountain.
    You are in confusion and unsettled
    And in the end will fall into the deep abyss.

The metaphor of the human body as a mountain was already widely current at this period; in this case, the querent's body is dessicated and nonnuminous. The Abyss, in Taoist lore, was the abode of demons and unshriven ghosts.[7]

Many oracles which begin on a harsh, pessimistic note conclude with assurance of betterment, if only the querent will repent and reform. This happy dénouement is often deferred to the last couplet, forming a poetic equivalent of the deathbed conversion:

30. You have sown evil deeds, and so obtained misery
    And your entire family is ill and suffering.
    More than one person is afflicted;
    Well may you worry lest your line die out.
    All this is due to causes from previous lives,
    That have brought you to this peril.
    If you can only repent in your *present* life,
    Disasters and malefices will all be banished hence.

Among the most insidiously disquieting responses are those that detect the
Bad Seed at work:

> 28. You have several children;
>   Each has the five refractory evils,
>   They are creating ill-fortune and disaster for you,
>   And are constantly offending others.
>   The tumult they cause gives rise to sins;
>   Devils and phantoms repeatedly come and misbehave.
>   These illnesses are not to be cured by spells,
>   And you may as well throw away your drugs and decoctions.[8]

Might these "children" simply be metaphorical, perhaps standing for the
passions? One can only hope so. Yet our oracle was well aware that some
families are irredeemable:

> 40. In your household are ten persons.
>   They are rebellious and refractory, without change.
>   Their tongues are constantly set against each other
>   And the sound of their contentious voices never ends.
>   Your management of affairs has not been advantageous;
>   In nurturing them you have not been kind.
>   The evil that they harbour will never be extinguished,
>   And Brahmā therefore will not bless them.

For if children may do harm to their parents, the evil deeds of a parent have
the most direct and dire effect upon his children:

> 50. If father and mother do what is not good,
>   Many among their children and grandchildren will die.
>   At the very last they will give birth to a child
>   Whom in his turn someone will murder.
>   Thus they will languish alone, without support,
>   Weeping and sobbing, pained in their innards;
>   Steadily onwards the inauspicious comes,
>   And they will go on to meet more misery and disaster.

The uselessness of medical treatment against morally induced illness, just
seen in 28, is a theme found more than once:

> 62. In your household are many goods and possessions,
>   The cause of deception and recrimination.
>   Today you have caught a grave disease—
>   All this the result of doubts in a former life.
>   Drugs and decoctions are unable to affect it;
>   This disease cannot be treated,
>   Great and small are disordered, in confusion,
>   And none of the spirits are protecting you.

63. The plagues afflicting your six sorts of domestic animals
    Cannot be treated by human agency.
    All follow as requital for your own karma.
    For twisted words and deceptions,
    For disobedience to master and to father,
    And for forever entertaining doubts,
    You will go directly into the prisons of earth [hell]
    And stay there a million kalpas without emerging.

The good, though, are to be coddled and reassured—and sometimes a precise term is appointed for their due reward:

19. In the past you have shown kindness and compassion,
    "Cutting off your own mouth" to feed the starving.
    You have saved the lives of the old and emaciated,
    And given all of your strength in others' service.
    Since you have so devoted yourself to living beings,
    And succoured others, you are always poor.
    At last you are to obtain your happy reward:
    It will be next year, in the Spring.

No. 41 also promises favorable requital, in the form of high official promotion, in "the coming year," whilst 71 confidently predicts disaster within the same brief term.

In addition to the expected concern regarding illness and eventual rebirth, frequent allusions to trade and material wealth forcibly remind us that our text dates from the fifth century, when we also begin to find the first fully explicit evidence for Chinese Buddhism's "economic aspects." We have already observed what can be expected if one does not take proper care of others' investments (33). Some people, though, are karmically predisposed for profit:

38. You wish to trade in various goods:
    All that you undertake will prosper.
    You need only be zealous and diligent—
    Your goods will be just as you desire.
    Cattle, horses, pigs, sheep, dogs,
    All will increase and flourish.
    Demons of pestilence will obtain no ingress,
    For the Good Spirits are keeping your accounts.

The oracle's barnyard menagerie suggests an orientation more rural than urban, and the countryside, or native village, emerges favorably in the following counsel to a prodigal:

41. The sense of this oracle: here is a man;
    What is he doing among the rivers and lakes ["on the road"]?
    He should return to his own village,
    Where he will spontaneously attain high promotion.
    Though today he has still not attained it,
    It will of a certainty arrive next year.
    His whole family will be overjoyed;
    Then they will have faith in Brahmā.

As the concluding line suggests, our oracle is not above a bit of self-promotion, which we also find in some of its modern analogues.

32. In bearing and nurturing, all is success and fortune;
    Boy or girl, the child will be sharp and clever.
    God Brahmā expounds the spirit-tablets
    And devilish maleficks cannot come to be...

49. What you seek is blocked by many impediments.
    The illness from which you suffer cannot be cured.
    Day and night this causes you great sorrow,
    And you weep and sob like clouds and rain.
    The spirit-tablets bring you through the world's troubles,
    As has been authorized by God Brahmā.
    Fast, keep the precepts, attend the Law's assemblies
    And what your heart seeks will be all arranged.

55. If a person is consumed by great sorrow,
    It must be owing to his evil thoughts.
    On this account his goods will be dispersed,
    And all be lost as time goes on.
    The spirit-tablets expounded by God Brahmā
    Are entirely good, and have no doubtful auguries.
    In all three worlds they save the suffering,
    And release them from the eight directions' snares.

"God Brahmā has expounded the spirit-tablets/ They are entirely auspicious, and do not deceive" (93)—a sentiment echoed in the final verses of the entire sequence (100).

Brahmā's personal interest in the users of his oracle is indicated by the construction of an opening verse which is found in five sets; he expresses his "earnest worry" or "concern" (*nien*) for the subject of the ensuing rhymes—and so confirms that the oracle texts consistently present themselves as Brahmā's own words, enunciated in the Buddha's presence:

7. I am concerned for you, the young orphan,
   Hobbling to a noble gate.

35. I am concerned for you in this present life,
    Enlisted in the army.

69. I am ever concerned for the incriminated sinner—
    He will receive as recompense a curtailment of his life.

75. I am concerned for this person without understanding
    Who drinks poison in the hope of obtaining Life.

83. I am concerned for this deserted orphan,
    Who will spend his whole life in the army.

Prospective childbirth was mentioned in 32; discussion of marriage, a very common theme in many modern oracles, is also found:

66. Earlier, when you took a wife,
    You thought yourselves a pair of mandarin ducks.
    In harmonious union you established a household
    Which would surely endure safely a long time.
    Suddenly, in the middle of the road,
    You have begun to do one another harm.
    There is no truce to your wranglings and disputes,
    And your goods and chattels are also all dispersed.

Nos. 86 and 88 are highly cautionary with regard to marriage prospects.

Besides householders and merchants (or entrepreneurs), there are verses directed to those on military service:

35. I am concerned for you in this present life,
    Enlisted in the army.
    Your superior officers will look after you,
    And protect you there, from start to finish.
    When you enter the ranks of battle you will always obtain the victory,
    And your courage will certainly be rewarded.
    This is due to Brahmā's aid,
    Which strongly endures and never fails.

65. What is there to envy in the army?
    Weapons are all about your head.
    On every side you can see nothing,
    Only piles of human bones.
    Yet simply concentrate on the Tao and its Virtue,
    And what sorrows can then remain?
    You will return in safety to full security
    And your strenuous efforts will not have been in vain.

83. I am concerned for this deserted orphan
    Who will spend his whole life in the army.

Far separated from his old ancestral village,
Going this way and that, in pursuit of an alien wind [or, foreign customs]
Although he may be in other, far-off regions,
Brahmā and Śakra will nonetheless raise him up.
In time he will return to safety and security,
And his friends and kindred will all rejoice.

The orphan state is mentioned in no. 7, as well.

Ordinary society provides the oracle's basic theater of operations. A single set of verses addresses itself to one who turns his back on civilization and betakes himself into the mountains in quest of unusual *pharmaka*. If he but preserves total equanimity, leopards and wolves will give him a wide berth (94). Otherwise, for all their Buddhist piety, our oracle's clientele are assumed to be essentially wordlings. It comes then as no surprise to discover that official rank and promotion loomed large in importance. The very first response contains assurance of high official promotion; "high promotion" echoes no. 41, whilst "official appointment" (2, 7) also occurs with reference to the future careers of the querent's progeny (32, 97). These worldly ambitions are found elsewhere in the sequence formulated as "official emolument and office" (15), "status (or rank) and office" (76), "felicity and official emolument" (78), and "good fame and emolument" (10).

For those not so favored, however, local officialdom posed one of the most redoubtable threats. In keeping with other Buddhist prophylactic and therapeutic ritual texts of the period, our oracle guarantees to the good immunity from official interference and rapaciousness (a *locus communis* in the *dhāraṇī-sūtras* as a group, and found in the Indian prototypes). In the opening set of verses, we find the assurance that "local officials will not oppress you," and again in 79, "Only concern yourself with performing good deeds/ And take care not to carry out the five refractory acts./ Then, though the factotums may hale you in/ The prefectural officials will be unable to charge you." The despotic inclinations of these troublesome functionaries are thus frustrated in the cases of the pious. Yet it is precisely these local representatives of the secular order who are held up as chief bogeymen to the wayward and wicked. Should you be so rash as to make fun of a monk, for instance,

6. When you go out on the road you will meet an official
   And be bound up straightaway by his factotums.

The descendants of an apostate who abandons Buddhism to return to the "Way of Devils" (*mo tao*) will suffer greatly from illness and be constantly snared by officials (70), and disputes, especially those within the family, backbiting and slander, will bring disastrous interference from the same quarter (73, 87).

"Fortune and advantage," in good oracular style, are several times promised (2, 42, 53, 76); their absence is threatened in 50. As we have noted, riches and fame are also frequently at stake. There are three references to celestial ascent in one's next life: "mounting" either to the Hall of Heaven (*shang t'ien-t'ang*, 4, 87) or to the Palace of Heaven (*t'ien-kung*). Another set holds out the prospect of "being reborn from life to life among the people of heaven" (*t'ien-jen chung*; presumably devas, if not (either) among gods or men—which though by no means optimal in a canonical Buddhist schema is still a good deal better than some of the other possibilities; 14).

It will already be obvious that specifically Buddhist references abound, as befits the oracle's scriptural setting. Most frequent of all are mentions of the great ensemble of the Three Treasures (*san pao*): Buddha, Law (Dharma), and Community (Saṅgha). This triad one must have faith in (3), meditate on (5), take refuge in (12, 82, 90), revere and exalt (18), do obeisance to (26, 29), worship (39, 44), incline toward (78, 98), do homage to day and night (95). One should repent transgressions with reference to the Three Treasures (20), never fail to have faith in them (74), and never deride them (80).

Of the Three Treasures, the Buddha himself is most frequently named: once as "the Buddha" (Fo, 11), once as "Hero of the world" (*shih hsiung*, 3), and eight times as "the Perfect Awakened One" (*chen-chüeh*, 32, 37, 43, 54, 59, 67, 68, 72).

The second member of the trinity, the Buddha's Law, is to be regarded as pearls and jade (43, 51); one is to worship the True Law (*cheng fa, saddharma*, 53, 58, 93—accept no counterfeits). The wicked do not trust in the True Law (92), do not act in accordance with the Law (71).

As for the religious community, to make mock of monks results in a long series of disagreeable rebirths, rebirths in which one is seized by the intrusive, ever-eager local officials and their minions (6).

These functionaries are here characterized as willing agents of demonic powers—much as if secular officials and the bureaucracy of hell were to be seen as interchangeable, functioning as they do in comparable modes on a single terrestrial plane; "Why, this is hell, nor am I out of it."[9]

Apart from monks at large, though, our oracle places a special emphasis on respect for one's own teacher; in the context, it seems quite safe to assume that a Buddhist Master is intended.

57. Serve your Master in accordance with the Law;
    Speak no words of indolence or disrespect.
    Do not rebel against him, or treat him casually,
    Or curse him, or have doubts about him.

63. The disobedient man who goes against Master or father
    Will always harbour doubts and hesitations.

46. You state that you have faith in the Tao and its Virtue,
    And practice zealously, always maintaining yourself in quietude.
    Yet within your heart you cherish the inauspicious,
    And after this life you will fall among hungry ghosts.
    You curse and revile without rhyme or reason;
    You call your Master an old dotard.
    Transmit this to people in your future life:
    A Master's benevolence is not to be despised.

I may err in taking *tzu shou,* "maintain or preserve oneself," to refer to contemplative practice (as in the analogous Taoist *shou* + noun constructions: *shou i,* and so on; cf. 97). Other Buddhist technical terms, by no means numerous in these verses, are also found; none of them, nor their sum total, will have been beyond the ken of even modestly instructed laypersons. The *parlando* tone of the entire oracle is quite consistent with the other parts of the *Book of Consecration.* We come upon "The Supreme Tao" as the equivalent of *anuttarasaṃyaksaṃbodhi* (supreme and perfect Enlightenment)—a frequent adaptation (11, 38, 68). "Equanimous contemplation" is enjoined upon the observer of disparities between rich and poor (48), as are the "four equanimities" (*ssu teng, catur-apramāṇa*— kindness, pity, joy, and indifference) recommended to the seeker after medicinal herbs in 94. A single mention of *wu-wei,* "le non-agir" (10), reminds us that this hallowed term was early used to render the Sanskrit *nirvāṇa.* We also find among *termina technica* shared by medieval Buddhism with Taoism *chen cheng,* "the perfect and true" (= the Tao; 23, 61, 78, 89, 90). The hope of liberation (*mukti*) is also held out to the faithful (8, 20; from the snares of the eight directions, 55; from the sufferings of this present life, 59). *Wu-chang,* the important idea of the nonduration of perceived phenomena, is mentioned (26; also 45); the Spenserian theme of Mutabilitie also informs no. 88. The Six Perfections (*pāramitā, liu tu*) occur, 93; so does, separately, the "perfection" of patience or forbearance (*jen-ju, kṣānti,* 36). *Kleśa,* or "defilements" (*fan-nao*), also crop up frequently.

Of the ritual actions that the oracle enjoins, a number may be implicitly subsumed under the injunction to revere or incline oneself before the

Three Treasures. Otherwise, penitence and contrition are several times recommended. "Repent of your transgressions before the Three Treasures" (20);
"Repent of your transgressions and wash your evil heart" (58); "Repent in
this present life" (30); "Expiate and repent, and burn various sorts of incense" (4). Incense and flowers, the two basic offerings of Buddhist cult,
are explicitly mentioned in no. 26. Over and above these fundamental cultic
acts, no. 35 counsels the merit-producing activities of making or sponsoring
scriptures and images.

Among deeds performed outside a cultic setting, in society itself, the most
important is surely charitable donation. A deserving recipient will serve as a
"field" (*kṣetra*) in which you "sow" your own merit (*puṇya*) through gener-
ous donations:

> 24. If with equanimous heart you bestow largess (*shih*) on others,
>   You will achieve a recompense unlimited.
>   You will sow them in a field of merit (*fu-t'ien, puṇyakṣetra*)
>   And diminish and eliminate your own traces of Self.
>   In stinginess, grasping, covetousness, possessive desire,
>   You will stay home guarding your goods and die.
>   But bestow largess (*pu-shih*) and maintain the Pure Precepts (*ching-chieh*)
>   And from life to life you will emerge from karmic causality.

> 45. Goods and chattels cannot be preserved;
>   One never knows when they may be dispersed.
>   Covetousness and cherished jealousy
>   Will spell disaster for you, life after life.
>   If you are stingy and decline to bestow largess,
>   You will stay at home, guarding your chattels, and perish.
>   If you wish to avoid this path, do not act thus,
>   For such behaviour is what is termed "inauspicious."

Ample charity might even result in the donor's achieving the most coveted
status of Master or teacher, and becoming an exemplar to the entire community of the faithful:

> 25. You have a fine field of merit,
>   which will bring you fortune and honor hereafter;
>   It causes others to revere you even now;
>   How resplendent is your virtuous behaviour!
>   You stand out loftily, without compare,
>   A great Master within the multitude.
>   Your lifespan, too, will be greatly prolonged.
>   You are the equal of the host of saints (*chung sheng*).

The recipient of an oracle is also supposed to observe the precepts (*chieh*): "Only concern yourself with the scriptures and precepts/ And no devilish maleficks will be able to trouble you" (43); "This person exerts zealous spiritual effort/ And also maintains the precepts quite completely" (52). "If you carry out retreats, maintain the precepts and participate in ritual assemblies,/ You will obtain in due order all that your heart requires" (49). But "If you break off your retreat and offend against the scriptures and precepts,/ Your words constantly giving out ugly tones,/ And you are insolent to the spirits (*shen-ming*: a hapax in this oracular sequence)/ Their requital for your sins will be hard indeed to bear" (39).

The precepts intended are the five meant for lay devotees—injunctions against killing, stealing, debauchery, lying, and drunkenness, still something of a test of Buddhist commitment throughout Asia.[10] Emphasis on the Three Refuges (*san kuei*, homage to the Three Treasures) and the Five Precepts is characteristic of an entire body of fifth-century Chinese Buddhist literature directed toward the growing lay community. The *Book of Consecration* elsewhere discusses these basic requisites in a chapter significantly entitled "Spirit-spells of the Three Refuges and Five Precepts borne at the waist to protect one's person."[11]

It was the thesis of this Buddho-Taoist, proto-Tantric compilation that acceptance of the Refuges and Precepts by a lay disciple also involved the infusion into that person's body of a cohort of protective spirits—exactly as was the case with the contemporary transmission of talismanic spirit-registers (*lu*) within the Taoist communion. These guardian "spirits of the precepts" (*chieh shen*) are mentioned in the oracle: "The spirits of the Three Refuges and Five Precepts/ Of them there are thirty-six./ They always follow and protect you,/ So that you will not be humiliated in what you undertake" (52). "If you practice good actions without forming evil predestination (*yüan*)/ The spirits of the precepts always protect and guard you" (93). "You have obtained the good, with no evil karma (*yüan*)./ The spirits of the precepts always protect and guard you" (100). In fact, we know from Book Three of the scripture that the thirty-six spirits were, duodecimally, attached to the Three Refuges; their uncouth names are listed there.

The spirits of the precepts properly speaking were twenty-five in number, and are named directly afterwards. They are called there the "good spirits" (*shan shen*)—a designation that also occurs in the oracle. In the oracle, their protective role is alluded to on five occasions; they will protect the good and all their possessions in all circumstances, at home and abroad (38, 43, 77, 87, 94). The other guardian spirits named throughout the sequence are the high gods Brahmā and Indra. Brahmā, the oracle's enunciator, is mentioned with fitting frequency in no less than twenty-two verses, as protecting, sustaining, predicting, and feeling concern. In eight of these he is joined by Śakra Devendra, alias Indra, King of the Gods, who only merits one independent mention on his own (4). We find a single reference to another divine instance, the spirit-mother(s), or divine mother(s): "The spirit-mothers will grant your desire,/ All that you undertake will be as you wish" (76). Might these goddesses be the same as the two "spirit-generals" mothers mentioned in the *Book of Consecration*'s eighth chapter? We have already encountered the "host of saints" (*chung sheng*)—one way of referring to the community of monks, but also possibly intending arhats or bodhisattvas (25, 68, 84, 98).

We are prepared to find that actions performed in previous lives are regularly adduced to explain present misery or happiness. Sins of all sorts "result from causes in previous existences" (8); "causes in prior existences" bring one into peril in this present life (30). One is inextricably bound up in the consequences of misdeeds performed in previous lives (*su shen*, 96); one must now make restitution for sins committed in previous lives (*su tsui*, 96, 99); one's present wealth or poverty result from previous lives (*su ming*, 48); every current action is still determined by residual karmic causes (*yü yin*, 61); and—apparently much more rarely—all the good things coming to you and your descendants are the consequence of benevolent acts performed in previous existences (47). Karmic recompense ("reciprocation of deeds," *yeh pao*) is mentioned (34, 90); *yeh-yüan pao* (63); *thoughts* and actions are both accountable (34, 90). An awareness of one's own previous lives (when all the present and future was determined) is among the boons promised to recipients of no. 64.

Most commonly adduced among evil deeds are the Five Refractory Acts (*wu ni*, *pañcānantariyāṇi*): parricide, matricide, killing an arhat, shedding the blood of a Buddha, destroying the harmony of the Saṅgha. There are variations on this list, but the importance of the term has given it a place in nine mantic stanzas (13, 28, 34, 36, 40 (var.), 61, 79, 81, 92). It is twice associated with cheating or deceiving one's father (34, 36). Next most frequently mentioned among sinful deeds is the taking of life (*sha sheng*, 54, 56, 64, 74). Other references specify that this reprehensible act takes place in conjunction with the worship of demons—the slaughter is that of sacrificial animals (69,

75). Like their Taoist confrères, Buddhist monks found this crime doubly detestable. The pollution incurred by murder was bad enough; that it should be done in the service of the pagan gods heaped insult on injury.[12]

"One who practices the Five Refractory Acts will be childless. One who sacrifices to the gods of this world may go to all ten ends of the earth, but he will still not obtain what he desires" (81). Like all the Buddhist and Taoist sources of its time, the oracle is quite explicit on the futility of offerings to the ordinary Chinese pantheon, who are in reality spirits of the dead, not *true* gods at all. *Extra ecclesiam nulla salus*—far from responding favorably to your prayers, these untoward spirits are themselves the active agents of disease and misfortune. The oracle's demonology is straightforward and uncompromising. For if you are imprudent enough to have left yourself karmically open to attack, there are several classes of ill-omened beings that will lose no time in taking advantage of your vulnerability.[13]

First in line are the māras, or devils (*mo*); under the ultimate leadership of their chief, Māra himself, they are often described as a host of devils (*chung mo* 43, 75, 76); they may test or tempt you (*shih*, 69).[14] If your spiritual concentration is sufficiently great, you will never enter the devils' grove (97). The supplicant is berated for assisting "the little māras" (48). And, connected as these devils are with a Buddhist interpretation of local Chinese cults, the reader is warned against acting as a "devil Master, teaching people to slay living beings" (12). The backslider who abandons Buddhism to take refuge once more in the Tao of Devils is courting ineluctable disaster (70).

The māras are also found in conjunction with other comparable demonic agencies, such as phantoms (*mei*)—"devils and phantoms" (or devilish phantoms) occur (28, 81). Independent *mei*, or bands of *mei*, are not unknown (18; sacrifice to the hundred *mei*, 20). Devils match with demons or spectres (*kuei*; *mo-kuei*, 78; observing retreats and keeping the precepts destroys devils and spectres, 93) . . . and *kuei* mix with *mei* (59). But are any of these quite so ubiquitously troublesome as the *hsieh*?

Hsieh, maleficium or "wraiths," is also a term that applies equally to the human and the spectral worlds, to pathology and demonology and even to theology. The *hsieh*, maleficks, are insidious pathogens that manifest in a wide spectrum of disease symptoms. They are closely linked to the māras (*mo hsieh*, 5, 18, 43, 44, 59), and there are even persons whose Buddhist resolution is so feeble that "in their delusion they put their trust in devils and maleficks" (20). Brahmā's exposition of the present oracle keeps devils and maleficks from being born (32). If you make fun of monks, the maleficks will seize you (6). A baleful house is infested with maleficks, phantoms, and spectres (31); effective repentance in this present life will drive away all the calamitous maleficks that have been afflicting you (30).

All these reflect good native Chinese usage, for *hsieh* were presumably around before Buddhism arrived in China's green and pleasant land. It is significant, though, that this term (the opposite of *cheng*) should have been chosen to express Buddhist conceptions of heresy or heterodoxy. The resulting expressions are rich in pathological implications. In our oracles we come across the common *hsieh chien*, for which "perverse views" is a standard translation. Also found are malefick reflections (90) and malefick heart (69, 90; "Your malefick heart pursues untoward practice," 61). Malefick actions (80) cover a host of sins against the Three Treasures. The malefick spectres in whom he puts his trust will be unable to help the miscreant (12), and the reader is warned not to have faith in malefick masters (37), for they delude their victims and slay living beings (54).[15]

Who or what else remains in the demonic casting-studio? There are pestilent envenomizations (4) and pestilential spectres (38). Twice are mentioned "evil dreaming-awakenings," which I believe designates disturbing oneiric visions of one's own deceased ancestors; they are mentioned as well in the Shang-ch'ing documents, and in the medical literature; perhaps the ancestor prophesies ill.[16]

We have already seen that malefactors can expect medicines to be quite ineffectual against their own well-merited diseases; similarly, they are twice informed that when calamity comes there will be no way to buy it off, or make a deposit on credit against just retribution (44, 71). Doubts in the omniscience of the Buddha or the efficacy of his Law were, as we have seen, culpable in themselves, and might easily lead to ill-omened apostasy. But any form of mental distress is potentially perilous, as it distracts you from mindfulness of the ultimate Goal and makes you weak-willed, hence more vulnerable to pathogenic agents (49, 55, 91).

And sorrowful indeed was the fate of one who exited his present life under any of these inauspicious conditions. There were the prisons of earth, the hells, for him to fall into (16, 20, 61), enter at death (39), enter "forever" (63), wander back and forth in (13), in an "earth-prison body [= life]" (8). The evildoer enters the dark invisible world (12), falls into the deep abyss (31), falls into the snare (33), falls among hungry ghosts (46). The good, however, are reassured that *they* will not enter the hells (39).

Apart from rebirth into one of the hells (and there is no mention of any of their picturesque tortures, though these were already known in China), other disagreeable incarnations might lie in store. Rebirth as a slave signified that you had defaulted on a debt in a prior life, which you were fated to repay by this means (96). An unregenerate practitioner of evil is told that he will be reborn as an animal (92). A thief is promised the same retribution, to redeem in the barnyard sins committed in a previous existence; he may also anticipate a whole series of rebirths with no freedom, his body covered with shackles (99). An especially vivid response addresses itself to one who will die by drowning and join the entourage of the Lord of the River (Ho-po). The misery will be hard to bear, and he will demand all sorts of offerings from his surviving family, thereby contributing to their utter ruin (60).[17]

Many theories have been devised to account for divination and to rationalize the effect which it supposedly has upon its users—an effect apparently great enough to justify the expenditure of time and money and perpetuate the oracular genre. The theoreticians often sound the leitmotif of "reassurance"; it is frequently suggested that the set procedure and often oblique responses somehow serve to bolster morale, confirm the querent in a projected course of action, or simply ratify views or intuitions that the querent already holds. We have already sampled the views of certain anthropologists, psychologists, and medical anthropologists, and a much larger florilegium could easily be gathered. The sociologist C. K. Yang also emphasizes the consoling function of temple oracles, and seems to make even greater claims than many other scholars for their psychosomatic efficacy: "Through divination, the Confucian doctrine gave therapeutic assistance to minds in distress."[18] After close examination of this fifth-century oracle, it should be amply clear that such simple rationalizations are relevant, if at all, to only a small portion of its contents. The forthright, outspoken nature of many of these "spirit-tablets" hardly accords with the childish psychologizing of many social pseudoscientists. For a better understanding of the oracle's significance, we will have to attempt to view it in the context of medieval social history.

7

LA TRAHISON DES CLÉROMANES: DIVINATION IN A BUDDHIST SETTING

Brahmā's oracle has made it possible to carry the origins of the mantic sequence back some 500 years from the earliest literary references cited by Banck, and fully 800 years prior to the *T'ien-chu ling-ch'ien* of ca. 1250. Moreover, we have found these precocious stanzas in the legitimizing context of a Buddhist scripture. In one sense this confirms a Buddhist prehistory for the oracle as we know it—but it also indicates a prior existence in other milieux. The *Book of Consecration* was intended as a comprehensive vade-mecum for the Last Age of the Dharma. Hence, many practices presumably already common throughout the Lower Yangtse region first make a formal appearance in its uninhibited pages, and in adapting, for example, certain Taoist rituals, the scripture's compiler often notes particulars of practice that even Taoist authors have failed to record.[1] If the oracle first appears in this book, it is surely because such oracles already flourished in the outside world.

We have more than its antiquity and intrinsic interest to justify the detail we have lavished on this oracle's contents. We have already found evidence for the transmission of such sequences in a Buddhist context, from the Sung down to the present day. It is remarkable, however, that of the oracles now circulating under Buddhist auspices, whether in areas of Chinese culture or in Japan, none are particularly "Buddhist" with respect to content. This is true even of the T'ien-chu Monastery's influential thirteenth-century exemplar, for all the panache of its opening sequence. That sequence and all its "Buddhist" fellows are singularly devoid of Buddhist technical terms or allusions to doctrine, and the ethical systems they embody are general, not sectarian, in tone. By contrast, our scrutiny of Brahmā's fifth-century oracle has shown that it is thoroughly rooted in the lay Buddhist movement of its time. Its stanzas hymn the moral drama of mankind and demons, the Buddhist vision of the Good Life and its dreadful antithesis. The Buddha's own voice speaks in each response uttered by his mouthpiece, Brahmā. How did this Chinese creation mesh with the practice of Buddhism in the fifth century? And what are the links between this innately spiritual fifth-century oracle and the Sung exemplars, which in their comparatively bland generality herald—and in two cases, at least, have actually become—the oracles of modern times?

It might at first seem odd that a Buddhist source of the early medieval period should be fostering a Chinese divination system. Theoretically, it might be equally strange were the authorization Taoist. As stated at the outset, both communions were initially outspoken in condemning mantic arts—an attitude that they to some degree shared with the secular authorities. There is a certain irony in the Taoist injunctions, since Taoism fully accepted common Chinese notions of hemerological determinism, and the same practitioners who were forbidden to divine for prognosis of an illness or the orientation of a tomb were as strictly enjoined not to eat the flesh of black animals on a *ping-tzu* day, or have sexual intercourse (or even share a bed with a woman) on a *keng-shen* day, or get drunk on an *i-mao* day.[2] But the sexagesimal apportionment of time and space, with all its implications for matter and morality, was for the Taoist simply a "given"; it was the symbolic manifestation of the very fabric of the cosmos. What they so staunchly objected to at this early, hypersensitive stage was the attempt to learn about or fiddle with destiny through outside, extra-Taoist means: spirit-mediums, physicians, geomancers, and diviners were all reviled as meddlers and interlopers in what should properly be unified Taoist territory.

Canonical Buddhism need not, in theory, have got mixed up with sexagesimal matters at all; yet it would not have made much progress in China without coming to terms with Chinese cosmology. Nonetheless, Buddhist monks were strictly forbidden to practice or have recourse to mantic arts, and this not only in Indian Vinaya but in its Chinese adaptations, as well.

The classic Indian scriptural tirade against all forms of divination and prophecy is in the *Brahmajāla-sūtra* (*Fan-wang ching*) of the *Dīrghāgama* (*Dīrghanikāya,Ch'ang a-han ching*, T. 1). Chapter fourteen of the Chinese version, nineteen in the Pāli, it is all but exhaustive in its frenetic concern to leave truly nothing to chance. It bans recourse to omens, portents, physiognomy, dreams, signs from rat-gnawings, fire-oblations of various sorts (divination by Homa-fire smoke is still common in Indian ritual), and various interpretations of celestial phenomena. From this profusion, Anne-Marie Esnoul has drawn forth and systematically arranged the classes of practice condemned: ouranoscopy (astrology and horoscopy); meteorology; human physiognomy and teratology, and comparable data from animals; inanimate objects and alterations wrought upon them; presages regarding human activities; divination from the progress of ritual; the study of dreams, both spontaneous and induced; and the application of divination to medicine.[3]

The canonical Indian *Brahmajāla-sūtra* inspired a Chinese work of the same title, composed in Chiang-nan sometimes between 430 and 480. This Chinese *Fan-wang ching* (T. 1484) became the authoritative source on the Bodhisattva Precepts (*P'u-sa chieh*) and the primary "code du mahāyāna" in China. It is no less outspoken than its Indian forerunner against mantic practices, and condemns physiognomy, oneiromancy, magical arts, the concoction of potions, along with a gaggle of games, as well as divination by fingernails, milfoil stalks, poplar twigs, bowls, and bones.[4] Another representative Chinese code, the *Ten Precepts for Novices, Together with Their Deportment* (*Sha-mi shih-chieh fa ping wei-i*) categorically forbids the novice "for the terms of his natural life" to study or practice fate-calculation, spirit-healing, the way of *ku* magic, to select lucky days or hours or divine good or evil fortune. Neither may he make calendrical or astronomical calculations, nor draw portents from phenomena celestial or terrestrial, whether deriving guidance from them for the coming harvest, or for epidemic pestilence, for the strength or weakness of the State or the fortunes of armies in battle.[5]

Under these circumstances, it is curious indeed to discover a blatant oracle occupying a whole chapter of Buddhist scripture—and just at the time when the Chinese *Brahmajāla-sūtra* was written. How did *this* come to slip through Brahmā's net, to be presented by Brahmā himself? Having entered the Buddhist Canon, why was it not speedily expunged? No doubt the point is precisely that Brahmā's is a Buddhist oracle. If the Chinese must need to be addicted to divination, let it at least be moral, Buddhist divination. It was in a similar spirit that the R. P. Joseph de Sainte Barbe devised his edifying "Spiritual Card Game with Hearts Trumps, or the Game of Love" in 1666.[6]

Moreover, Brahmā's was not the sole method of divination to be naturalized in the Buddha-realm at this time. Significantly, Hui-chien, author of the *Book of Consecration*, was also credited with another work that embodies a mantic element. *The Rite of Inviting Piṇḍola (Ch'ing Pin-t'ou-lu fa)* is directed toward the arhat of that name who, like the Wandering Jew of Western Tradition, roams the world until the coming of the Lord—in this case, the future Buddha, Maitreya. His presence at any ceremony is an assurance of good fortune, which is why people always leave the door open at such times. During the rites for inaugurating a new house or, it may be, a new bed, special arrangements are made for inviting Piṇḍola to be present. Afterwards, the next day, one may observe the signs of his visit: the special cushions set aside for him will show the imprint of a body; flowers previously scattered on the seats will not be withered; there will be indications that someone has used the bath—all this an augury of happiness and good fortune.[7]

For how could Buddhism possibly bar its Chinese votaries from a fuller knowledge of destiny—Buddhism, especially, which had after all taught them that there was so much more to know than they had ever dreamt? Not only did the future stretch before them a sequence of new lives in an infinity of forms and in realms of kaleidoscopic variety, there was also the past, the nightmare past in which all present and future lets and hindrances would find their ultimate explanation. It was scarcely sporting to open these dizzying vistas and then deny the means of access, replacing the urgent need for knowledge with the passive anodyne of faith. And how might one ever know one's standing in the giddy tumbrel of fate? True enough (as every sermon reaffirmed), to be born a man in an age when one might hear the Buddha's Law was already a considerable advance. But who could ever be certain of the next act in the cosmodrama? Unless gifted with the miraculous power of vision bestowed by the Buddha on Mu-lien (Mahāmaudgalyāyana), able with a single glance to sweep from the highest heavens to the bottommost pit of hell, what guarantee did one have of the posthumous condition of departed family members? With its direct mode of address to the Buddhas, gods and saints, divination was bound to be surer, and certainly far swifter, than any tentative computation of one's familial karmic account.[8]

It was to bring some system into this vast lottery of fate that another man-tic method was given *droit de cité* in Chinese Buddhism, toward the end of the sixth century. It is expounded in a scripture entitled the *Book on Divining the Requital of Good and Evil Deeds* (T. 839). It is appropriately under the patronage of Kṣitigarbha, the psychopomp in monkish form, and is desig-nated for a time of the world when "the True Law has already vanished and the Counterfeit Law is approaching its end, at the ingress to the Final law": in short, the second half of the sixth century, according to the calculations then in force, seen by the Chinese of the time as an epoch of unparalleled apocalyptic travail. The book directs the faithful to employ the "divining method of the wooden wheel" to inspect the good or evil karma remaining from their previous lives, which explains the joy and suffering, weal and woe of their present existence. A good, veracious method is this, the text assures us—and we are not to abandon it in order to run after any or all of the vulgar, profane ways of divining fortune that are current in the world.[9]

Essentially, what the scripture has in store for us are tops: three sets of tops. The first group of ten tops enables you to determine the different sorts of good or bad deeds committed during previous existences. On each is written one of the ten good acts (*shih shan*) with its antithesis on the opposite side. The second group of three tops are respectively inscribed with "body," "speech," and "mind," the three modes of meritorious or culpable action. From the falls of these three tops you may learn the relative distance and strength of the particular karmic residues. The third set of six tops indicates the various forms of retribution for this karma, in past, present, and future lives. The determination is made by adding up the numerals inscribed on the top's faces. A table of the 189 possible outcomes is provided; nos. 1–160 refer to the present, 161–171 to the past, and 172–189 to the future. The scripture gives very exact instructions for making the tops, lengthy invocations to be employed during the proceedings, and detailed directives on interpretation. Such an intriguing series of operations could not fail to attract the curious—as we shall also see in the case of the medieval and Renaissance "Books of Fate" in Europe. The system was much in favor in China, even attracting the disapproving notice of the authorities, and spread to Silla, where it enjoyed great success among the Saṅgha.[10]

All this suggests a massive incursion of Chinese (as well as Indian) rit-ual and custom into Chinese Buddhism, an ungovernable trend that contin-ued well into the T'ang and beyond. Promising patrons were never lacking among the famous Indian bodhisattvas or patriarchs; in particular,

Nāgārjuna (Lung-shu p'u-sa), magician and alchemist, gained extended fame
and repertoire as a divine sponsor of occult arts in China and Japan.[11]

In this context, we may recall Gibbon's observation on the status of divination in Christianity: while councils continued to condemn it, prelates
continued to practice it. Do such commonplace contradictions represent a
species of "cognitive dissonance," or are they simply a product of institution-
alized hypocrisy, in Rome as in Ch'ang-an? At all events, a basic distinction
must be made in the Chinese case. The scriptural canon of Buddhism (as
that of Taoism) can be said never really to have closed. We are dealing, then,
with direct additions to holy writ, rather than simple custom or convention.
Though European clerics might cite references in scripture to the practice
of divination, and though they might employ scripture itself as their *sortes
sacrae*, it is unlikely that they would have succeeded should they have attempted to pass off a handbook of sortilegium as the very words of Christ
himself. In medieval China (and even thanks to spirit-writing in present day
Taiwan), the enterprising author had a far broader field open to him. The
author of the *Book of Consecration* was contributing to the corpus of the
Buddha's own pronouncements (*buddhavacana*). If he chose to install or
Buddhicize an extra-Buddhist system of divination, he achieved legitimacy
by presenting it as the gift of a non-Buddhist, though Indian, deity. In this
way he established a "canonical" precedent for oracular verses, and this borrowed authority continued to protect the custom. Subsequent oracles were
deemed to be the work of incarnate bodhisattvas, and thus direct additions to
the body of revelation. This undoubtedly explained their uncanny accuracy,
as the eminently respectable thirteenth-century *Chronicle of the Buddhas
and Patriarchs* relates. Once acclimatized in a Buddhist scriptural and social
context, the poetic oracle and other mantic systems might be endorsed at all
levels of the hierarchy—despite certain clerics' pained outcries of dissent.

In the steady, relentless appropriation of Chinese spiritual culture by
Chinese Buddhism, it is sometimes hard to discern just what is being
appropriated and transformed. Often, the elements in question have barely
appeared in the written record prior to their Buddhist adoption. There may
also be a convergence and synthesis of independent, though analogous,
Indian and Chinese components.[12] We can demonstrate some of the
complexity and ambiguity by examining the two paramount elements in the
modern temple oracle ritual: the means of access, and the oracles themselves.
We shall begin with the first element, the sticks, lots, or other numbering
devices. Then we will consider the collections of mantic stanzas.

Both divining sticks and gnomic verses project us immediately into the ambit of the *Book of Changes*, the *I-ching*. In many ways, this great prototype of Chinese divination remains considerably more obscure than any of its progeny. It is perhaps sufficient for our purpose to recognize that Chinese temple oracles, too, ultimately issue from this fecund source. Like other archaic techniques that achieved canonical status in ancient China—medicine, for example—the *I-ching* continued in use down the centuries. And as it still continues, vast changes in application and interpretation are veiled, to a degree, by the perpetuation of time-honored terminology as well as substance. Access to the *I-ching* might be gained by various means, but the prime method involved the manipulation of sticks, in patterns of odd or even, to construct a figure of six solid or broken lines, which in turn gave access to an oracular response and an ever-growing number of commentaries.[13]

More generally, the sticks carry us into a world of fragmentary allusions and references to kleromancy, rhabdiomancy (rather than rhabdomancy, following the useful distinction made by Toufic Fahd), and belomancy—the relevant mantic categories.[14] Analogous Western sources, for example, include Herodotus on the use of lots among the Scythians, Tacitus on comparable activities among the Germans, Ammianus Marcellinus on the Goths; they are cited again and again in this connection.[15] The crucial element, I think, is that there should be writing on the lots, making them into a distinctive series. China's apparent locus classicus is of a military nature. Early in the first century C.E., a Chinese general, obliged to send a detachment on a perilous mission, writes each of his commanders' names on a separate bamboo writing-slip, which he puts into a basket for drawing.[16] The formal record of this practice is interesting though hardly momentous. In early imperial China, most of the writing was done on bamboo slips and so the convergence of ordinary writing and inscribed kleromantic tablets was probably inevitable. Perhaps the alignment between script and divining sticks was even closer in Han China than in any other culture. Yet the archeological record to date shows that all the original ancient bamboo slips or strips which bear texts on divination are simply descriptive, and not themselves intended for direct drawing as lots.[17]

Another term, besides *ch'ien* and *chiu*, that occasionally designates oracular lots is *ch'ou* 籌. The *Shou-wen* defines this graph as "arrows in a vase"—the counters in the once much-loved, subsequently often-discussed, game of pitch-pot (*t'ou-hu*). Handsome depictions of pitch-pot in full swing have been preserved from Han times. The Chinese wrote a number of treatises on the game, some emphasizing the moral values supposed to be exemplified in it.[18] Joseph Needham has included pitch-pot in his masterly survey of "the magnet, divination and chess," and believes that it also functioned as a means of divination.[19] Richard Rudolph observes that the Han-period regulations for playing *t'ou-hu* show that drinking was an integral part of the game.[20] This at once brings to mind a whole series of Chinese drinking-games, some still current at the present day—but perhaps most spectacularly illustrated by an archeological discovery in 1982.

In a recent article, Donald Harper has studied the eighth-century game-set found at Tan-t'u, Kiangsu. Designed for use at drinking-parties, it consists of an elaborate container: a lidded cylinder mounted on the back of a tortoise, all in beaten silver and gilt. Included were fifty silver lots, each inscribed in gold with a line from the Confucian *Analects* (*Lun-yü*). On the cylinder stands the name of the set: "*Analects* Jade Candle" (*Lun-yü yü-chu*). Like the pitch-pot counters, the lots are termed *ch'ou*. One end of each lot is tapered to form a handle, by which it could readily be drawn from the cylinder. Each participant would presumably be invited to draw a lot, read out the literary quotation, and pour liquor in accordance with the instructions given on the lot. Harper observes that such games are known from the post-T'ang period, but this find represents the first T'ang evidence. No mention of this particular version, a bibulous parody of Confucian pomposity, has survived in written sources.[21]

In noting that all this apparently began with arrows in a pot, one is impressed by the perspicacity of Stewart Culin. Writing in the heyday of speculation, Culin was wont to derive the origins of virtually every game of chance or skill from the primitive manipulation of arrows.[22] More recently, Needham has summarized the matter with characteristic brilliance and verve:

> Some social anthropologist will produce some day a fully integrated and connected evolutionary story, quite biological in character, showing how all these games and divination-techniques were genetically connected. It would only need markings or numbers on the arrows to have an object which by compression would become a cubical die, and this again by extension or unfolding would give rise to dominoes on the one hand and playing-cards on the other.[23]

The challenge, I think, is still out.

André Caquot has stressed the proper distinction between divination by lot, kleromancy, which may include the *drawing* of arrows from a quiver or other container, and belomancy, the *casting* or *throwing* of arrows. He demonstrates the antiquity of using arrows as divinatory lots, observing that the word for arrow in Ugaritic, Phoenician, and Hebrew is related to one of the words for "fortune."[24] In pre-Islamic Arabia, kleromancy and belomancy were both highly esteemed. "Among the pagans of pre-Islamite Arabia, there were ordinarily seven arrows used in consulting the oracle of Hubal. On these arrows were written certain fixed responses, from which some sort of oracle could be gathered in any matter whatever that might be referred to the idol. Appropriate to the rude condition of those benighted heathen, the inscriptions were: the price of blood; yes; no; it is yours; stranger; water—or so at least medieval Muslim savants inform us."[25] In fact, a complicated nomenclature developed by stages around the arrows of Hubal's mantic cult at Mecca, as Toufic Fahd has shown.[26] At the conclusion of his excellent study of all facets of early Arab divination, Fahd remarks that "tous les procédés de la divination arabe se présentent comme des succédanés de l'oracle. Un antique refrain rhythmé qui était récité avant la consultation bélomantique à la Ka'ba le dit clairement. S'adressant à Hubal, le consultant lui disait: 'Si tu ne veux pas parler, fais-le, du moins, par les flèches!'" The inscribed arrows replace the now-mute voice of the god.[27] ·

As the recipient of the instruments of the divine will, even the quiver in which the arrows were kept was invested with sacred significance, and had its special priestly guardian.[28] Attention should be given to the Chinese divining sticks' container, as well. The luxurious T'ang drinking-game provides the most eye-catching known example, but Donald Harper has pointed out that it belongs to a larger class of tubular containers, t'ung. "Its uses were manifold: the cylinder used to hold the yarrow stalks [in I-ching divination] was a kind of t'ung, various documents could be stored in a t'ung for safekeeping, and when sūtras were to be buried on a holy site they were sealed inside a t'ung."[29]

Although most modern accounts describe the querent as taking up and shaking the recipient until a lot comes forth, there are indications that some of the containers are far too grand or heavy to permit this. Morgan writes of a metal recipient much too heavy to be shaken, and Pas describes "huge oracle containers three or four feet high, made of dark green marble, extracted from Hualien mountain quarries," in the larger temples of Peikang, Taiwan. Unable to lift such gigantic vessels, the querent simply shakes the sticks themselves, and then chooses one. We can better appreciate their grandeur when we read, on one of the responses in Werner Banck's collection, "These transcendent divining-tablets have grown old with heaven and earth;/ Inside the 'pot' (*hu*) are a separate Celestial and Terrestrial (*ch'ien k'un*)." The pot-like vessel, the "pot" of the pitch-pot game, assimilated to the gourd (from which it perhaps originated, and itself a primitive container for Taoist scriptures) and in turn equated with the gourd-shaped caverns of paradise beneath the earth, is seen here ultimately to represent a universe in miniature—like the alchemist's prototypical cucurbit, which it resembles in form and name, as well as (we now perceive) in function.

The word *ch'ou*, "lot," also stands for "counters" generally, often in connection with lot-drawing on a very large scale.[30] The lottery, indeed, is one of Yang Lien-sheng's "four money-raising institutions" in Chinese Buddhist history. Yang cites a report of 1288 in the Yüan collection of government statutes, the *T'ung-chih t'iao-ko*, on the Chiang-nan practice of holding public lotteries for profit in the monasteries: *nien-chiu she-li* is the vivid phrase, conjuring up an orgy of riotous profiteering by greedy monks. Thousands and tens of thousands of wooden lottery-slips (*ch'ien-ch'ou*) would be manufactured and farmed out to powerful local clans for sale. Yang also quotes the important collection of Ch'an monastic regulations, the *Po-chang ch'ing-kuei* (edition of 1336/38) on the way in which a lottery (*chiu-nien fa*) had come to supplant the older custom of public auction (*ch'ang-i*) as the preferred method for disposing of a deceased monk's effects: The lottery, it was said, "reduces the noise and confusion."[31]

Lot-drawing, then, was a conspicuous feature of Chinese Buddhism by the thirteenth century. The T'ien-chu oracle is contemporary with these reports, and should therefore be viewed within a larger context of Buddhist entrepreneurship that exploited various aspects of gambling. That urban, mercantile China should be the setting seems perfectly understandable, and we might be tempted to see lot-drawing as merely an extraneous feature of Buddhism—a natural ceding to temptation, at one of those sensitive points of contact where the world flocked to the monastery's gates and monks met men. Yet this proves to be only one part of the story. Sortilege in fact turns out to have a long prior history in Buddhist monastic custom.

The word *ch'ou* was also used to render the Sanskrit *śalākā*, "counting stick." In a remarkable study, Hubert Durt has reconstructed the Buddhist history of the term and its associated practices.[32] Like *ch'ou*, its Chinese equivalent ("arrows in a vase"), *śalākā* apparently derives from the same

root as śalya, "arrowhead." In the early Indian Buddhist community, counting sticks were employed ceremonially to determine the number of monks
in residence, or in attendance at rituals, and this custom continued in the
conservative Chinese Vinaya-lineage (lü-tsung). Counting sticks were also
used in allotting goods, serving as meal-tickets on the occasion of ritual
assemblies, as well as for the distribution of clothing. Indeed, as Durt has
shown, the use of such sticks as lots in disposing of a deceased monk's effects
is both ancient and Indian, being prescribed inter alia in the Vinaya of the
Dharmaguptakas as well as the Mahāsaṅghikas. The procedure appears to
have involved a casting, rather than a drawing, of lots: belomancy rather than
kleromancy. This is what we find being done in T'ang China.

As early as 626, the great Vinaya master, hagiographer, and visionary,
Tao-hsüan (596–667), spoke out on the subject of auctions then held in
monasteries for disposing of a deceased monk's effects among the assembled
monks, nuns, and novices. These auctions gave rise to unseemly tumult and
jocularity; they were, he claimed, contrary to the Law and the discipline. In
order to distribute those of the dead monk's belongings which he had not
bestowed upon specific heirs, the number of monks and nuns present should
first be counted, and the goods then divided into a corresponding number
of portions. "The lots are then thrown, to obtain one's own portion" (chih-
ch'ou ch'ü-fen).[33]

All these instances represent what Durt has termed the quantitative aspect
of Buddhist monastic counting-stick usage. Their qualitative employment is
of considerably greater ideological significance, being one of several procedures ordained for resolving conflict within the Saṅgha. In such cases, voting
by means of counting-sticks served as a last resort, since recourse to majority
rule might all too easily have led to the dread disaster of Schism. Durt has
learnedly evoked the solemn associations of the technique, its institutional
significance, and the related growth of authoritarianism within the monastic
community.[34]

There can no longer be much doubt that a broad diversity of factors
contributed to the creation and promotion of Chinese Buddhist oracles. To
the profusion of various indigenous mantic systems must now be added
the canonical status of sortilege in Buddhism. If Chinese customs made the
development of such oracles all but inevitable, even in Buddhism, Buddhism
actually did furnish a happy precedent. The Chinese oracle in Buddhist vestments is not only an exemplary case of Sino-Indian convergence, but also
illustrates the complexity of these cross-cultural studies.

WRITING AND CHINESE RITUAL

"If you do not wish to speak, speak, at least, through the arrows!" The decline of oracles, the withdrawal of the gods, is a theme at least as old as Plutarch.[1] How can this mechanical alchemy of the sticks ever replace the powerful immanence of the divine voice? Only the second component of our oracle, the mantic verses, can possibly bring us an answer.

The bond between poetry and prophecy is primordial. *Vates* and vaticination are linked, functionally as well as etymologically, down through the Indo-European tradition and just about everywhere else as well. Rhymed, rhythmic, or assonantial verse has at all times been a vehicle for the gods, whether as a direct conduit for oracular voices or through the medium of a divinely inspired poet. This function of poetry precedes and subsists beside its later, derived function of entertainment—though some would grant precedence to the not necessarily numinous work-song or dance-song.[2] Be that as it may, formal literature retains clear traces of the inspired poet's divine gift of knowing the future as well as the past.[3] Even the suave Virgil maintained the vatic persona. Yet an inspector of the modern East Asian mantic tradition, in which poetry is still formally wedded to prophecy, must be struck by the relative poverty of its poetics. There are flashes of force and insight, but much of this is small beer indeed. In some instances, the divine afflatus seems to be fizzling out into doggerel, and even doggerel has been debased, in certain oracles' interminable elucidations, into turgid prose. If the range of topics touched upon is often limited to the base concerns of mired wordlings, the technical scope of the verses is usually no less narrowly restricted. They bring to mind Alfred Jarry's dictum, "Clichés are the armature of the Absolute." Among the trivial and expected, we are doubtless closer to God.

Yet, has it always been so? Or may we discover a progressive decline of the genre? There is already a fair sampling of historical material against which to test hypotheses. We now have one oracle from the fifth century, seven more produced between 1225 and 1445, and another prior to 1607 (and at least three of these are still in use today). Werner Banck has been dating the oracles in his collection accordingly as they are cited in other, dated literature, and so matters of chronology and regionality should soon become far more precise for the corpus as a whole. Still, a decided reduction in compass appears to be characteristic of the very system. Our temple oracles after all represent a channeling and simplification of both phases of the two-step mantic process. Rather than being the result of studied, protracted specialist manipulation, the initial procedure for selecting the critical stick (singular rather than plural: a basic simplification) is left to fate, chance, and the god. The stick's very uniqueness is determined by the structure of its container, or by a stringent rule of selection. And, passing to the second phase of consultation, the oracular verses are already extant, as if independent of human agency, in printed form, often already accompanied by a full panoply of interpretation. On first inspection, all this might seem quite sterile: like the printed oracles themselves, literally cut and dried. Rather than a "spiritual" phenomenon (in our rather hazy sense of the term), it seems much more an outgrowth of that innate craftsmanship which many observers have attributed to the Chinese: "Le peuple chinois est artisan-né."[4] Is there still room for inspired poetry in such a closed mantic circuit?

Systems comparable to the one we are studying still exist in Africa, although they represent an oral, not written, tradition—much less a printed one. The most famous example is the Ifa corpus of mantic poetry from West Africa. Under the divine patronage of the god Ifa, the Yoruba of Nigeria have perfected a system of divination that admits of interesting comparison with certain East Asian developments. Ifa consultation, like our temple oracles, is in two stages. First a figure (odu) must be obtained, by a combination of the manipulation of implements and fairly elaborate mathematical operations. There are 256 possible figures, and each figure has a number of literary pieces associated with it. There is apparently no certainty regarding the extent of the total corpus, but it is said that a practicing diviner must know at least four pieces for every *odu*; good diviners are said to know about eight pieces for each of the 256 figures and many more for the sixteen most important figures.[5]

So extensive a mantic corpus must obviously be the property of highly trained professionals; divination occupies a central place in Yoruba life, and the owner of the Ifa priesthood is correspondingly great. Here then is a system that structurally approximates our Chinese temple oracles, first, because it does not operate through spirit-possession or trance-states, and second, because it too is a two-stage process: a reduction of choice through manipulation of material objects, followed by the appropriate response in literary, often poetic, form. The immediate contrasts, of course, are of complexity (the figure has to be formed step by step) and scale (the number of associated literary pieces, or potential "responses," is far grater). Also, since all this falls within a living oral tradition, we might imagine that the contrast in content and quality between this vital oracular force among the Yoruba and the puny, contrived Chinese stick-and-paper game would be overwhelming. Yet what do the authorities tell us? The Yoruba themselves admit that "Ifa speaks always in parables—a wise man is he who understands his speech," and it appears that a large part of the god's utterance takes the form of maxims or precepts, "sometimes a veiled utterance, but sometimes merely a reflection."[6] Ruth Finnegan notes that "This type of mantic poetry tends to be highly conventional, with little emphasis on the individual creativity of the performer."[7] The Yoruba, too, appear to be born craftsmen. Perhaps our Chinese oracles are not such a sorry lot after all. In extended mantic versification, ingenuity is seemingly even more serviceable than inspiration—doubtless it is inspiration—and the Chinese material is very strong on ingenuity.

Therefore, it seems clear that the written aspect, the book, is certainly not the sole factor prompting standardization over sublimity. We may even wonder if it is that great a contributing factor. Any "system" must necessarily involve stasis. And, in any case, it is unlikely that the supposedly crucial moment when a living oral tradition was first fixed in writing actually came in the fifth century. On the contrary, we can show that even in the 450s, the author of Brahmā's oracle was already working within a long literary tradition.

The evidence lies in a later Han work in the wash of the *I*: the *I-lin*, traditionally attributed to Chiao Yen-shou (first century B.C.E.), but more

probably composed ca. 25 C.E. by Ts'ui Chuan (according to Yü Chia-hsi).[8]
Perhaps the most thorough critical study of this intriguing book is by Suzuki
Yoshijirō, in his *Kan'eki kenkyū*.[9] The *I-lin* contains verses for each of the
permutations of the *I-ching* hexagrams. According to Suzuki, there are a
total of 4,096 sets in all, in verses of four syllables; of these, two-thirds are
quatrains, and the remainder run from two to nine verses.[10] There is no
doubt about the intrinsic interest of this material; the literary value of much
of the work's contents was recognized by Wen I-to, who collected over one
hundred poems from it into his *I-lin ch'iung-chih*.[11]

The term by which the verses or sets of verses are designated is *chou–tz'u*.
The graph 繇辭, prounounced *yao*, does sometimes stand for 繇 / 謠, and it
would be tempting to see here a reflection of the ambivalent *t'ung yao* 童謠 of
ancient renown.[12] But philologists seem agreed that in this usage, and with
the pronunciation *chou*, the graph is a borrowing for 籀 or 籀, connected
with reading, reading out loud or chanting, intoning, and with reading out
the results of divination. Also, we are here once more in the graphic realm of
the bamboo, and the character is sometimes also explained as meaning "draw
forth." Suzuki cites the *Cheng-i* commentary to the *Tso-chuan* (Chuang,
22), to the effect that "by hymn 頌 is meant the *chou* 繇. The words which
the diviner obtained in divination were termed by the ancients *chou*. Their
phrases were made as he looked at the mantic manifestation; they emerged
from the divination at that moment."[13] If correct, this explanation would
suggest that there may have been an extensive corpus of mantic experience
directly enshrined in verse. Whatever the reality lurking behind the archaic
use of the term, it was deemed appropriate to the verse sets of the *I-lin*,
and it is interesting to find it employed for comparable mantic stanzas in
later times—for example, the poems composed by Fu Yeh in 1225–27 for
the oracle sequence of the King of Chiang-tung (HY 1294) are also called
chou-tz'u. A single specimen from the *I-lin* must suffice to illustrate its style;
I borrow a congenial example from Glen Dudbridge:

A great ape from the southern mountains
Robbed me of my beloved wife.
For fear, I dared not chase him.
I could but retire, to dwell alone.[14]

Absit omen; but the passage is noteworthy as the earliest reference to a
mighty theme, as Dudbridge has so well shown.

One hundred twenty-four (or 125) stanzas of four-syllable verse, contained in a book as absorbing as the *I-lin* and even more mysterious in origin, comprise another mantic system that closely parallels our temple oracles. Like the *I-lin*, the *Ling-ch'i ching*, or *Book of the Empowered Draughtsmen*, is found in the Taoist Canon (in a Sung recension, HY 1035). The introduction gives directions for carving the twelve round tokens that provide the material means of selection. They are cosmically inscribed, four representing Heaven (and marked *shang* 上), four embodying Man (*chung* 中), and four standing for Earth (*hsia* 下). To draw the cosmic analogy even tighter, they are thrown on a round board termed *shih*, like the Han diviner's board. The Tao-tsang text assigns names to the various figures, or *kua*, formed by the tokens' permutations. The oracular verses are followed by several prose commentaries. Four manuscript fragments of the *Ling-ch'i ching* are among the Tun-huang texts, and so we will discuss this work in the context of other systems documented in Tun-huang collections, below.[15]

Research on written and oral literatures should involve more than "compare and contrast." We are beyond the stereotyped romantic formulation that spontaneity and truth lie in the oral, as opposed to the artifice of the written, tradition: that authentic inspiration somehow favors illiterates. Arguments indeed might be made for an entirely contrary view, especially when it comes to Chinese calligraphy. More interesting questions revolve around the neurohormonal effects of sound, the mnemonics of sound, homophones, and visual puns. All these questions are beyond our compass here. Suffice it to say that a relationship between oral and written has long existed, in a variety of forms, and writing has in fact exerted a determining influence on what are usually thought to be the oral creations of nonliterate societies.

This area of research has been explored most thoroughly by Jack Goody. Much of his analysis throughout a long series of books and papers is germane to the Chinese case.[16] Here I will cite a single example of the many on which he draws. It is, once again, the Ifa oracle of the Nigerian Yoruba. The Yoruba were not traditionally literate, and were "pagan" rather than Muslim. Their exceedingly complex system of divination therefore was seen as falling naturally into the category of oral literature, and was studied accordingly. Yet in neighboring kingdoms the influence of Islam, a religion of the Book, and the writing associated with it, has long been evident. As Goody points out, "the area in which the influence of Islam on non-Islamic, non-literate cultures is most immediately apparent is that of magico-religious activity."[17]

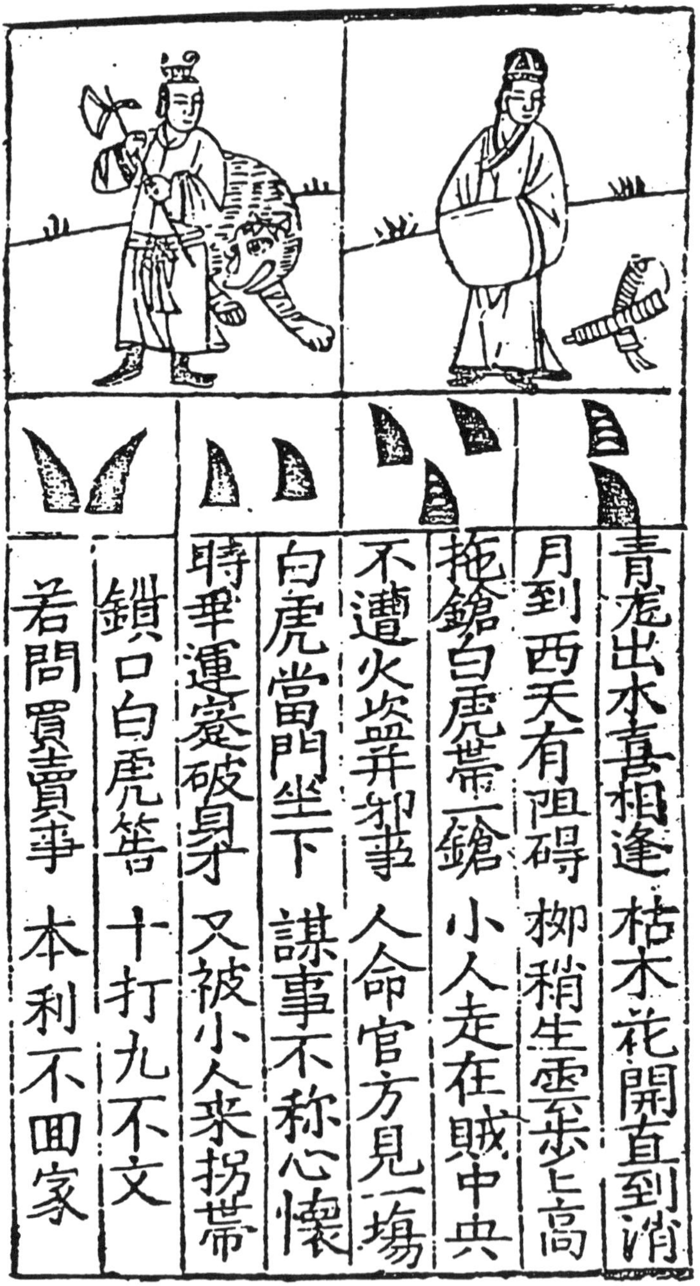

青龍出水喜相逢 枯木花開直到消
月到西天有阻碍 柳稍生雲步上高
拖鎗白虎帶一鎗 小人走在賊中央
不遭火盜并邪事 人命官方見一場
白虎當門坐下 謀事不称心懷
時乖運蹇破身 又被小人来拐帶
鎖口白虎筶 十打九不文
若問買賣事 本利不田家

FIGURE 24. A page from the *Ch'ing-lung kao*, "Blue Dragon Divining-Blocks" (Sung); cf. note 15 of Chapter 8.

The magic and ritual transmitted by Islam emanate from the Mediterranean cultural region, and there is now widespread recognition that Ifa, the Yoruba oracle, is a product of this influence. The procedures are those of Arabic geomancy—*al-raml*, "sand-divination": the same system known throughout medieval Europe as *ars notoria*, or *Punktierkunst*. There are other related forms throughout West Africa, and the *sikidi* divination of Madagascar also derives from the same source. The name "Ifa" may itself be an indication of outside origin, possibly representing the Arabic *al-fa'l*, "auspice"; Orunmila, a synonym for Ifa, may be the Yoruba vocalization of the Arabic *al-raml*.[18] There will be more to say about all this in the following chapter on diffusion. Already, though, it is clear that if the "oral" corpus of Ifa oracular pronouncements tends toward formal constraints rivaling our printed Chinese examples, it is also hardly exempt from the molding influence of a long-written tradition. In fact, it proves to be only another idiosyncratic twist in a literary catena—and one which, as we shall see, stretches across all Eurasia.

As we proceed, there will be still less eluding the conclusion that the written word has been dominant and determinant throughout the entire oracular spectrum. In China, writing has in fact held a central position in ritual generally, from the very beginning. Its association with divination is no less archaic. The earliest Chinese writing is found on oracle bones and mantic tortoise-plastrons, to which heat or fire was applied to produce significant cracks. Their patterns were interpreted as answering the written questions: the inscriptions are queries, the craquelure, an occult response.[19]

Writing has maintained a focal role in Chinese ritual and divination ever since. Might this be because, of all the world's great writing-systems, China's was the last to be created? The civilization and its unique script are virtually identical. Despite all the conventional jeremiads about its pedagogical impracticality and its "elitist" character, Chinese writing has decisively formed the culture of all East Asia, molding the minds of persons at every level of literacy, and affecting millions of nonliterates as well. Toward the end of the third century B.C.E., both script and State were standardized into forms which they were more or less to maintain into the present century. In China, script and State have kept in step for well over two millenia; they are coextensive and coeval. Small wonder, then, if writing is omnipresent and omnipotent in China, even among the nonliterates; even communication with the gods is expressed ideally in writing, and in official terms.

The earliest Taoist rituals, from the second century C.E., fully embody this presupposition. They also reflect the archaic association of script and fire. To gain the deities' attention and assistance, a formal document was to be drawn up and submitted—by burning it in the flame of an incense burner. The officiant simultaneously visualized a little cohort of spirits, formed from the vital breaths within his own body, carrying the memorial heavenwards and presenting it before the tribunal of the appropriate celestial agency. Healing was a primary function of early Taoism. Taoists were instructed to eschew ordinary secular medicaments; their panaceas were prepared in the same manner as their communications with the pantheon. The officiant drew a talismanic seal, incinerated it, and mixed the ashes with charmed water, which he gave the patient to drink. The talisman was a command to the spirits; through burning it was realized, actualized. Ingestion and incorporation guaranteed its microcosmic efficacy, even as the written memorial, once burned, was released as a gigantic script in the heavens, bearing a request that could move the gods.[20] So potent was this ritual formula that it became indispensable to the performance of all major, classical rituals in China, even those of Buddhism. It has even infiltrated the otherwise conservatively Indian Homa ritual—the Tantric Buddhist fire sacrifice—as it is now performed in Japan.[21]

Here then is "sacral" writing as communication and command. Prayerful, petitionary, in heaven-bound requests; stern and monitory in commands to lesser gods and demons; prophylactic and therapeutic in talismanic seals (these written, or printed, in variations on archaic "seal-script"): indeed, directly efficacious as medicament. If writing is the favoured ritual means, it follows that all writing is somehow ritualized: charged, weighty, to be treated with respect. It is significant that "waste" paper is always incinerated in China. Yet the intact Chinese character may also be an icon.[22]

Even explicitly "oral" forms were transmitted principally in writing, as recognized literary genres. We have already mentioned the *t'ung-yao*, prophetic ditties chanted by unselfconscious children, and sedulously collected and written down by government agents. They soon came to form part of an ever-burgeoning body of politically significant prophetic literature, the *ch'an*. In medieval Taoism, a master transmitted his most secret teachings to a single chosen disciple; they were termed "orally transmitted instructions" (*k'ou-chüeh*), but as early as the fourth century, we find this as a prominent Taoist literary genre. Such coveted auricular directives are regularly appended, in black and white, to the hagiographies of their fortunate original recipients. Somewhat later, Zen (Ch'an) Buddhism adopted the genre for its own very similar purposes. It is as if even the vitally oral had first to be written, before it could truly exist.[23]

If this is so—if the oral must be written, and even ritual action hinges on writing—what then is "ritual" for the Chinese? The answer is disarmingly simple. It is Law. Or at least it is *fa*, usually translated "law," but also meaning "model," "pattern," or "method." In common parlance nowadays, a Buddhist or Taoist ritual is referred to as *fa-shih*: if one likes, an "affair of the Law." Westerners with Buddhist leanings would fain render *fa* as Dharma, and *fa* was of course the Chinese word chosen to represent that crucial Buddhist term. But chosen, not invented; and chosen, I think, precisely because it was even then the Chinese concept that most closely paralleled the Sanskrit word. Both Dharma and *fa* are "law" if one takes the term as signifying a corpus of customary, necessary practice: a pattern of action not merely conventional, but essential, since reflecting cosmological norms. Action according to such patterns is essential to the smooth functioning of the world and society; it is, in a word, ritual.

Many sinologists may well find this equation of *fa* with ritual problematic. For scholars of Confucian leanings, reflections on ritual at once evoke a very different picture, and a different word: *li*. For my purposes, *li* might best be glossed as "ceremonious good behavior," or even just "high politeness." It is not that we should allow ourselves to be impaled on minor points of terminology. The true problems here are two. First, in the literary tradition, *li* and *fa* are seen as opposing, mutually hostile categories. *Li* is the suave ceremonial of the Confucians who (according to later Confucians) can do no ill; *fa*, the fell tactics of the Legalists (*fa-chia*), who would replace the rituals of ancient sage kings with severe statutes and vicious mutilating punishments.[24]

In the literature of the early Empire, then, the contrast between *fa* and *li* assumed a polemic quality afterwards maintained, I think, more in the writings of the learned few than in the practice of the many. Perhaps *li* could be viewed as the power-granting ritual of that "religion" in which the Emperor was Pontifex Maximus and the Confucian Classics served as preceptorial texts. For it does seem that social exclusion was a vital part of the concept of *li* from early on. Is it perhaps always situational, in contrast to *fa*'s infinitely more inclusive claims? Whatever its relation to *li*, it appears that for Buddhists, Taoists, and all those in between, medieval Chinese ritual was deemed to "work" because it conformed to the Law—because it *was* the Law. And unlike India, in China the majesty of the Law was conspicuously bodied forth in writing.

The term "Master of the Law" (*fa-shih*) has a long history in China. It is early attested in Buddhism and Taoism alike. "Masters of the Law" were to be chiefly responsible for the wide diffusion of the influential *Lotus Sūtra* (*Saddharmapuṇḍarika*), and such "preachers of the Dharma" (*dharmabhāṇaka*) have been credited with a major role in the dissemination of Mahāyāna scriptures, legends, and doctrines.[25] The same title is found amongst the Taoists, at least by the fourth century, if not before. Masters of the Law were evidently Masters of Ritual: chanting, processing, preaching; also doubtless, healing, and casting out demons, their title seems, above all, to suggest ritual action.[26]

The title lives on in Taiwan today. "Masters of the law" (Hokkien *huat-su*) are still highly active—but outside both the hereditary hierarchy of Taoism and the Buddhist cloister. The term now designates the red-coiffed vernacular priests or exorcists, whose contrasts and complementarities with the gild of Taoist masters have been lucidly analyzed by Kristofer Schipper.[27] There have been earlier attempts to explain the term by rendering *fa* here as "magic"; these drudges *extra ecclesiam* would then just be vulgar magicians.[28] Though "magic" is certainly one facet of Dharma and ritual, it seems more likely that the Taiwanese exorcists have simply inherited a lofty title from by-gone days—much as their vestments and ritual implements can also be shown to be hand-me-downs from well-established Buddhist and Taoist prototypes.[29]

Apart from direct intervention in time of illness, these modern *fa-shih* also handle immanent manifestations of divinity on earth—quite literally, as they control both the marionette theater and living spirit-mediums. In both cases, *fa-shih* are puppet-masters, interpreters of the divine presence. The mediums—"oracle-youths" (Hokkien *tang-ki*, Mandarin *chi-t'ung*)— are, when possessed, the gods themselves come among men; they represent the last living oracles. Through them, the voice of the gods can still be heard directly; while oracle-lads still draw breath, what need to scrabble among crabbed fortune-papers?

Or so the innocent anthropologist might believe. Here at long last we seem to have stumbled on a truly oral Chinese tradition. Neither mediums nor their masters necessarily get high marks for literacy, and such ritual handbooks as the *fa-shih* own are usually written in an ill-kempt vernacular jargon. Yet what issues from the medium's mouth is more usually blood than language. He cuts his tongue, for blood to smear on written or printed talismans. He pierces his cheeks, flails his back—talismans are pressed to him, stuck to him, and for all his tortured ecstasy, the rain of blood only serves to quicken written matter.[30]

Spirit-possession is pandemic in Taiwan, and it does not always take such violent forms. There are temples and chapels where gods regularly descend into the bodies of their worshippers, in order to prophesy and instruct. In the light of all we have so far seen, it seems fated that these communications should be in writing. Often the possessed here work in pairs. Each holds one handle of a forked divining stick, with which (as the spirit moves them) they trace characters on a flat surface, or in a tray of sand or ashes. One character rapidly follows another; they are at once read out by nonentranced interpreters standing alongside, and written down by one or more scribes. In this manner, entire books of revelations have been composed, scriptures that circulate in Taiwan and other bastions of traditional Chinese culture.[31]

Certain temple oracles may owe their genesis to comparable procedures. All the verse oracles represent the visible, legible voice of the gods, and it should now be obvious that the frozen form, in writing, in no way diminishes immediacy or power. On the contrary, where script and civilization are coextensive, the highest authority must necessarily be a written one. In a sense, the written temple oracle represents a lofty goal toward which every twitching medium, even the least literate, is somehow obscurely groping.

9

VISIONS OF DIFFUSION: CENTRAL ASIA AND THE WEST

In China, then, writing and authority were peculiarly identified. The dominant forms of Chinese divination have always been based on writing, viewed as the voice of authority from the unseen world. This powerful amalgam of writing, authority, and divination could hardly be kept within China's borders. And indeed, as it spread, it was instrumental in molding neighboring people and states into approximations of the Chinese model. We have already alluded to the permeation of written oracles into the surrounding cultures: among Koreans, Japanese, Tibetans, Mongols, and the people of Southeast Asia. Like their ultimate arcane prototype, the *I-ching*, latter-day Chinese temple oracles have been an inextricable part of the overall "civilizing" process of sinification.

Yet written oracles of this sort are by no means confined to the immediate sphere of obvious Chinese influence. Closely similar texts and procedures are found at the Western as well as the Eastern end of Eurasia, and at all points in between. The Tibetan case, with its intriguing variety of oracular texts, offers a great challenge, but at least the Chinese model was never far away. However original the Tibetan variations, the main Chinese themes were still being sounded close at hand. The patterns of mantic inspiration or dissemination seem to parallel the example of Tibetan storytelling. Alexander Macdonald

has shown that Indian frame-stories were used to enclose Tibetan tales.[1]
Tibetan divination, like Tibetan narrative, reflects the irresistible influence
of both China and India. What the Tibetans fashioned from their outside
models properly belongs, in its turn, to the history of Tibet. In this case,
the analysis of diffusion and its limitations has clear boundaries, as well
as an intrinsic plausibility. Broadly speaking, Tibetan culture was created
by Tibetans through an original synthesis of many elements: Tibetan, Indian, Chinese, and others. Yet what are we to say when we discover works
closely resembling Chinese (or Tibetan) temple oracles in fifteenth-century
Germany?

Medieval and Renaissance Europe

Before we can utter a word, there is a good deal of scholarly literature
to be considered. This in itself is heartening; though in the Chinese realm
such studies have only just begun, they are already well developed among
European medievalists and folklorists. Most of the work has been done by
Germans, and much of their attention has been focused on German "Books
of Fate" (Losbücher). These in turn are closely related to earlier French,
Italian, and Latin examples. German scholarship is thus a natural point of
departure for a very cursory survey.

The first major study of the subject was published by Sotzmann in
1850–51: "Die Loosbücher des Mittelalters." He observed that the genre
had been unjustly neglected, and began by describing in some detail several of the earliest printed texts. These were Lorenzo Spirito's *Libro delle
sorte* (Vicenza, 1473?), Sigismondo Fanti's *Trionfo di Fortuna* (Venice,
1526), Francesco Marcolino da Forli's *Giardino di pensieri* (Venice, 1540),
and *Le dodechedron de fortune*, attributed to Jean de Meung (Paris, 1556).
These examples are all richly illustrated with figures in numerical series: for
example, ancient kings, symbolic animals, signs of the zodiac, and planets,
in Spirito's *Libro delle sorte*. The verse oracle itself is accessible by means
of three dice, and is presided over by an imposing pictorial series of Old
Testament figures. The later works are even more elaborate. Fanti's *Trionfo
di Fortuna* includes seventy-two categories of questions, covering not only
problems of daily life (love, friendship, children, travel, death, and so on) but
political, philosophical, and meteorological matters as well. This is strikingly
similar to the long lists of comparable categories in many Chinese printed

oracles, diligently tabulated by Werner Banck. Fanti's questions and versified responses, though, are only the oracular nucleus around which blossoms a tumultuous pictorial cosmology and history. Popes, emperors, kings, queens, legendary heroes, artists, scholars, and writers all appear; nor (as the work proceeds) are sibyls and astrologers forgotten. The heavenly bodies all have their place, as do the palace facades of the twelve leading families of Italy. Fortune triumphs through glorious inclusiveness (Figures 25–27).[2]

In presenting these remarkable texts, Sotzmann got the study of "Books of Fate" off to a good start. But the printed works mark the culmination of a long tradition. They are supremely refined, elaborate, and complex not only in iconography but in their means of access as well. Apart from dice (two may be used, as well as three), some employ wheels of fortune, and many of the images are arranged in wheel-patterns throughout. The French *Dodechedron de fortune* makes use of a single twelve-sided die, whence its name. As we might expect, all these elements prove to have a long prior history. In the second part of his study, Sotzmann went to examine a number of German Losbücher in fifteenth-century manuscripts. He distinguished three basic categories. First there were Losbücher proper, which furnish prophetic responses to definite questions regarding fate. They conduct the enquirer to the proper answer through a labyrinth of pictures or even simply names of persons and objects. Such works, he claims, were the only ones to be carried over into print in their independent form, among the three types.

The second category he terms "Lucky Books" (Glücksbücher), since they assist the querent in finding lucky and unlucky days. A verse-element enters here, too, since the nefast *dies aegyptiacae* of the Roman calendar came to be marked, in the Middle Ages, with poetic tags; for example, for January, *Prima dies mensis et septima truncat ut ensis*, signifying the first and twenty-fifth (that is, seventh from the end) days. Such works either fell gradually into abeyance or were absorbed into the Losbücher themselves.

The third category comprises oracle games. Here no questions are specified; one simply obtains a saying, which is then to be applied as circumstances warrant, and this "response" may be accompanied in the texts by objects that are either pictured or merely named. The most usual mode of access to this type of "oracle" is dice, though each object and related saying may be written on an individual card, which can then be drawn from the pack. The other types of oracle are accessible through casting dice, drawing cards, or spinning a disc—a wheel of fortune. But Sotzmann also found a parchment

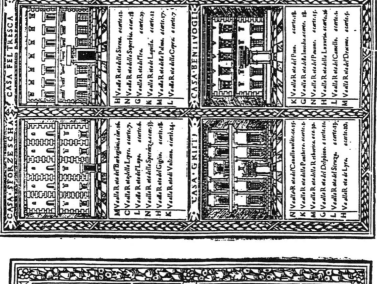

FIGURE 25. Sigismondo Fanti, *Trionfo di Fortuna*: Fortunes and Noble Houses.

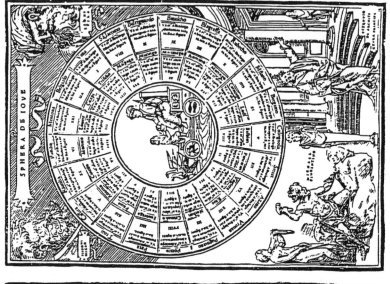

FIGURE 26. *Trionfo di Fortuna*: Wheels of Fortune and Sphere of Jove.

FIGURE 27. Francesco Marcolini, *Le Sorti intitolate Giardino di pensieri:* "Fear" and "Plato"

manuscript Losbuch that used sixteen figures composed of different arrangements of dots or points. These are the sixteen basic figures of geomancy, or Punktierkunst, on which there will be more to say below.[3]

Sotzmann's three categories extend over a range of functions already familiar from our Chinese examples. There are serious responses to questions, furnishing guidance for daily life: the temple oracles, as well as those contained in separate booklets. There are numbered sequences of calenderic, meterological portent, like the verses found in chapter 18 of the Taoist *Spirit-Spells of the Abyss*. And there are playful sequences, like the wine-lots studied by Donald Harper, and even like the Chinese-inspired American game contributed by Louise Paige (see above).

In 1858, Ignaz Zingerle published selected verses from a splendidly illustrated and decorated parchment codex Losbuch, dated 1546. We find there once again the set questions, the biblical patriarchs, kings and prophets, the planets, and the apostles.[4] And in 1867, the field was enlarged by an edition of a thirteenth-century Provençal *sortes apostolorum*, "Las sortz dels apostols," together with its Latin original, by Bruno Dusan. Camille Chabaneau brought out a more satisfactory edition of both texts in 1880.[5] Chabaneau observed that the Latin manuscript had already been published in 1687 in a collection of the posthumous works of the distinguished scholar, Pierre Pithou (1539–1596).[6] This discovery opened a path back into the earlier Middle Ages, and to the Latin models for the vernacular Books of Fate that abounded during the late Middle Ages and the Renaissance. It also provided matter for assessing a problem that has proved of interest in regard to our East Asian oracles: the faithfulness of tradition and translation, and the role of inventiveness, or improvisation, in the oracular genre. Comparison of the thirteenth-century Provençal manuscript with its Latin source allowed Chabaneau to establish that the translation was often inaccurate or garbled; that three of the fifty-six responses were absent from the Provençal version, whilst three others were new, not found in the Latin; that some of the Latin oracle's answers had been arbitrarily split into two parts, and still other, distinct responses had been fused into a single answer, and so on. The Latin text is preceded by a short set of instructions, setting forth the ritual conditions under which it is to be employed; it is an infallible and entirely Christian oracle, to be consulted only after fasting on bread and water for three days. On the third day, the Office of the Blessed Trinity is to be chanted, then in the greatest humility with prayers and weeping you may ask of the oracle whatever it is you require. These instructions are lacking in the Provençal version, which does, however, open with the text of a long prayer. From all this, Chabaneau deduced that the translator was working with a Latin text that differed substantially from Pierre Pithou's manuscript. He found this hypothesis more likely than the alternative, that the differences are due to the translator's whim, haste, or misunderstandings. After our review of East Asian parallels, I should say that this latter possibility seems at least equally plausible. One thing is clear: texts of this sort were never meant to exemplify a tradition of scribal fidelity. They were, in a sense, alive—hence constantly changing, despite the basic conservatism of the genre.

The Latin text was designed for use with three six-sided dice. Each die bore the numerals I., II., III., IIII., V., and C., and each response was keyed to one of their threefold combinations: hence the total of fifty-six responses. Chabaneau rightly observed that such oracles of the saints or apostles could be traced back to the practice of the early medieval Church, as had been described in 1678 by the prodigious Sieur du Cange (1610–1688) and elaborated by Jean-Baptiste Thiers (1636–1703) in his *Traité des superstitions*.[7] Yet although (as in the case of Chinese Buddhist and Taoist oracles) the Church conferred a pious tone and an apostolic benediction, it did not originate the practice, which had indeed been known to the Greeks. Apart from the most highly publicized oracles of antiquity (at Delphi, Claros, Didyma, and so on) that were emitted *viva voce* by inspired priests and priestesses, there were also written verse oracles—numbered sequences made accessible, most usually, by casting dice or "knucklebones" (*astragalia*). The term "rhapsodomancy," often applied to this form of divination, well brings out its poetic and recitative character (though like most Greek terms used to classify the various mantic systems, it was created only much later, by Renaissance humanists).

Graeco-Roman Antiquity

In 1879, the year before Chabaneau's publication, Bouché-Leclerc had brought out the first volume of his great *Histoire de la divination dans l'antiquité*. Chabaneau was thus opportunely able to cite him on ancient precedents and reinforce the link between ancient and medieval, pagan and Christian oracles that had already been noted by du Cange (as well as the early Church Fathers). Bouché-Leclerc treated several similar mantic procedures under the general rubric of kleromancy, and observed that kleromantic practices had traditionally existed at Delphi as well as Athens before the installation there of Apollo's oracle. For that matter, such methods continued to be employed there, alongside the living, spoken oracle. "Far from disappearing with time, kleromancy imposed itself, as it were, to the oracles that had not been able to discredit it." Nor was kleromancy confined to temples, or to private matters. "Simple, expeditious, and theoretically impregnable, since it leaves to Providence an absolutely free choice among a certain number of agreed signs," it proved ideal not only for selecting chiefs and champions in battle (attested in Homer), but even the political leaders of a self-consciously "free" society: "Thus, later on, democracies answered to all objections raised against electoral competence of the masses and held in check ambitious desires by having their magistrates designated by fate, considered as divine will": divination in the service of democracy.[8]

Bouché-Leclerc would term the division of kleromancy that here concerns us—the application of chance to language—*clédonisme*. In a later volume, he gives an account of the famous Italic oracles of Caere (Cerveteri) and Falerii (Falleri)—inscribed tablets bound together in a bundle, which became prophetic only when drawn forth. They might also speak of their own accord, the bundles becoming spontaneously loosened, as happened at Caere in 218 B.C.E., and a fateful tablet might even fall out, as at Falerii the following year—to announce the approach of Hannibal. In the ancient Italic world, no oracle of this type was more revered than the one found in the temple of Fortuna at Praeneste (Palestrina). According to a legend, it consisted of tablets of oak inscribed with letters of the primitive alphabet, found (in response to a series of increasingly stern dream-directives) inside a rock. They were kept in a coffer of olive-wood, under the protection of the goddess Fortuna Primigenia. Her assent had to be obtained before any consultation, no doubt by means of a sacrifice, but very likely also through a visible sign— a movement by her statue. Then the receptacle was shaken and a child drew forth the wondrous tablets. With regard to the oracle in another great temple of Fortune, at Antium (Porto d'Anzio), Bouché-Leclerc speculates that the statue's auspicious movements (often mentioned by ancient authors) may have been connected with some mechanical device for selecting the lots.[9]

Bouché-Leclerc surmised that the letters on the tablets may have been used to form words comprising the goddess's response. (In fact it is more likely that each letter gave access to a verse, as in the fragment published by Buecheler.) The Greeks, too, knew such primitive written oracles, but preferred to obtain their responses from preexisting verse texts: hence their penchant for "rhapsodomancy." Homer and Hesiod were drawn upon, as well as the collections of spoken oracular poetry. As Bouché-Leclerc puts it, the official and unofficial oracles as well as the great poets might be considered to have amassed sufficient truths so that advice for every circumstance of life could be discovered in their writings. The process might be made even more convenient by fixing the responses in advance, and correlating them with the throws of dice or knucklebones. Bouché-Leclerc concludes his kleromantic section by referring to an epigraphic fragment from Attalia (Antalya) in Pamphylia. Each of its ten responses is in three hexameter verses, and each is headed by the name of a god and a fivefold numeral. Responses were obtained by a simultaneous throw of five four-sided dice. The ten surviving answers must then derive from a set of fifty-six, the full number of possible variations in such a system.[10]

Since Bouché-Leclerc's day, much work has been done on Greek oracles of this sort, greatly stimulated by explorations and discoveries in Asia Minor. Before Bouché-Leclerc's 1879 volume, the Antalya inscription had been published by Hirschfeld (1875) and Kaibel (1876).[11] A number of more substantial texts were found and edited from 1880 on. They formed the subject of a comprehensive dissertation by Franz Heinevetter (1912), who published them all in full, traced their historical development, and clarified their relationship to dice and knucklebones.[12] Most often either five or seven dice were used (a seven-dice throw implies 120 different responses). If the oracular tables were inside a temple, the dice would lie there, ready to hand. But such epigraphic sequences were often found along the public way, and the querent would then need to carry his dice with him. Several surviving inscriptions address the wanderer: ὦ ξένε. An oft-cited passage in Pausanias indicates that when the locus was a shrine, dice would be cast (after a prayer) on a table before the deity's image. The throws were all listed on a separate chart.[13] Heinevetter illustrates other surviving polyhedrons, chiefly "Eikosaeder," twenty-sided dice inscribed with the letters of the Greek alphabet from A to Y. There are also dodecahedrons with their sides numbered A to IB, and these recall the *Dodechedron de fortune* printed in Paris in 1556.

The dice-oracles studies by Heinevetter all came from southwestern Asia Minor, and were normally written in hexameter verse. Those to be queried with five dice comprised fifty-six responses of four verses. Working from seven incomplete examples, Heinevetter was largely able to reconstruct the original poem of 224 verses that had generated the entire regional group. Apart from the dice-oracles, his dissertation also dealt with letter-oracles

(Buchstabenorakel). Bouché-Leclerc had simply mentioned these in passing, but Heinevetter published two examples, one obviously a variation on the other, or both perhaps covariants on some single archetype.[14] Such sequences are composed in trimeters, and the first word of each verse begins with a different letter of the alphabet, in order. Hence there are twenty-four verses in all. Access might be either through dice (since twenty-four numbers could be obtained by using five astragalia) or, in a temple, by drawing from an urn one of twenty-four stones or sticks, each inscribed with a letter of the alphabet. The priests could then instantly recite the response; it is almost like our Chinese temple oracles.

Some of these epigraphic oracles may still be viewed *in situ*. Northwest of Antalya, high in the mountains of the ancient Roman province of Pamphylia, stand the ruins of the Pisidian city of Termessos. Here was found the most nearly complete sequence among the five-dice oracles studied by Heinevetter, the seventh in his edition. It was inscribed on a pillar 1.86 meters high, next to the ruins of a small temple. The same site yielded up Heinevetter's seven-dice example, which was described anew by George E. Bean in 1968, on the basis of a visit to Termessos. The main ancient road of access, constructed in the second century C.E., passed by a gate through the outer fortification. The beginning of the oracle (all that has been preserved) was inscribed on the inner east wall of the gateway. Bean noted that the inscribed blocks were, in the mid-1960s "lying among the jumble of stones at the roadside." Professor Bean did not approve of oracles, "these curious monuments to human credulity." "There is a remarkable sameness about the responses, and it seems that the client was expected to ask only about the advisability of some course of action; the god's advice is in effect confined to two alternatives: 'Go ahead,' or 'Wait'." He quoted two examples:

> 44466   24   Cronos the Child-Eater
> Three fours and two sixes. This is the god's advice:
> Stay at home and go not elsewhere,
> Lest the destructive Beast and avenging Fury come upon you;
> For I see that the business is neither safe nor secure.

> 66661   25   The Light-giving Moon-God
> Four sixes, and the fifth a one. This is the meaning:
> Just as wolves overcome lambs, and mighty lions subdue
> Horned oxen, so shall you overcome all,
> And with the help of Hermes son of Zeus shall have all your desire.[15]

Bean later described the site of the Lycian Olympus, near which the mysterious flame of the Chimaera still burns. In the extensive necropolis, two of the tombs "are inscribed, in addition to the usual epitaph, with letter-oracles." "Some of the verses are the same on the two tombs, others are different. Here again the advice offered is virtually confined to the two alternatives: 'Go ahead' or 'Wait.' The responses are conceived as given by the heroized ancestor, and the consultants would be members of his family."[16] In spite of Professor Bean's disdain, it is clear that the epigraphic oracles promoted familiar and respectable access to the counsels of the invisible world, from departed forebears as well as from the gods.

One might not expect much movement from oracles graven in stone (though in fact such Greek texts have been found from Cyprus to Thrace). But some twenty years after the great epigraphic sweep of Asia Minor had got into stride, the rubbish heaps of Egypt began to yield up quantities of Greek papyri, including oracles. Early in 1897, Grenfell and Hunt made the first of their remarkable discoveries in a rubbish mound at the site of the ancient Oxyrhynchus (Behnesa), 120 miles south of Cairo. "The flow of papyri soon became a torrent it was difficult to keep pace with."[17] A familiar, personal tone was already evident in the oracles inscribed at temples, on the public way, or at tombs. How much more intimate might such a text be, when written on papyrus—and also, how much more portable and transmissible.[18]

Mikhail Rostovtzeff was most impressed by the value of such destiny-linked materials, particularly the numbered lists of questions that were to be addressed to an oracle. He felt that they furnished "an excellent bird's-eye view of the chief preoccupations of average residents of different classes" in Egypt toward the end of the third century C.E. There are general, neutral questions regarding marriage and business prospects. But in at least eight of the twenty-one questions preserved in one such papyrus, Rostovtzeff saw a clear reflection of social conditions specific to the time and place. Two concerned the possible confiscation of property: "Shall I be sold up?" and "Is my property to be sold at auction?" Others were "Shall I become a beggar?", "Shall I take to flight?", "Shall I become an envoy?", "Am I to become a member of the municipal council?", "Shall my flight come to an end?", "Shall I receive my salary?", and so forth. In contrasting these questions with similar second-century lists, Rostovtzeff suggests that they reveal that the peril threatening a man's career came from the state's increased intrusiveness in the life of the individual.[19] Potentially significant lists of questions or question-categories are present not only in the later Western tradition, but in the Chinese oracles as well. The Chinese data have been efficiently tabulated by Werner Banck.[20]

To what sort of oracles may these suggestive question-repertories have been linked? In 1939, Gudmund Björck reviewed the full range of what he termed "Heathen and Christian oracles with ready-made answers."[21] Following Heinevetter, he described the dice-oracles and the letter-oracles, and went on to compare the old Italic inscribed *sortes*. These latter were a priestly monopoly; perhaps the Hellenic specimens too, before their popular diffusion, had been a sacerdotal speciality. He noted (as others had already done) Apuleius's account of the itinerant priests of the Syrian Goddess. Apuleius tells how these self-serving charlatans had a single oracular answer with which they would respond to every query: *Ideo coniuncti terram proscindunt boves/ut in futurum laeta germinunt sata*; "The patient oxen plough the soil,/ And harvests rich repay their toil" (Farrar). Questions of marriage, property, travel, success in battle, all could be happily resolved in the querent's favor by judicious application of these inspired verses.[22]

In describing the priests' trickery, the mss. of Apuleius read: *sorte unica per casulis pluribus enotata consulentes de rebus variis plurimos ad hunc modum cauillantur*. The emendation for the meaningless *per casulis* is usually *pro casibus*: to every question they gave but a single response. In his third edition (1931), however, Rudolph Helm opted for a different reading: *(sem) per cartulis*.[23] Now the rascals have but one oracular jingle on their entire set of "papers," or papyrus-strips—and so whenever the *sortes* are drawn, the same uplifting message emerges. This reading advantageously reflects a knowledge of mantic practice. Björck remarks that strips of papyrus or little wooden tablets could have been drawn directly, or else consulted by means of dice. They were in any case ideally portable, and he suggests that the oracles graven in stone may have been associated with a host of sequences on more perishable media, which may in part have borne the same verses as the stones.

Björck perceived that if the answers to this new form of oracle were fixed in advance, the questions must be too. A whole series of answers might be linked to a single question, and the dice or some other randomizing method would determine the one to be applied. The client would have the set of questions, but the responses would probably have been held by the diviner alone.

In contrast to earlier, sententious oracles, these responses would necessarily have to be more specific, and directly related to the question. Björck recognized that two such sequences have survived from early Christian times. One, in Greek, is attributed to the pseudonymous Magian or Phrygian, Astrampsychos (*Sortes Astrampsychi*). The other, in Latin, is contained in a St. Gall palimpsest (*Sortes Sangallenses*). They are clearly related, and though the prototype must have been Greek, Björck believed that the Latin version represented the more primitive form. Here then are oracles of Late Antiquity that have entered the medieval manuscript tradition. This is of special significance, for (as Björck discovered) the answers in the Astrampsychos oracle correspond perfectly with the questions in the third-century papyrus that so impressed Rostovtzeff as testimony to social conditions in Roman Egypt.[24] Björck also usefully demonstrated the process of mantic translation, from paganism to Christianity. In responding to an unlimited array of questions, commonplace sayings are called for, and Björck was thus drawn to compare the proverbial tags figuring in many epigraphic responses with similar phrases in the ideally Christian *Sortes sanctorum apostolorum*. He found four responses in the Christian sequence that corresponded closely with six passages in the oracles published by Heinevetter.[25] Continuity between ancient and medieval, pagan and Christian, stone and manuscript seems well established.

After this excursus on ancient precedent, we may return to German research into medieval and Renaissance Losbücher. In 1903, the folklorist Johannes Bolte edited a Losbuch by the sixteenth-century writer of popular romances, Georg Wickram. First published in 1539, this work went into more than twenty-four editions, easily surpassing all prior German efforts in the field. At the end of the volume, Bolte added an appendix on the history of Losbücher, which has been the outstanding survey of the subject ever since. It is divided into two parts, extra-German (31 pp.) and German (40 pp.). Chinese temple oracles are mentioned briefly in a note, as one of those related forms of divination that Bolte intentionally left out.[26] Otherwise he seems to have omitted little, and describes specimens in all the major classical languages: Greek, Latin, Sanskrit, Arabic, and Hebrew, as well as medieval Latin and most of the European vernaculars.

Writing long before Heinevetter or Björck (and not cited by either of these classicists), Bolte established the necessary relationship between the dice- and letter-oracles of Greek antiquity and the three chief early medieval examples:

the Astrampsychos sequence, the *Sortes Sangallenses*, and the *Sortes apostolorum*. The latter is mentioned as a separate book by Pope Gelasius in 494; the title refers to *Acts* 1.26, "And they gave forth their lots; and the lot fell upon Matthias; and he was numbered with the eleven disciples." Their own company completed by sortilege, the twelve apostles subsequently counseled the faithful by the same means. The apostles' sequence is organized just like the Greek dice-oracles, with fifty-six responses to be obtained by a simultaneous throw of the dice—only here, rather than five four-sided dice, three six-sided dice are required. The contents for the most part counsel faith, prayer, and patience, and Bolte is able to cite only four more vivid similes, when the impatient querent is likened to a blind young dog, and the unreflective inquirer compared with a traveler in a trackless forest, a captain who puts out to sea in a storm, or a hunter who tries to catch a running deer. This is the *Sortes apostolorum* that was translated into Provençal in the thirteenth century (and published by Chabaneau, with the Latin, in 1880). Bolte observes that instead of requiring dice, the Provençal manuscript was written on a piece of parchment that could be folded up, with a colored thread attached to each response. The questioner chose a thread and the diviner read out the corresponding answer. Bolte also found a previously unnoticed rhyming translation of the *Sortes* into Old French, in a thirteenth/fourteenth-century manuscript—a version more faithful to the Latin prototype than the Provençal.[27]

Ancient India

Having documented the connection between ancient and modern Europe, Bolte moved on to India. The standard Indian dice-oracle, the *Pāśaka-kevalī*, had already been studied by the Sanskritists Albrecht Weber (1859) and J. E. Schröter (1900).[28] Bolte found many similarities to the ancient Greek system and observed that the oracle's contents were for the most part banal. The most curious feature in forty-two of the sixty-four responses was the confirmation of the answer by a particular sign. This sign could be either some disfigurement on a secret part of the querent's body or a subsequent dream.

The earlier study by Albrecht Weber provided a complete translation to the *Pāśaka-kevalī*. It began with an invocation to the goddess Durgā, and specified that all is to be prepared on Saturday for a Sunday consultation, when a maiden (*kumārī*) is to cast the dice. Weber associated the Goddess's presence with accounts in literary sources of her pleasure in dicing with Śiva, her spouse. Three four-sided dice are used, cast sequentially rather than all at once, and the names of the various throws are sometimes given in the oracle text, just after the threefold enumeration. In Weber's manuscript, the author's name was given as Garga, described as a Jaina, but Weber declared the work's contents to be, if anything, Śaivite. He then speculated that the Buddhists may after all have been responsible for it, or at least for its diffusion. He noted a similar Tibetan oracle found in the *Vaiḍūrya dkar-po* (second half of the seventeenth century). It too comprises sixty-four responses, also obtained by casting three four-sided dice—though on these, instead of numbers, stand the syllables A YA VA DA. He dated the Sanskrit manuscript used for his translation to the sixteenth century.[29]

On this showing, the congruence with Greek examples may be striking, but need not have been ancient. Yet evidence soon appeared that carried the Indian dice-oracle back at least to the fifth or sixth century, and also spoke for its considerable diffusion by that time. In 1890, a Lieutenant Bower found a substantial corpus of manuscripts in the ruins of a Buddhist stūpa near Kucha, in Chinese Turkestan. They were in a rough Sanskrit interspersed with Prākritisms, and their contents were mostly medical. Rudolf Hoernle published them in full, together with a complete translation and thorough commentary. He was inclined to date them to the fourth century, though more recent scholarship places them between the fourth and sixth centuries.[30] The collection includes a treatise on garlic, and another on the therapeutic use of the myrobalan. It also quotes and copies from many of the standard Sanskrit medical compendia. All the more significant, then, is that we also find substantial data on divination. Just as in the *Book of Consecration*, written during the same period, and just as in Chinese practice still today, a written oracle provided the manuscripts' possessor with a ready mean of diagnosis and prognosis.

The Bower Manuscript contains two dice-oracles. The first is nearly complete, lacking only four out of sixty-four responses. The second is much more fragmentary; of the sixty-four, a mere twenty have been preserved. The two sequences are quite different works, and the latter's responses are notably fuller than those of the former.[31]

The first text opens with salutations to various forms of Śiva, to Māṇibhadra and his fellow Yakṣas, to Prajāpati, Vaiśrāvaṇa, and the Maruts, among others. "Let the dice fall for the purpose of the present object! Hili! Hili! Let them fall as befits Kumbhakārī, the Mātaṅga woman!" Mātaṅgīs, like other outcaste women, were regularly associated with magic and mantic arts.[32] The first response runs, in Hoernle's translation, "444 Salutation! Janārdana [Viṣṇu] is well-pleased with thee who art an excellent man. All thy enemies are killed. What thou shalt desire, that shall be done." Or again, on a less hopeful note, no. 7: "344: Thou contemplatest a meeting, but the fair one does not join thee; thy body is heated with desire, but thou shall obtain no enjoyment."

The second text starts off with an obeisance to Janārdana, "the lord of the world, by whom the truth of this (art of divination) has been decreed..." An invocation to the Goddess follows: "Oh thou pure, pure, stainless Devī! Oh Devī! That which is true, that which is well, all that do thou show to us. Though the human eye may fail, the divine eye will prevail; though the human ear may fail, the divine ear will prevail; though the human smell may fail, the divine smell will prevail; though the human tongue may fail, the divine tongue will prevail. Oh thou Garlanded One, thou Garlanded One! Svāha!" The first two responses may be quoted:

> 441: Twice four and one,—if thus the dice have fallen, then assurely loss of friends, trouble, and great pain will be thine; most keenly thy stars are opposing thee: neither thy ancestral nor thy own business will prosper, nor that which thou, in thy great anxiety, has marked out in thy heart: think of some other object: that one will not be realized. Thou wilt be in trouble for five years only, and not be able to rejoice. And this shall be for a token to thee: there is a mole at the base of thy back.

> 144: When one comes first, and then twice four, then thou wilt attain progress in all thy business and wealth: thy family Deva, Maheśvara, the great Deva, will be favourable to thee: give praises to him and worship, and keep his vigils. Very great will be thy gain: there is no doubt about it. And this shall be for a token to thee: there is an ulcer on thy buttocks: also in thy sleep thou talkest much.[33]

Here we have the physical symptoms that confirm the oracle's omniscience, the feature that so struck Bolte in Weber's rendering of the *Pāśaca-kevalī*. In the Bower Manuscript, such signs come up far more often than in the later text. They are numerous even in the remaining fragments, less than one third of the original sequence, and include "a mole at the base of thy back," "a mole at the base of thy anus," "a black mole in thy private parts," "at the end of thy side there is a black spot," "on the back of thy neck there is a mole," "on thy left thigh there is an ulcer, and on the right thigh there is a small mole," an oneiric sign ("in thy dream thou are held fast by thy wife, and thou speakest sounds... "), and a fairly obscure sexual allusion, suggesting that the querent's disappointed wife is ripe for adultery.[34]

Yet if the early manuscript is richer in such picturesque details, in other ways it is remarkably close to its modern counterpart. It is indeed virtually the same oracle, as these two responses, in Weber's translation, will show. They correspond to the Bower Manuscript's first two answers, given above, though the falls of the dice are differently arranged in the two texts:

4.4.1. Zweimal Vier, Eins zuletzt, hier ist ein schlimmer
Wurf gefallen dir.
Verwandten Verlut, Heimsuchung, grosse Qualen im
Herzen dein.
Auf wen sich dies (dein) Werk bezieht, dessen Stern wird
gepeinigt sehr.
Fünf Tage, 'nen Halbmonat lang hast du Qual; keine
Freud' ist dir.

1.4.4 Eins zuerst, zweimal Vier sodann; jetzt fiel dir ein
stierkräftiger Wurf.
Aller Geschäfte Vollgedeih, Getreide, Reichtum kömmt
dir zu.
Und welches Ziel du hast im Sinn, das wird zu Theil
dir werden ganz.
Und im Traum wirst du sehen Gott des Nachts,
nicht sei ein Zweifel dran.[35]

In 1907, Heinrich Lüders brought system and critical acumen into the domain of ancient Indian dicing, in a densely rich monograph on *Das Würfelspiel im alten Indien*.[36] Primarily concerned with royal dice-games in Vedic times and their reflection in works like the *Mahābhārata*, Lüders did not disdain the humbler medieval dice-oracles, and neither Weber, Schröter, nor Hoernle was safe from his basilisk glare. Among the earlier opinions that he demolished: the shape of the dice was not that of a four-sided pyramid, making the face that lay on the ground the decisive one (as the unfortunate Schröter had maintained, and Bolte innocently repeated). Rather they were (and still are) right-angled, four-side prisms, ca. 7 centimeters long and 1 centimeter broad. Only the four sides were numbered, not the ends, and there was no chance that the prism might accidentally come to rest on one of the unnumbered ends (which Schröter's hypothetical pyramid had been designed to prevent).[37]

Ancient literary sources refer to golden dice, but Lüders observes that only fairy-tale kings have objects fashioned exclusively from gold and silver. Most people are content with less precious substances, and the *Pāśaka-kevalī* mentions dice made of ivory or *śvetārka*-wood (*Asclepias gigantea*). In oldest times, however, according to the poems of the *Ṛg-veda* and the *Atharva-veda*, the preferred dice were fashioned from the nuts of the Vibhītaka tree (*Terminalia bellerica*; the dried fruits are still used today to treat cough and eye diseases).[38] As for the number of dice used, the Bower Manuscript is of significance, since the oldest literary texts give no information on this point. The oracle clearly requires three dice, but unlike his Indological predecessors, Lüders is by no means convinced that they were cast seriatim. He sees no obstacle to a simultaneous throw, providing only that the triad were distinctively marked to determine precedence. He believes that marks were a pot, a discus and an elephant, and thus he understands the opening phrase of the Bower Manuscript's first oracle: *kumbhakārīmātaṅgayuktā patantu* (more dramatically rendered by Hoernle as "Let them fall as befits Kumbhakārī, the Mātaṅga woman!"). In an earlier article, Hoernle had proposed this interpretation himself, only to abandon it later. All three objects are auspicious royal symbols. In the later *Pāśaka-kevalī*, only a single die is referred to, indicating that it was cast three times to determine the oracle's response.[39]

Lüders is scathing on poor Schröter's hypothesis of a chart or table of throws (Bolte took this over, too), and describes the technique of the throw from literary sources. He provides a wonderfully full account of the names of throws, in which the oracle data are naturally included. He also suggests an intriguing explanation of the presence of female figures at the oracle's outset. In the *Atharva-veda*, the Apsaras are said to love dicing, to be good players at dice, to take their pleasure in the dice-game. They anoint the player's hands with ghee, and bring his opponent into his power. Two hymns specifically entreat their assistance in the dicing. Lüders began his study of dicing with the *Vidhurapaṇḍita-jātaka*, which describes the dice-game of the King of the Kurus. As the game is about to begin, the king meditates on the Goddess and recites: "All rivers go in curves, all trees are made of wood, all women sin, when they find a seducer." As Lüders remarks, this has nothing to do with the Apsaras; it is a spell designed to assure success, since a true and virtuous wife brings her husband luck in gambling. The *Pāśaka-kevalī* specifies that the die must be cast by a pure maiden: has this virgin come to stand in for the faithful wife? At all events, whether virgins, wives, or goddesses, female figures envelop the opening stages of play as well as sortilege.[40]

The Indologists so far quoted all describe the dice as being numbered, 1-2-3-4 in the older versions, with variations in the modern. We have noted Weber's reference to a Tibetan oracle in the seventeenth-century *Vaiḍūrya dkar-po*, which employs three four-sided dice, each bearing the syllables A VA YA DA. Lüders only mentions this in passing, in a footnote; there were apparently no ancient Indian data.[41] But dice of this sort are much more widely known. Anne-Marie Esnoul describes the present-day use in India (the region is unfortunately not specified) of a manuscript book called the *Abhavapraśna*. It contains predictions written on both sides of its palm-leaf pages, and in the margin beside each response is found a combination of three letters, drawn from the four letters A, BH, Y, and D. A wooden die, attached to the manuscript, bears one of these letters on each of its faces. The die is thrown on the ground three times in succession, and careful note is taken of the letter on the uppermost face each time. The corresponding combination is then sought in the manuscript, and the response read out.[42]

The lettered dice are current elsewhere, as well. A resident of Meshed in the province of Khorasan, Iran, in the 1930s, Bess Allen Donalson described a mantic practice in use there, attributed to the Imam Ja'far as-Ṣadik. "A wooden die on the four faces of which are written the letters of the word *abjad* (a b j d) is thrown three times, the letter on top is noted each time, and the resulting combination is looked up in the book on *raml* [geomancy], and the result is worked out by the geomancer."[43] No doubt a good deal more evidence could be found for the widespread use of such dice with their four letters. Here we need only note their obvious Greek origin—in the Greek numerical alphabet. For of course they represent its first four letters, or numbers, duly syllabized when they entered, first, India, and then Tibet. A VA YA DA, A BH Y D, and A B J D all derive from α' β' γ' δ', and thus whether they are seen as "letters," syllables, or numerals is really all one. The true question concerns their age and mode of transport. As we have seen, the Indian dice-oracle is ancient and certainly Hellenic. Were such dice as these its instruments? What would be more at home in a soldier's kit than a set of dice? Did they form part of the baggage borne to India in Alexander's wake that included genethliac astrology, Greek medicine and mathematics, catoptromancy, and icons (with their theurgy no doubt as well)?[44] Or were the transmitters Muslims, centuries later, bearing their own

Hellenistic legacy—of which the Greek letter names and alphabetic order form an obvious part? Is the dissemination of these significant letters only another minor feature of the great wave of Islamic geomancy that over-whelmed much of Asia, Africa, and medieval Europe? Whatever the answer, with the Indian texts, we have tracked Hellenistic oracles to the frontiers of Tibet and beyond; and the Bower Manuscript has carried the tale deep into Central Asia.

The Islamic World

In his 1903 survey, Bolte followed the Indians with the Arabs, and so shall we. Earlier we had occasion to consider their ancient custom of divina-tion with inscribed arrows. In time, written verse oracles also made their appearance in the Islamic world, consulted either by means of dice or by the considerably more elaborate procedures of geomancy: *al-raml*, the art or science of sand. As early as 1861, Gustav Flügel had published a study on "Die Loosbücher der Muhammadaner."[45] Challenged by Sotzmann's re-marks, ten years before, on the probable Islamic origins of European Books of Fate, Flügel undertook to survey the evidence. He drew attention to the magical power of words in pre-Islamic Arabia. Words overheard casually were among the most significant *omina* portending future events, and this continued even after the Koran had provided a corpus of uniquely sacred language. The Koran itself became the primary oracle throughout the Islamic world, employed in the way that the texts of Homer, Virgil, and the Bible had been: opened at random to foretell destiny and aid in making decisions.

Flügel was soon to distinguish himself as editor of the massive bio-bibliographical encyclopaedia of Islamic culture, al-Nadīm's *al-Fihrist* (com-pleted ca. 989, in Baghdād), and it was in this work that he found the earliest references to Arabic manuals of divination.[46] These date from the ninth cen-tury, and may have included Losbuch-like examples. In the titles of these lost works, *fāl* divination is found together with auguries from the flight of birds, astrology, and the occult significance of numbers. Later, in Persian and Turkish, Losbücher were to be called *fāl-nameh*. Flügel notes that the Persians' special interest in this domain is already indicated by a title such as *Fāl-book Composed for the Inhabitants of Persia* (or *The Fāl-Buch in Cur-rent Use Amongst the Persians*). Unlike Arabic, Persian was not a sacred language of Islam, nor were the Persians at all strict about the prohibition on representing the human form. Naturally it was among the Persians, somewhat later, that the Books of Fate were expanded and perfected to include all manner of poetic and proverbial wisdom, as well as elaborate illustrations.

Persia's most prestigious oracle was in fact to be the collected poems of Hāfiz (died 1390). His *Diwan* even came to be known as "the Tongue of the Secret." Ultimately Hāfiz was to inspire Goethe's *West-östlicher Divan*. Goethe envied the happy destiny of a poet whose writings had become an oracle for his people, and even composed a curious Losbuch of his own, the *Weissagungen des Bakis* (1798).[47] Yet though Werther may have driven hundreds to suicide, it is doubtful whether Goethe's works ever achieved such mantic status as that accorded to Hāfiz's poems. Persian scholars compiled testimonies to their miraculous efficacy, such as were written elsewhere for icons of the Virgin Mary or the text of the *Lotus Sūtra*.[48]

Flügel goes on to describe a second stage of Koranic divination, which represents an interesting development of the letter-oracle. The Koran would be opened at random, and the first letter of the seventh line of the right-hand page noted. This letter would then be sought in a special *Fāl-nameh*, in which the responses were arranged according to the twenty-nine letters of the alphabet. The saying inscribed there, with or without a Koranic verse, would be the answer to one's question. The letter itself might well prove to be significant, since special powers were deemed to emanate from each letter (or numeral) of the alphabet, though only the initiate was aware of all the secret meanings and applications of letters and numbers.[49]

Among extant Persian Books of Fate, Flügel found that one attributed to the Imam Ja'far as-Ṣadik came fairly close to the form taken by many later European Losbücher. It consisted of thirty-two pages, each bearing a response, and each opening with a combination of three letters. These corresponded to the letters (rather than points or dots) borne by three dice. European libraries contain many Persian and Turkish texts belonging to the same group. (The dice-oracle attributed to the Imam Ja'far is the one recorded by Bess Donaldson as still current in Meshed.)[50]

Still another type of Persian text involves a preliminary list of fixed questions. Flügel describes an example with four question-categories: on a prospective journey, a profitable business undertaking, a threatening enemy, and whether or not an ailing person will die. This particular text was used as a Koranic oracle, and letters standing in certain positions on a page of the Koran opened at random were to be selected, depending on the question.

The magical power of the letters and their relevance were then to be assessed according to the presence or absence of diacritic signs, the particular vocalization of the consonants, and so on. At the end of his study, Flügel publishes and translates two short letter-oracles.[51]

As a supreme example among Persian Losbücher, Flügel adduces a large and richly illustrated manuscript in the Dresden Library. Its opening pages are missing, so the title, author, and date are unfortunately unknown. The text often cites the names, honored in mantic tradition, of Daniel, Naṣiraddin Ṭūsī, and the Imam Ja'far. As for the full-page paintings, they depict "Ali and descendents, including Mohammed and the twelve Imams; ancient and mythological kings and worthies (Cyrus, Alexander, and others); the prophets and sages (Abraham, Ishmael, Moses before Pharaoh, Lokmān, Joseph in and out of Egypt); and even such exemplary pairs as Adam and Eve, Cain and Abel, Leila and Majnun." All these are intermingled with illustrations of Koranic texts: the Seven Sleepers, the two judges of the dead (Munkar and Nakīr), the Prophet's camel. The planets Mars and Mercury are shown, as well as the Ka'ba with angels, and more.

All this is strikingly reminiscent of late medieval and Renaissance Losbücher in Europe. Flügel appears indeed to have succeeded in his quest for the Islamic prototypes posited by Sotzmann. We should quote Flügel's impressions, as he gazed upon all this with the fresh eyes of a discoverer. The work's Shi'ite inspiration was obvious, and it was certain, too, that this great manuscript's illustrator had been a Persian. In tolerant Persia, such an iconographic project could be readily undertaken without troubling one's religious conscience; there too the artist "leider aber in ihrer Ausführung nur zu sehr chinesischem Geschmack und chinesischen Mustern sich hingab."[52] Coming upon this remark in the alien wilderness, the weary sinologist's sorrow is turned to joy, his tears to laughter. Chinese influence is certainly plainly visible in medieval Persian art of all sorts: ceramics, figure-painting, bronze mirrors.... But might there have been a more precisely identifiable influence on the illustrated book—especially on the illustrated Book of Fate?

In 1854, during a summer's sojourn in the mountains of the Antilebanon, Johann Gottfried Wetzstein purchased the Arabic manuscript of a Book of Fate from an itinerant bookseller. The game-like oracle came as a welcome diversion from the loneliness of the isolated spot, and Wetzstein translated it for his wife's amusement. In later years friends often urged him to print his verse translation, but he resisted. It only appeared in 1929, revised by

Gotthold Weil, who prefaced it with a survey of the genre.[53] Weil began with
Assyro-Babylonian belomancy, and went on to the Greek dice- and letter-
oracles studied by Heinevetter. He described the oracle of Astrampsychos,
with its fixed list of ninety-two preliminary questions, and observed that
in some editions certain answers are attributed to persons or places known
from the Old Testament, for example, Abraham, Rachel, or Egypt. He then
examined the *Sortes apostolorum*, the other notable Christian extension of
the ancient oracle book.

Passing to the Arabs, Weil reviewed the procedures known to have been
current before Islam. Like Flügel, he noted that although Mohammed banned
most pre-Islamic forms of divination, he did authorize the long-standing
custom of drawing omen from human acts and speech: "Bird-augury (*ṭijāra*)
is forbidden, but the interpretation of human acts and words as an omen
(*fa'l*) is permitted."[54] As in the Christian West, in Islam recourse was also
had to sortilegium in deciding disputed legal cases. Meanwhile, the fixed
written oracle became ever more prominent—the Koran serving as the initial
prototype. Mantic consultation of the Koran was made more complex by
a growing number of "tension-producing" procedures that involved rules
for choosing a letter or series of letters, which then might give access either
to another book of answers, or to an esoteric disquisition on alphabetic
mysteries—or both.

In these systems Weil saw the essential elements of the later, more compen-
dious Book of Fate; though distinct from the *Stechbuch*-aspect of Koranic
consultation, they too were accessible only by means of detours through
numbers, letters, or dice. The term *kur'a* was used to designate dice-oracles
and the entire literary genre of Losbücher. Even as the Latin terms *sortes*
and *sortilegium*, originally denoting cleromancy, were in time applied to all
sorts of experimental divination, so the word *kur'a* was extended to cover a
wide variety of mantic exercises as Books of Fate became the most popular
divinatory medium.[55]

Weil observes that similarities between mantic systems in different cultures must often be attributed to the nature of divination itself. Thus many
resemblances between Arab divination and practices of the Graeco-Roman
world should not be taken an evidence of borrowing—especially since like
phenomena are also to be found elsewhere, at great remove, throughout the
world. Yet he admits that for the Arabic Books of Fate the situation is entirely different. "In their structure, arrangement, equipment, and maxims,

they are so amazingly close to the corresponding Greek Books of Fate that there is no longer any question of a coincidental similarity." And Weil goes on to remark that a clear indication of their direct derivation from Greek literature is present among the Arabs themselves, since the oldest Losbücher mentioned in al-Nadīm's tenth-century *al-Fihrist* are attributed to Pythagoras and Alexander the Great: to Pythagoras as the method's discoverer, and to Alexander as the one who made use of the oracle, and whose great success bears witness to its veracity. The same august patrons in fact appear in the Greek oracle of Astrampsychos.[56]

Having admirably set the stage, Weil goes on to present the three chief types of *kur'a*. The first is ascribed to the Prophet Daniel and is called *Kur'at al-anbijā*, "Kur'a of the Prophets." It is the most primitive of the three and shows no dependence on Greek sources. It opens with a table of thirty-two boxes, in each the name of a prophet, from Adam to Daniel and Mohammed. This is followed by thirty-two responses of the most general import, each attributed to one of the prophets. The fated answer is to be found by laying one's finger at random on the table of names.[57]

Next comes the system already described by Flügel, the dice-oracle attributed to the Imām Ja'far. Weil has no doubts regarding its Greek provenance. He notes that although Western Losbücher generally consist of fifty-six responses (based on selected five-place combinations of six different signs), this *Kur'a al-ga'farīja* always gives the full set of sixty-four possible variations, formed by the permutations of four letters in groups of three places, as aaa, aab, aac, aad, and so on. He sees the use of four letters as unquestionably deriving from Greek *astragaloi*. The oracle's responses are all very general in tone, as befits the unrestricted range of potential questions. In the fullest editions, each response includes a text in prose opening with a verse from the Koran; this is followed by verses. In smaller texts one finds only the prose, and sometimes even only the Koran verses.[58]

Tradition ascribes the third sort of Losbuch to the Caliph Ma'mūn, and it is therefore termed *al-Kur'a al-ma'mūnija*. The revealers of the responses here are birds and kings, and the genre is consequently also known as *Kur'at aṭ-ṭujūr* or *Kur'at al-mulūk*. The oracle translated by Wetzstein belongs to this species, and Weil thus chose to name it *Die Königslose*. This example comprises thirty-six sets of answers, but Weil knew two other manuscripts of this type, one counting but sixteen sets of responses, the other sixty. The various versions differ, too, in the quantity of material (or number of obstacles), which they place between the question and the oracular response—material that Weil felt was added to heighten the thrill of the chase. Yet however different in detail, all oracles of this third, Caliph Ma'mūn type, open with a fixed list of question topics. One of these must be chosen and submitted to the oracle, then the dice are cast or a number is determined by other means. The main portion of the book is occupied by the answers, in verse, classified under each category of questions, with each set of answers placed in the mouth of an historical or mythical personage. Owing to the relative specificity of the initial questions, the answers could be fairly forthright—in contrast to all other Losbuch forms. This accounts for the popularity of this type of oracle in daily life, until (Weil suggests) its use came nearly to assume the character of a religious exercise.[59]

Weil proceeds to explain the method of consultation: how the querent selects the object of inquiry from one of the first six "wish-circles," then the same object from one of the second six wish-circles (in which all thirty-six items are repeated); next puts together the two letters which stand in the middle of the respective circles; then on to the next two circles, each of which contains eighteen constellations. Numbers are inscribed around the rims and, beneath each number, one of the two-letter combinations. The querent finds his two letters and casts the dice for a number from two to ten. The number obtained, he moves that many sectors forward, that is, to the right, from his place on one of the two circles of constellations. The sector he reaches by these means bears, like all the others, the name of a constellation and a number. Here (if he likes) the querent may stop, and go to the oracle to get his response, since the number is the same as that of the king who will later deliver his pronouncement. But the excitement is enhanced by the various intermediate procedures that have been inserted here. From the thirty-six constellations one goes to the thirty-six birds, which in turn bring one to the thirty-six cities, which for their part name thirty-six kings: one of them holds the answer. Each king announces nine responses, each of which bears a number from two to ten. The suitable answer is the one corresponding to the number obtained by casting dice at the outset.[60]

Weil notes that this Oracle of the Kings shares with the Greek Astrampsy-chos text the feature of giving fixed alternative responses to predetermined questions. This alone, though, would not guarantee that it was Greek-derived. Yet a closer scrutiny of the initial questions themselves makes such a derivation very probable, since Weil has determined that all the thirty-six questions in the six wish-circles of the Arabic text are found in closely similar Greek versions among the ninety-two questions of the Astrampsychos oracle. (The far greater number of questions in the Greek results from the subdivision of individual inquiries, for example, "inheritance": from one's mother, one's father, one's wife, one's friend, and so on.) The two lists also share the designation of each question by a particular number; in the Greek text they are numbered from 1 to 103, in the Arabic by thirty-six combinations of two letters.[61]

Thus the two major Arabic Losbuch types are unquestionably based on Greek models. Yet they had been vastly, fantastically enhanced, and later examples are of course even more elaborate than these. In divination as in other sciences, Arabs and Persians worked from Hellenistic templates, but their absorption in the task was no sterile routine. When in due course the Greek oracles returned to Europe, they had been wonderously enriched. Virtually everything coming between the question and the answer was Islamic—if it was not indeed Chinese.

In 1925, in the middle of his work on the mammoth *Anmerkungen zu den Kinder- und Hausmärchen der Brüder Grimm* (1912–1932), Johannes Bolte turned once more to the Books of Fate. His concise survey, "Zur Geschichte der Punktier- und Losbücher," represents his views twenty years after his 1903 study. The article's most conspicuous features were the diagrams with which it opens: first the lines by means of which a geomantic figure is constructed, then the sixteen figures themselves (each consisting of from four to eight points, differently arranged), and then the sixty-four hexagrams of the *Book of Changes*. In 1903, Bolte mentioned Chinese oracles only to exclude them from his survey. In 1925, he adduced the great-grandfather of them all: the *I-ching*. He owed his knowledge of it to the German translator, Richard Wilhelm. After reviewing the principles and practice of geomancy, Bolte was convinced that the Arabs found their inspiration in Chinese mantic practice. "Man braucht nur diese Trigramme und Hexagramme mit den vierzeiligen arabischen Punktierfiguren zu vergleichen, um zu der Erkenntnis zu gelangen, das die Araber die Punktierkunst wohl systematisiert, aber nicht erfunden haben."[62]

We have seen that one of the Losbuch manuscripts mentioned by Sotzmann in 1851 gave, for access to the oracle, the sixteen geomantic figures made up of differently arranged dots or points. Bolte's 1903 study contains a summary of information based on a number of European texts. They represent what he termed the new stimulus given to the Losbuch genre by this Islamic science from the twelfth century on. And it is indeed into the History of Science that this subject brings us. Paul Tannery (1843–1904), whom George Sarton called the first historian of science, wrote a lucid study of geomancy and its introduction to Byzantium and Europe (only published posthumously, in 1920).[63] Copious information on the subject is found throughout the two vast surveys, Lynn Thorndike's *History of Magic and Experimental Science* (1923–1958) and Sarton's *Introduction to the History of Science* (1927–1948). One of the major medieval Latin treatises, the *Experimentarius*, by Bernard Sylvester of Tours, is available in a modern edition.[64] In Germany, at least, the practice continued into our own century, and modern instructions for use can still be found. The quantity of available descriptions and analyses fortunately relieves us of that task. There is also now, in English, an exhaustive book on the subject, Stephen Skinner's *Terrestrial Astrology: Divination by Geomancy*.[65]

Skinner is mainly concerned with actual techniques and calculations, History is his weakest suit; he feels the system should simply be attributed to Muslim North Africa, and does not speculate on the theory of origins further to the east. He does bring together the European data with ethnographic reports from West Africa and Madagascar. It is certain that the great Ifa oracle among the Yoruba and the *sikidy* of Madagascar have a common source in Islamic *al-raml*, "Sandkunst"—the same foundations in the dust that ultimately regenerated the European Losbuch.[66] All this is useful in suggesting how new methods of access might expand and enhance the form and content of oracles—whether written, as throughout Eurasia and North Africa, or oral, in West Africa and Madagascar. It also unveils a tableau of vast diffusion certain to dazzle the innocent sinologist, perched at Eurasia's easternmost rim. In all this seething interchange, can China really have been out of bounds?

Following Bolte's 1925 survey, another general account of Losbücher was produced by Fritz Boehme, in the fifth volume of the indispensable *Handwörterbuch des deutschen Aberglaubens* (1933).[67] Boehme took Bolte's two studies as his model, and had access to Bolte's own annotated, updated copies of them, as well. He was also able to make use of G. Weil's introduction to Wetzstein's *Königslose*, which had been published in 1929. The result is a clear, intelligent presentation. When read in conjunction with Boehme's article "Los, losen" in the same volume, it offers a very useful conspectus of the field. For Boehme, though, the question of the Greek originals of Arabic and Persian oracle books was not yet settled. It is precisely in this connexion that he adduced the problem of possible Chinese influence. (Wilhelm's translation of the *I-ching* had been published in 1924.) Here again one confronts yet another formulation of the old Asia-against-Europe hypothesis, all too familiar since Herodotus, where it is always "us" against "them," and the East is not only permanently exotic but also strangely homogeneous. Clearly, possible Chinese contributions must be isolated and anatomized individually and step by step in the way that Greek contributions have been.

Central Asia: Turks and Sogdians

Novel in Bolte's 1925 article and carried over by Boehme are a number of oracle texts discovered in Central Asia. Even as the late nineteenth century had seen first the systematic exploration of ancient Greek sites in Asia Minor, and then the spectacular papyrus finds in the dust heaps of Graeco-Roman Egypt, the early twentieth century thrilled to the reports of those who sought out "traces of Hellas in East Turkestan."[68] A series of expeditions by Aurel Stein, Paul Pelliot, and Albert von Le Coq brought renown and booty to collections in London, Paris, and Berlin. Among the hoard of statuary, wall paintings, banners, hanging scrolls, and manuscripts were these Central Asian Books of Fate. The largest, most complete example, written in Turkish runic script, was found at Tun-huang by Aurel Stein in 1907. Vilhelm Thomsen, who published and translated it in 1912, believed that it probably dated from the early ninth century.[69]

The oracle consists of sixty-five responses, written on fifty-eight sheets of thick yellow Chinese paper, folded and glued together to form a compact booklet, 13.6 × 8 cm. It is a dice-oracle, and above each response the corresponding throw stands depicted in three series of small black circles filled with red: the permutations of three four-sided dice. The initial answer reminds us forcibly that we are at Tun-huang, the Chinese gateway to the Silk Road (or, coming from the West, the entry to China):

(1) I am T(ä)n si [T'ien-tzu, Son of Heaven:
the Chinese Emperor]. Early and late I enjoy
sitting on the golden throne. Know ye this. This
is good.

(2) I am the Way-God [yol t(ä)ṅri] on a piebald horse.
Early and late I amble [?] along. He met a two-month-
old child of man. The man was afraid. "Fear not; I
will give you blessing," said he. Know this. This is good.

Each response is generally an independent vignette, and many of them depict animals:

(15) The fog was hanging above, the dust was lying below.
The young bird went astray while flying; the young
deer went astray while running; the child of man went
astray while walking. By the blessing of heaven they
all met again in the third year, hale and hearty. They
all rejoice and are glad. Know ye this. This is good.

(22) A monk dropped his bell into a lake. In the morning
it tinkles, in the evening it jingles. Know ye this.
This is painful. It is evil and bad.[70]

(25) Two oxen were bound together with one fetter. They
stand without being able to move. Know this. This is
bad.

(31) A tiger went out in search of game and prey. It found
its game and prey, and after having found it comes
to its den rejoicing and glad. Know this. This is good.

(33) The felt is put into water. Still beat it, tie it
tightly. Know ye this. This is bad.

(51) I am a bold black-eagle. A green rock is my summer
abode, a red rock is my winter abode. I enjoy staying
on that mountain. Know this.

As Thomsen observes, "several of the details are so closely connected with the mode of living of the Turks that . . . it is impossible to conceive that they are translations from another language." Once again, the imported form has been fleshed out with indigenous elements to make a properly Turkic oracle.

Yet this was not the only Book of Fate in circulation among the region's Turks. In 1909, von Le Coq published a "Christian manuscript-fragment" which he had found in 1905 in the ruins of Bulāyïq, north of Turfan. It too was the remnant of a little booklet, 13.5 × 9.5, written in greyish ink on rough brownish-yellow paper. Its editor deemed the contents Christian, "but apparently apocryphal, and a literal translation from the Syriac." He gives text, transcription, and a word-by-word translation.[71] Seventeen years later, Willy Bang reexamined this short text, translated it anew, and set it in its proper context. Rendering his German:

> O my son! This is thy path. Now hear God's command!
> Do not go forth upon that path at this time. Should
> you without obeying [nevertheless] go, you will fall
> into the great pit. If you ask why, [it is because] the evil
> fiend awaits you and will destroy you.

> 18th Commandment. Favourable. So speaks
> the Apostle Zawtai: You resemble, O son of man,
> that cow which called from afar to her calf that had
> strayed. When the calf heard his mother's voice, he
> came running quickly back and was comforted. Even so
> will you immediately be reunited in great joy with
> your loved ones who are far from you.

> 19th Commandment. Unfavourable. So speaks
> the Apostle Luke: You son of man, wash your hands
> clean! Have no fear of evil [but fight it bravely]!
> Keep your thoughts pure! Everything that your love of God
> inspires, do it completely! If [you do not
> do it] completely . . . [72]

Bang recognized that this fragment must be part of a book of divination, like the one published by Thomsen in 1912—but in this case, a Christian book. Yet he too imagined that it must have emanated from some Syriac collection of noncanonical sayings of the apostles. After Bang's article appeared, the Cambridge scholar F. C. Burkitt wrote informing him that the text evidently came from a version of the *Sortes apostolorum*.[73] Thus another western *Losbuch* has appeared on China's frontier—though unfortunately, there is no information on the method of consultation. Another fragment has since turned up, however, this time in Sogdian. Discovered among the Chinese manuscripts acquired by Aurel Stein at Tun-huang in 1907, it had long been overlooked, but was at last published by Nicholas Sims-Williams in 1976. It originally formed part of a scroll. In Sims-Williams' translation:

> . . . *Thus says the Apostle* Simon: "You are like
> the cow [that had] strayed from the herd. A
> lion was lying in the road, very hungry and

thirsty. Thus he wished: 'I shall eat her';
[but] God delivered the cow from the lion's
mouth. So will God deliver you too from the
... thing which has come upon you."[74]

Sims-Williams finds that this Christian Sogdian text is closest, among the published Central Asian Losbuch manuscripts, to Le Coq's Christian Turkish fragment, and he quotes Bang's version of the anecdote concerning the cow and her calf. Animals are indeed remarkably prominent in all the Central Asian texts examined so far.

In 1929, Bang and Annemarie von Gabain published the remains of a very substantial Turkic Losbuch, found at Yar Khoto.[75] In this case, a Chinese presence is manifest, since each of the responses includes a hexagram from the *Book of Changes*, though they do not follow the normal order. Bang and Gabain believed the work to be "a translation or at least an adaptation of one of the numerous Chinese popular Books of Fate which are ultimately based upon the archaic *I-ching*." The text itself provides no instructions about obtaining a particular response. The editors supposed that the method may have been the same as that ordinarily used by the Chinese in *I-ching* consultation, with milfoil stalks.[76] They were also uncertain regarding the text's date, but its language seemed very archaic and very close to that of the ninth-century Turkic inscriptions.

As a specimen, herewith the first two responses:

You have become .... The service of all lands has emerged. Divine luck and victory have of themselves settled in front of you. In your time the splendor of the sun has risen and shone forth. The countenance of the brown earth turned green and beautiful. A white cloud rose and it rained. The dust settled. In the East and in the West the lands are according to your wishes. In the South and in the North cities and empires are according to your heart's desire. You improved your lowly name; you elevated your paltry name. Who could disobey you? Your bundles of ware are on the way. Your ... commands have been carried out. If you have desired a child for a long time, you will conceive and receive it right away. [The] sickness has disappeared ... Let your heart rejoice. Heaven and earth shall offer joy.

If this sign called 'coincidence' should occur, it expresses by its word the following: grim, stern, ferocious words have emerged in your presence. Endless roaring winds have blown [without end] around your house. If at the time of sickness [on the occasion of sickness] you ... see

· ·

· · · · · · · · · · penetrated you, to wound you. Sickness persecuted you, to torture your body. Sickness entered the upper arm; [now] there is pain [there]. It has to be nursed. Fire [i.e., worries] entered your heart; [now] grief inhabits it; from this danger one has to liberate oneself, No path is evident for you. Peace and joy cannot be found. The sun god entered the earth, his shining was hindered. The bird that flew under the blue sky could no longer fly. The sovereign is tortured, without finding a deal [?]. Ärklig-Qans commands *arqulayu turur* in your house. Deceptive people deceive you in your presence. They work to hinder the splendor of the sun and the moon. They exert themselves to cut off the path of good people. Five demons battle against each other. Three ghosts beat each other. Cease all dealings! Do meritorious good works! The loathsome will dissolve, the Good will approach. (Ibid., pp. 245–46)

Here the querent is provided with a comprehensive analysis, couched in sententious Chinese parallel style (which the German translators admit greatly helped them in their work). The translations of hexagram-names correspond to the Chinese originals, and the responses also reflect familiarity with the symbolic interpretation of the hexagrams' particular structure; it may all very well have been taken over from some Chinese prototype. Might the various weather-signs mentioned bring this oracle into some closer relationship with the other Central Asian texts? Here, a white cloud rose, it rained, the dust subsided; in Thomsen's response no. 15, "the fog was hanging above, the dust was lying below"—but such lines are found in Chinese sequences, too. A surer indication: birds and animal are scarcely mentioned. "Der Schwan flog auf, auf seinen See lässt er sich nicht nieder" ["The swan flew up, it does not settle upon its lake"] (11. 215–16)—but bird-life does as much, or as little, in Chinese oracles. Many responses deal programmatically with their applications to precise circumstances: "Wenn du seit langem ein Kind wünschst, so bekommst du es sogleich. Wenn du Hab und Gut wünschst, so bekommst und erhältst du es sogleich. Die Krankheit ist gewichen ... "[79]; or again: "Deine dich umgebenden Feinde wurden zahlreich. Dein Vorteil und Ehre nahmen ab. Deine Habe verminderte sich. Von Reich und Qan gibt es Leid. Um deinen Körper herum gibt es Gefahr. Ein Weg, der für dich Vorteile verspricht, zeigt sich nicht ... " (11. 58–61).[80] One thinks immediately of the systematic applications, category by category, which follow each response in certain Chinese sequences. One also thinks of

Astrampsychos and his progeny—but in this case, there can be no doubt of a Chinese origin.[81]

Medieval Tibetans

Among all the Central Asian texts then newly emerging, Tibetan, too, was represented, and several torn Tibetan Losbuch pages were published in 1924 and 1928 by A. H. Francke.[82] He considered their handwriting to belong to the oldest, eighth- or ninth-century stratum of Tibetan script. Francke initially edited three leaves, two brought back from Turfan by the Prussian expedition, one found by Aurel Stein at Mazār-Tāgh.[83] In them we encounter elements with which we are already familiar:

[First leaf]

    I. 1. The camels went to drink water, and the day turned hot...

        2. The moon rose. Then it turned night. Then the sun rose...

        3. At the meeting with... the heart rejoiced. So also you, man...

        4. It will happen in accordance with [your] thoughts. Surrender the joyless mood!

○ ○ ○

   II. 1. From the mouth of the interpreter of signs: You, man, [will become] a Glorious...

        2. In accordance with this it will come about, it will be fulfilled...

○ ○ ○

   III. 1. The Rākṣasa spoke: Not becoming rich [or a rich man], wealth...

        2. ..... neither by the tambourine invited...[84]

The second leaf is fearfully lacunose; but the first line concludes, "Das Los ist gut" (*mo bzaṇ*), as does VI. 3.

[Third leaf]

   IX. 1. ..... high are... even if the mountain of the gods is ridiculed, [it still will remain] a high mountain.

        2. ..... glory [?] does not spread, remaining firm... thinking...

3. .... longing for the mountain of the gods, up on high sun and moon display [their splendor].

4. .... cold wind in open field, does not greet a bright day.

○ ○ ○

X. 1. Even if the king of arrows is lame

2. the wild birds do not know to save themselves and do not know to

3. fly. Even though antlers would be of benefit to the gentle stag, it does not show them when it is disturbed.[85]

Here the whole menagerie is back again, and Francke is certainly right in detecting close analogies between this Tibetan oracle and the Turkish one published by Thomsen. Both contrast with the stern injunctions to purity found in the Turkish *Sortes apostolorum*, with its "Son of Man, wash your hands clean!" and other such cheerful sentiments. Like Thomsen's text, the Tibetan oracle is a dice-oracle, and the little circles above each response depict the triple throw. Responses in both oracles often end with a judgment: here, "Das Los ist gut" in Turkish, "know this: this is good," or "Know ye this: this is bad." Francke adduces several Turkish responses that seem particularly close to the Tibetan fragments. Thomsen's no. 26: "The morning dawned. Then the earth brightened. Then the sun rose, and the light shone over everything. Know this. This is good," he compares with Tibetan I. Tibetan II he finds similar to Thomsen's no. 55: "A brave man's son went to the army [in the field]. When he was at the seat of war a messenger prodded him, saying: 'When [a man] comes home he himself becomes famous, and his horse comes rejoicing—[?].' Know ye this. This is evil and good."[86]

By 1928, four years later, Francke had identified three more pages of Tibetan dice-oracle in von Le Coq's collection. All three are fragmentary and in poor condition, and all are written on the back of Chinese Buddhist texts, on sheets of varying size: paper was scarce in Central Asia. From these additions to the corpus, it is clear that many of the responses were placed in the mouths of particular deities. Earlier we had *Phyvai zhal-nas* ("Aus dem Mund der Zeichendeuter"; *phya* itself means "lot," "fortune," but Francke now identifies it as one of a class of Bön deities, "fates" or gods of good fortune).[87] There was also *'dre phon srin*, at first translated by Francke as "Der Rākṣasa," but which now causes him to hesitate.[88] In these new pages we find a response uttered by Pho-lha, "the male god," one of a set of deities born at the same time as the person whom they accompany and protect throughout life.[89] A "Great King" whose mutilated name ended in *mtsho*, "Ocean," Francke believes is probably a Nāga. An inauspicious answer ("O Mensch, es ist niemand unglücklicher als du . . . ") issues from the mouth of Lha rol-mo-chan, "Der Gott mit dem Musikinstrument." On dPal-lha, his "Gott des Ruhmes," Francke has no further information, but wonders if he does not indeed stand for the Bonpos' supreme god. In any case, these oracular personages form a very special set of "Apostles."

Francke refers the reader to published photographs of dice recovered from Central Asian sites by Aurel Stein.[90] He also quotes the 1907 study of ancient Indian dicing by Lüders, whose reconstruction explains the way the Tibetan oracle worked. Going back to Weber's 1868 translation of the *Pāśaka-kevalī*, Francke tabulates (among its sixty-four responses) the good (41), the bad (11), and the mixed, half good half bad (12), according to the respective throws. Only two of the Tibetan fragments still retain the depiction of all three dice in any one response. But these both correspond to their equivalents in the *Pāśaka-kevalī*, in that they are also attached to "good" answers. Francke takes this as an indication of consanguinity between the Indian and the Tibetan oracles, but it is hardly decisive, since the Indian work has nearly twice as many favorable answers as bad or indifferent ones (suggesting that its author was keen on reassurance). On the contrary, in light of the endless series of contrasts and congruences stretching across Eurasia, this particular Tibetan Losbuch does not seem especially close to the Indian text—particularly since (as Francke too observes) the *Pāśaka-kevalī* does not put its responses into the mouths of deities. And where in the Indian Losbuch is all the fauna that makes this Tibetan oracle so fitting a companion for its Turkish contemporary? Apart from the dice, it chiefly shares with the *Pāśaka-kevalī* the common dicta and old soothsayer's routines enshrined in the oracle genre across Asia.

Albrecht Weber had mentioned a dice-oracle in the Tibetan bsTan-gyur; he quoted Anton Schiefner's description of this work, entitled simply *Kevalī* in Sanskrit, *Mo-rtsis* in Tibetan (no. 5814 in the catalog of the Peking edition): it instructs the reader to carve three dice from the wood of the Sandilya tree (*Aegle marmelos*) during the third watch of the fourteenth night of the first month of spring—wood taken from the north or east side of the root. The four-sided dice are to be marked with the syllables A, YA, VA, DA; there are sixty-four combinations. The opening verse explains that this text emanates

from the school of Srī Raudhe, who was born in the land of Pārśika, north of
Nepal, in the endless north.[91] It is attributed to Śrī Śāntideva as author, and
Gautamaśrī, Rāma, Buddhaśrījñāna, and Ñi-ma rgyal-msthan dpal bzaṅ-po
as translators. Francke offers a rendering of one response:

Va-dava

> You who inquire, take note of this!
> You will reach these your goals almost completely!
> Why give medicine to the healthy?
> Pacify your heart! No more hatred!
> The goals will most likely be reached in a beautiful manner.
> The enemies outside will be repelled. Why
> fear the conclusion of peace?
> Therefore offer plenty [of praise] to your gods!
> Because you have done that, you will reach your goal and will have no
> enemies!
> And your enemies will depart humiliated.
> By this you will find benefit for your work and will really reach your goal.[92]

As Francke observes, the manuscript fragments certainly did not originate in *this* Tibetan oracle. After surveying the Sanskrit specimens (Bower
Manuscript and *Pāśaka-kevalī*), the *Mo-rstis* or *Kevalī* text in the bsTangyur,
Thomsen's Turkish oracle in runic script, and the Turkish *Sortes apostolorum*, Francke concludes that his Tibetan remains are closest to the Turkish
runic sequence.[93]

The next major publication of medieval Tibetan oracle manuscripts was
(posthumously) by F. W. Thomas (1867–1956), in his *Ancient Folk-Literature
from North-Eastern Tibet*. His sixth chapter is entirely devoted to "Mo-
Divination."[94] An introductory section describes the texts in relation to the
older studies by Weber, Hoernle, Francke, Lüders, Waddell, and Thomsen.
Thomas observed that Francke's Tibetan fragments from Turfan were in
prose, unlike the one from Mazār-Tāgh, in verse. The five Turfan specimens
also present a narrative element not found either in the Sanskrit *Pāśaka-
kevalī* or its later Tibetan equivalent. In this the Turfan fragments do indeed
closely resemble Thomsen's Turkic sequence (as Francke has pointed out),
and Thomas concluded that "the Turfan method was an adaptation to local ways of thinking, which from historico-geographical considerations and
upon the evidence of Thomsen's Turkī Ms. we should be inclined to conceive
as Turk" (p. 114).

Thomas gives in transcription and tentative translation a Tibetan verse-oracle from a ninth-century Tun-huang manuscript in the India Office Library. It was intended for use with three four-sided dice, and presumably comprised sixty-four responses (the total number of possible combinations), of which thirty-one have been preserved. Each verse response is followed by a prose statement regarding its application to a classified set of circumstances, depending on whether the inquiry concerns domestic life, personal warfare, friends, petitions, property, travel, trade, ailments, enemies, official position—but not all categories are represented in each case. In an addendum (pp. 140–157), Thomas notes the presence of similar manuscripts in the Bibliothèque Nationale and transcribes portions of two other, related dice-oracles in the India Office Library.

With regard to the systematic list of applications, Thomas remarks on a continuity in this respect with modern Tibetan dice-oracles as documented by Waddell, and takes this feature to indicate an ultimate Indian origin (pp. 115–116). He goes on to declare that "the practice illustrated by the Ms. is characteristically Tibetan. There is no trace of anything Chinese" (p. 117). Brave words from a Tibetologist. As we have seen, similar lists are found in written oracles throughout Eurasia, including China. Close comparison of such structural features wherever they occur may indeed eventually allow us to determine a common origin—but Chinese influence on these Tibetan texts is certainly not excluded.

Like Thomsen's Turkic sequence, one of Thomas's Tibetan texts is bound as a little pocket-manual. From this circumstance and from the curiously disjunct oracular phrasing generally, Thomas infers that such texts probably recorded the personal experience of individual diviners (pp. 117, 141). One need only compare the seemingly arbitrary responses of many other, printed oracles to see that the evidence does not warrant this conclusion. Yet it is all too easy to find fault with Thomas's pioneering work. His translations are not always fully intelligible, but his sustained engagement with these obscure, elusive texts is to be admired.

The year before Thomas's *Ancient Folk-Literature* appeared, A. Róna Tas made a suggestive contribution to Tibetan mantic studies. In analyzing the iconography of Lha-mo, "The Goddess," he observed two attributes that had not been adequately accounted for. Alongside the mule ridden by the deity hang two dice. Róna Tas linked these with oracle books of the sort that Francke has studied, and noted Lha-mo's prominent role in divination.

He returned to the equivalence, already remarked by Francke, of *mo* "dice" and *mo* "woman." The oracular formula *mo bzaṅ ṅo* might mean either "the augury is favorable" or "the goddess is favorable." He stressed the close connexion between divination and healing, and noted that Lha-mo consistently appears in the guise of a female fortune-teller in the *Bcun-mo bka'i thaṅ-yig* (Laufer's "Roman einer tibetischen Königin").[95]

Another, more puzzling attribute of the Goddess is a stick, sometimes notched, tucked into her belt (or held in her hand). This is called a *khram-siṅ* or tally-stick, and Róna Tas reviewed the original documentary and juridical role of such sticks, which are mentioned in Tibetan manuscripts from Tun-huang. Giuseppe Tucci has suggested that the later, iconographic significance of the tally-stick was as a record of sins. When a newly dead person was led before the Lord of Death (Gsin-rje), this monarch of the shades examined the tally-stick on which were noted the sins committed during that person's lifetime. Róna Tas observed that "Lha-mo repeatedly plays the part of a goddess of death, being at the same time the wife of the Lord of Death, Yama"; he believed that her tally-stick thus represented a "score of sins."[96] We should compare a trait of Chinese infernal iconography. In paintings of the ten kings (or judges) of hell, we sometimes see on each judge's desk two cylinders filled with notched tally-sticks, or oracular lots. The receptacles are labeled "fire-lots" (*huo-ch'ien*), or simply "lot-cylinders" (*ch'ien-t'ung*). Since there are two containers, the sticks are probably being used as counters of good and evil deeds, rather than adding an element of mantic risk to the fate of the wretches who are dragged before those dark tribunals.[97]

China at Tun-huang

From these eighth- and ninth-century texts discovered at Turfan and Tun-huang, it is a short step to the far more abundant materials in Chinese from the same period and region. If China has always been a sooth-sayer's wonderland, it was only to be expected that the 30,000-odd Tun-huang manuscripts should include a wide variety of mantic texts. Divination has been a prime focus of the Paris Tun-huang studies group, under the direction of Michel Soymié and Paul Magnin. There have been pioneering studies of dream-interpretation by Jean-Pierre Drège, physiognomy by Hou Ching-lang, and astrology by Jao Tsong-yi.[98] Closest to our concerns here is the research of Carole Morgan and Marc Kalinowski, on sortilege and numeromancy.[99]

Earlier, in reviewing other types of Chinese verse oracles, we briefly described the *Ling-ch'i ching*, the *Book of the Empowered Draughtsmen*. Carole Morgan has now studied the *textus receptus*, whose commentaries confirm it as a fourteenth-century recension, in the 1445 Taoist Canon. She has examined earlier fragments of the work in four tenth-century Tun-huang manuscripts, and has also had access to a Japanese manuscript of uncertain date and provenance in the Yonezawa collection. There are significant differences among all six texts, though Morgan has determined that the Yonezawa manuscript is closest to the version in the Taoist Canon, and thus far later than has been generally supposed.[100]

The instructions in the Taoist Canon direct one to carve the draughtsmen from the wood of a tree that has been struck by lightning, either catalpa wood or datewood or white sandalwood: round, 1.2 inches across by .3 inches thick. The several stages of production should be accomplished at twelve-day intervals: hew the pieces out on a *chia-tzu* day, inscribe them on a *ping-tzu* day, incise them on a *hsü-tzu* day, dust them with powdered cinnabar on a *keng-tzu* day, place them in a myrtle-wood box on a *jen-tzu* day. (The six *tzu* days may have been chosen because of the draughtsmen's analogy to *tzu*, "seeds" or little counters.) Next come directions for steeping, steaming, drying, and slicing the root of the medicinal plant *shang-lu* (*Phytolacca* species; poke-root) as an offering to the spirits—taken verbatim from the *Lei-kung Pharmacopeia* (third century C.E.).[101] The spirits are then formally invoked. They are the Twelve Asterisms (or Chronograms: *shih-erh ch'en*), to begin with. Then comes the Primal Sovran, the Most High, Celestial Father and Terrestrial Mother (*T'ien-ti fu-mu T'ai-shang yüan-chün*), followed by the sun, moon, five planets, Northern Dipper (Ursa major), and the remaining functionaries who preside over time and space: this little "maṇḍala" seems to reflect the face of the diviner's compass. After this one recites another spell, this time in Sino-Sanskrit (*Oṃ hūṃ hūṃ maṇi dari hūṃ t'o* command!), then casts the twelve draughtsmen and composes a *kua* trigram from the result—since four are marked with the character *shang*, four with *chung*, and four with *hsia*, representing Heaven, Man, and Earth, respectively.[102]

In the fourteenth-century Tao-tsang edition where these instructions are found, the falls of the draughtsmen are represented by ordinary Chinese numbers: 111, 112, 113, 114, 121, 122, and so on. Yet this was not the only way the trigrams were composed and classified. Photographs of the four Tun-huang fragments have been reproduced by Ōfuchi Ninji.[103] Among these tenth-century texts, Stein 557 and Pelliot 3782 have graphic *kua* composed of the *shang*, *chung*, and *hsia* characters themselves, in three ranks of varying numbers: the *shang* falls on top, *chung* in the middle, and *hsia* at the bottom. The student of trans-Asian mantic systems can only note the close resemblance in presentation between these texts and all the dice-oracle manuscripts, in Central Asia, India, Islam, and Europe.

Marc Kalinowski has pointed out that in the two other Tun-huang fragments, the *kua* are represented by counting sticks, depicted as superimposed horizontal and vertical lines (for example, the combination 2.1.4, in Pelliot 3782 and Stein 557 is shown as in Pelliot 4048 and 4984). Kalinowski also observes that Pelliot 4048 calls for square rather than round pieces to bring the dice-analogy slightly closer, although these square pieces, like the round ones, are inscribed on only one of their two faces (the blank face represents zero).[104]

In a remarkable study of "numeromantic texts" from Tun-huang, Kalinowski has drawn attention to a comparable system, *Maheśvara's Method of Divination, Mo-hai-shou-lo pu-fa* (Stein 5614). Each of this work's sixty-four responses is placed under the aegis of a deity. Most are drawn from the Buddhist pantheon, but others are of Chinese origin, like the Queen Mother of the West (Hsi-wang mu) and the god of the house (*chai-shen*). The ensemble is attributed to Śiva, the "Great God" (Maheśvara), who presides over the final, culminating response. Significantly, the same pagan deity sponsors an influential rite of divination by induced possession, preserved in the Chinese Buddhist Canon.[105] In the Tun-huang text, the querent is instructed to sit facing west, to state his name ("[I,] the child [of Buddha] so-and-so"), declare his wish, and set forth the circumstances of his request. Then he may either "throw dice or throw draughts-men" (*chih-t'ou chih-tzu*) three times in succession, though it is uncertain how many of these are to be thrown each time, or how they are shaped and numbered. From the total of sixty-four answers and the three successive throws, Kalinowski deduces that they may have been a single six-sided die with two faces blank (5 and 6), or four two-sided draughtsmen marked on one side with a distinctive number, sign, or color having the value "1" on one side and "2" on the other. Whatever instruments he used, the inquirer was told he should go on casting until he got an auspicious response. If the answer was unfavorable he might continue seeking for a total of three times (just as we found in Brahmā's oracle in the *Book of Consecration*). The procedure should only be used by those who have faith, and it will not be wrong even once in ten thousand times. It should not be given to anyone for the asking, even if he offers a thousand pieces of cash.[106]

Kalinowski surveys a total of ten different numeromantic systems documented in Chinese manuscripts from Tun-huang. Like Rostovtzeff before him, he recognizes in these oracles a valuable reflection of social life, "the vision of small urban communities of peasants and merchants concerned to make their patrimony fructify" ("la vision de petites communautés urbaines de paysans et de commerçants préoccupés à faire fructitifer leurs patrimoines"). And he adduces from one manuscript (Stein 2578) an instructive list of twenty-seven questions, worthy of being placed alongside the Astrampsychos Oracle's similar inventory. Among them are inquiries concerning one's own health and that of family members; the chances of recovering lost objects, domestic animals, or slaves; catching thieves; good fortune in the household; a sick person; travel and returning home; trouble with government officials and slander; borrowed objects; fishing and hunting; whether all would be well after a funeral; the sex of an unborn child; the prospects for happiness after a marriage; success in seeking a wife; the day of a traveler's return; the fate of someone carried off by brigands; good luck in buying and selling; the good or evil outcome of uncanny manifestations (*kuai*), and so on.[107]

We have seen that Maheśvara's oracle is at least nominally Buddhist. The *Method of the Empowered Draughtsmen* shows a Taoist penchant, and in time ended up in the Taoist Canon. Another fragment studied by Kalinowski (Pelliot 3803) includes a figure it terms "the *kua* of Lord Lao" (*Lao-chün chih kua*), suggesting a Taoist origin, and yet another work calls itself "Li Lord Lao's *Changes of Chou*"—*Li Lao-chün Chou-i shih-erh ch'ien pu-fa*, a "mantic method of the twelve sapeques" in which twelve coins are cast to obtain a trigram, which is next combined with another trigram to form a hexagram. Here the Taoism is purely nominal, though indigenous gods like the Lord of the Hearth (*tsao-chün*), Lord of the North (*pei-chün*), and Master of the Site (*t'u-kung*) do put in an appearance. For that matter, as Kalinowski remarks, the *Book of Changes* is cited chiefly for its prestige-value, since the "response" is simply a matter of determining the productive or destructive mutual relationship of the two trigrams composing the hexagram.[108]

One of the ten Tun-huang methods goes under the name of the Duke of Chou (*Chou-kung pu-fa*), another under the auspices of both the Duke of Chou and his admirer, Confucius. Still another is attributed to Confucius alone: "Confucius's Horse's Head Divining Method" (*K'ung-tzu ma-t'ou pu-fa*), which provided the list of questions quoted above. Seized by doubt in the course of an urgent errand—so the story went—Confucius suddenly dismounted, and leaning on his horse's head, with a foot in the stirrup, he resolved his perplexity by means of this simple, speedy oracle. It consists of counting-sticks lots, a mere nine of them, contained in a length of bamboo, which has been sealed at both ends. Only a small slot has been left at one end, large enough for a stick to emerge. Such receptacles are of course still in use for dispensing temple oracles in Japan. A noteworthy feature of this book is that the numbers of the lots correspond not to answers, as in most temple oracles, but to questions, and it is under each heading that one finds the question's nine possible answers. We have found other examples of this arrangement outside China.[109] Kalinowski has discovered a reference in the *History of the Sui Dynasty*, which attributes the *Confucius's Horse's Head Divining Method* to the court astronomer and mathematician Lin Hsiao-kung, active at the end of the sixth century. As Kalinowski notes, not only does this date the book, it also shows that if a man of Lin's stature could fashion such a simple system, the gulf between learned and popular divination must have been a good deal narrower than is often supposed.[110]

A final example is attributed to the famous diviner, Kuan Lo (third century C.E.), the *Kuan Kung-ming pu-fa*. This proves to be a variation on the Duke of Chou method mentioned above: a system of manipulating counting sticks so as to obtain sixteen figures. The first (in the Chou-kung manual) is named for the Duke of Chou, the second for Confucius, the third for the doomed poet-statesman Ch'u Yüan, the fourth for the immortal Ch'ih Sung-tzu, the fifth for the tyrants Chieh and Chou, the sixth for the King of Yüeh, the seventh for the martyred sage Chieh Tzu-t'ui, the eighth for T'ai-kung, and the remaining eight for the eight trigrams of the *Book of Changes*. Might these sixteen figures have some relation to the genesis of the sixteen figures of Islamic geomancy? If the origins of *al-raml* are indeed to be sought in China, I should be inclined to search for hints in one of these lesser, more readily accessible systems in general use at such cosmopolitan centers as Tun-huang between the sixth and tenth centuries. For the present, we need only record that this Kuan Lo oracle erects a Buddhist superstructure on its solid Confucian foundations; before divining for a figure, the querent must recite the names of the Seven Buddhas.[111]

Such eclectic diversity has been common to all our Central Asian examples. The Tibetan oracles stand under the aegis of Bön deities as well as members of the Buddhist pantheon. The Turkish runic oracle has been viewed as Manichaean, if not Buddhist. The Turkish fragment of the Christian *Sortes apostolorum* must not be forgotten, or the scrap of paper that attests its counterpart in Sogdian. And the Bower Manuscript, found in a Buddhist stūpa near Kucha accords much honor to Śiva, Viṣṇu, and the Goddess—though this certainly does not put it beyond the Buddhist pale, on the contrary. For that matter, we have even considered a Turkish rendering of some loose Chinese Capriccioso on the *Book of Changes*: just the sort of work that the Chinese Tun-huang manuscripts have revealed. Even as all the religions of Asia followed trade in and out of China, the abundance and variety of these oracles for laymen reflects a concern with prosperity and welfare inseparable from the commercial fortunes of travelers and merchants along the main Central Asian arteries.[112]

Conclusions? Or Enigmas?

So in time we do behold Greek and Chinese oracles meeting, and possibly merging. But was this their first encounter? It is of course the prehistorical diffusionists who have given diffusionism a bad name. The similarities among mantic systems in different cultures are patent and undeniable.[113] All may ultimately derive from some occult common parent, but such genealogies are always chancy and suspect. Yet the spread of ideas, images, techniques, and materials continues to intrigue historians as well as prehistorians. Surely there is no need to waffle or make a mare's nest between the Archetypes and the deep blue sea. Only give us a text, or better, a whole gaggle of texts, and we can establish clear filiations. Or can we?

In this case, the text is rather more than just another historical witness to thoughts or events. It is itself intended for manipulation, under prescribed ritual conditions and in conjunction with other objects and gestures: the separating out of counting sticks, the drawing of lots, the scratching of lines in the sand, the casting of dice, coins, or draughtsmen, the spinning of a wheel, and more. It is also a voice of quite peculiar intimacy, for the querent goes to it for counsel and it speaks to him or her directly. Considered in this way, there seem to be far too many oracles singing in the vast trans-Asian choir. How are we even to distinguish the ground bass and the descant in this gorgeous mantic polyphony?

I am not proposing to sort this all out—I shrink from taking up Joseph Needham's noble challenge of 1962 to produce "that fully integrated and connected story, quite biological in character, showing how all these games and divination-techniques were genetically connected." But I share his optimism that it can and should be done. Work toward that goal has meanwhile been going forward on other fronts. I need only mention Michael Dummett's impressive study of Tarot, which among many other achievements has shown that evolution does not always invariably move from ritual to entertainment. Tarot is not the only mantic system to have begun as a game and ended as a Mystery.[114]

What I would propose at this stage of our inquiry is a simple if sweeping formulation. I believe that every member of the extended corpus of oracles we have considered came into being in full awareness of some other member of the corpus. That there are overlapping relations of consanguinity I do not doubt. There may be consubstantiality—though I still lack the theology to define it. Yet the entire subject seems infected by the intrinsic chanciness of the fate it seeks to plumb. Whatever hypotheses of dissemination we advance, we may only be certain, with Mallarmé, that "un coup de dés jamais n'abolira le hasard."[115]

With regard to the history of the written oracle in China itself, we now see that the first Buddhist example, in the *Book of Consecration*, was contemporary with the Sanskrit Bower Manuscript from Kucha. It also circulated separately from its host scripture and thus forms part of the special mantic corpus from Tun-huang (Kalinowski excluded it from his survey only because it was a direct, one-step oracle, without a "numeromantic" means of access.)[116] The fifth century marks the beginning of the most intense period of Sino-Indian synthesis, and Brahmā's Chinese oracle well exemplifies the views and methods of many religious professionals during this formative phase of Chinese religion. The fifth and sixth centuries witness an extraordinary outpouring of original Chinese Buddhist literature in which Chinese and Indian elements were more or less artfully blended. In this mission of acculturation, no class of writings had greater importance than the so-called Chinese apocryphal sūtras, which conferred divine authority on a host of innovations. The fifth- and sixth-century scriptural corpus largely determined the course of Buddhist practice in later China and throughout East Asia. The next great period of production and diffusion came in the twelfth and thirteenth centuries, with printing as its agent. Present-day texts and practices all harken back to thirteenth-century prototypes—as even our modest sampling from the humble genre of oracle sequences have revealed.

From the early Middle Ages on, Buddhism, Taoism, and the secular administration all directed their efforts to the containment of native spiritual enthusiasm. Significantly, the only "heresy" on which earnest Buddhist monks, Taoist masters, and government officials could all agree was the religion of the people at large—stigmatized in literary sources as "licentious" or "demonic" cults. All three official institutions sought to interpose themselves between the people and their gods: in fact, to redefine the gods. Buddhists, Taoists, and officials strove to tame uncontrolled inspiration by establishing set forms for ritual. When they reduced action to writing, they made rituals repeatable and their outcome predictable. In this way they not only took control of the present, but set their seal upon the future, as well. Each Chinese written oracle reflects in miniature this larger process of social engineering. The oracles, too, are a product of the greater movement from revelation to routine.

Writing in 1869, the pioneer folklorist Robert Chambers remarked that in England "professional card-cutters ... always take care to point out what they term 'the cards of caution,' and impressively warn their clients of falling into the dangers those cards foreshadow, but do not positively foretell, for the dangers may be avoided by prudence or circumspection ... Consequently the fortune-tellers are the moralists as well as the consolers of the lower-classes. They supply a want that society either cannot or will not do."[117]

The inculcation of moral values is certainly the dominant feature of the earliest Chinese Buddhist oracle. Certain of the later examples, with their cryptic allusions and their invitation to historical role-playing, may superficially appear to justify Keith Thomas's view of divination's chief function as legitimizing random behavior.[118] Yet when commentaries and other data are available, it becomes clear that all this disparate material was being dragooned into service to bolster a prevailing ethical code. I believe that some of our earliest oracle sequences also represent the earliest *shan-shu*, or moral tracts, broken up and concentrated in stanzas, for maximum effect. They were designed to powerfully imprint the author's message under the mantle of a god, under ritual conditions at a moment of doubt or crisis—the querent's receptivity being further assured by his making an offering or paying a fee. For an understanding of this aspect of divination, a thematic analysis of the texts is only the beginning. The living context is crucial, and it is here of course that History must join forces with Anthropology.

Yet for the moment we do have an astounding array of texts to study and classify, texts that seem to form an entire, neglected subdivision of Comparative Literature. Their significance extends, as we have seen, into the History of Science and the History of Art. No other international genre better exemplifies the traditional mingling of play and faith, *Scherz und Ernst*. There is no body of literature more revealing of the relentless attempt by Authority to influence the people at large, nor more influential in spreading normative notions on morality and destiny throughout the Chinese *Kulturkreis*. He knows not traditional China, who only China knows.

NOTES

Introduction

1. R. A. Stein, *Recherches sur l'épopée et le barde au Tibet* (Paris: Presses Universitaires de France, 1959; Bibliothèque de l'Institut des Hautes Études Chinoises, 13), pp. 419–37. For Vedic enigmas, see Louis Renou, *Hymnes et prières du Veda* (Paris: Adrien Maisonneuve, 1938), and L. Renou and L. Silburn, "Sur la notion de Brahman," *Journal Asiatique* 1949: pp. 7–46 (esp. pp. 22–46, "Le *brahmodya* védique"); Wendy Doniger O'Flaherty, *The Rig Veda: An Anthology* (Harmondsworth: Penguin Books, 1981), pp. 71–83 ("The Riddle of the Sacrifice").

2. "The Context of Enigmas in the Tamang Buddhist Oral Tradition" (paper to the Csoma de Körös Symposium, Sopron, Hungary, 1987). Steinmann draws upon a distinction between "poetic" and "liturgical" enigmas made by Roger Caillois, *Art poétique* (Paris: Gallimard, 1958), pp. 149–64, "L'énigme et l'image."

3. Cf. M. Strickmann, *Mantras et mandarins: le bouddhisme tantrique en chine*, chap. 6 ("Les rêves et la divination")—where I also address the curious question of whether Buddhists divine the future or the past as well as the subject of lists and listing generally. Not only are the lists among the most precocious specimens of writing. They are also a fundamental means of promoting the illusion of control over cosmic multiplicity, hence their place in divination procedures.

4. T. C. Skeat and G. M. Browne seem to be the only scholars to have analyzed the process by which a particular oracle was actually constructed. Both studied oracles with predetermined questions as well as fixed answers: closed mantic circuits, which must be tightly organized. Skeat described an eleventh-century Latin specimen, and Browne has devoted much labor and ingenuity to the *Sortes Astrampsychi*, the third-century Greek oracle that appears to be the progenitor of the species in the West.

5. Adler and Zempléni 1972. In addition to the references given by Adler and Zempléni, one may consult the extensive bibliography in Stephen Skinner's *Terrestrial Astrology: Divination by Geomancy* (London: Routledge & Kegan Paul, 1980).

6. Ibid., p. 139.

7. Léon Vandermeersch, "Les origines divinatoires de la tradition chinoise du parallélisme littéraire"(*Extrême-Orient, Extrême-Occident* 1989, 11: pp. 11–33).

Chapter 1: Ritual and Randomization

1. The origin of the fortune cookie is still a keenly disputed topic in San Francisco. According to one local tradition, it was invented in 1909 by Makoto Hagiwara, who created the Japanese Tea Garden in Golden Gate Park. He sold his fortune cookies in the garden where they are still served, but failed to patent them. They were soon copied by local Chinese restaurant owners and the rest is history. Other guardians of tradition attribute their introduction to David Jung, in 1912. Jung is said to have been inspired by the custom, in his native Canton, of writing verses on slips of paper, which were then folded and placed inside cakes. The cakes were passed around at gatherings of the leisured and cultivated. Each recipient was expected to improvise on the theme (or possibly, in the rhyme scheme) of the cake-verse that fell to his lot. A parallel in modern Turkey is furnished by the predictions printed on the wrappers of bonbons and caramels: J.-P. Roux and P. Boratav, "La divination chez les turcs," in Caquot and Leibovici 1968, vol. 2: 317.

2. Stein 1961, vol. 5: 9–10, 19.

3. *rGyal-po bKa'-thaṅ*; Stein 1959: 251. On Tibetan divination generally, see Blondeau 1976: 302–4 ("Divination et oracles"), and Radha 1981. For medieval and modern Tibetan dice-oracles, see section on Medieval Tibetans in Chapter 9. On the latter-day Sino-Tibetan mantic idiom, cf. S. C. Vidyabhushana 1913.

4. Shoolbraid 1975: 46.

5. On the relation of the *I-ching* to divination using a tortoise plastron, cf. Léon Vandermeersch 1974.

6. See the studies by Marc Kalinowski listed in the bibliography. On discoveries which confirm that achilleomancy preceded the formation of the *I-ching*'s hexagrams (and thus, that the *I-ching* represents a system derived from achilleomancy), see Jao 1983: 13, n. 9; Diény 1986: 455–66. For good hagiographic and anecdotal background on diviners in the pre-Buddhist, proto-Taoist, cf. Ngo Van Xuyet 1976.

7. Cf. Harper 1982.

8. The most complete exposition focuses on the medieval Taoist ritual of sexual union: Kalinowski 1985: 773–811. Cf. also the very comprehensive study by Kristofer Schipper and Wang Hsiu-huei (Schipper and Wang 1986).

9. Cf. Strickmann 1979: 164–69.

10. For a description of the Canon's contents, cf. Demiéville 1953: 398–463; rpt. in Demiéville 1973: 157–222. On scriptures written in China, directly in

Chinese, though purporting to be translations, see the studies collected in Buswell 1990.

11. Elliot 1955: 38–39.

12. Bastian 1867: 125; this account was quoted by J. G. Frazer in his commentary on Pausanias (n. 6 of Chapter 9). See de Gubernatis 1878, 1: 204; Friend (n.d.), 1: 268; Lenormant (n.d.): 237–38. The special character of Chinese sortilege had already been described by the English merchant, Peter Mundy; see Temple 1919: 195, n. 3.

13. Michaux 1933: 152.

14. Doolittle 1966, 2: 333–34. Mantic birds in action are also described by Emily Ahern: "On the streets of San-hsia [a town in Taiwan] one can seek out an itinerant diviner who uses a pair of trained birds in 'bird biting lots.' Each of the birds pecks out a stick from a set of eight marked with characters and two cards from a set of sixty-four depicting well-known legends. Using the information on the sticks and cards, the diviner speaks to the question the client presents.... The diviner told me that before leaving for the day's work he presents the birds to the goddess *Kuan-im*, telling her that he is going to tell fortunes. Then, when the birds pull out the cards and sticks, the goddess's spirit is with them, directing what they do" (Ahern 1981: 49). "Snakes and turtles are used in much the same way, the direction of their head indicating which piece of paper is to be selected," wrote the American Presbyterian missionary John L. Nevius, who labored in Shantung (Nevius 1869: 189).

The Berlin folklorist Johannes Bolte reports having frequently seen similar exhibitions at German fairs. A seller of fortune-papers (Glücksbriefhandler) would have a green parakeet select from among a great number of printed slips for the prospective purchaser; cf. Bolte 1925: 191, n. 26. It is no accident that birds should figure so prominently in divination, being without peer as celestial messengers. Not only are their flight and their calls portentous, they may even be the living instruments of fate-selection, as these examples show. This association is further supported by the use of arrows in divination; see *infra*. On East Asian bird-divination generally, see Laufer 1914; Schafer 1963; and Morgan 1987c: 57–76. For important observations from Tamil Nadu, cf. Diehl 1956: 59 ff. ("Science of the Five Birds").

15. Lebra 1966: 63.

Chapter 2: Chinese Oracles In Partibus

1. Macdonald 1932: 126–27.

2. de Nebesky-Wojkowitz 1956: 462.

3. Heissig 1980: 100.

4. Waddell 1959: 465—using cards—and 466–70—using dice and a chessboard, or magic square. Cf. also Radha 1981: 17–18—with dice, using a book almost certainly of Chinese derivation.

5. Stein 1939: 297–372.

6. See Stein 1971: 497–547; Thomas 1957.

7. Ekvall 1964: 251–82, "Divination."

8. Courant 1894–96, vol. 3: 60; Government-General of Korea 1972: 387–90. In Southeast Asia, too, the story of Chinese temple oracles is raveled and complex. Piet van der Loon's collection in Oxford, assembled during the 1960s and 1970s from temples in Thailand, Cambodia, and Malaysia (as well as Hong Kong and Taiwan), includes specimens of all sorts, sometimes bilingual, in Chinese, Thai, Khmer, and Malay.

9. Ōba 1967: 695d, 512c.

10. The Ōbaku lineage played an important role in the transmission of Chinese popular culture to Tokugawa Japan. For their role in disseminating Chinese vernacular stories and novels, cf. Ishizaki 1967.

11. Yamada Etai has published a biography of Ryōgen: *Ganzan Daishi* (Hieizan 1959); on Ganzan Daishi's cult, see Murayama 1976: 61–75.

12. Like all other Buddhist "clans" or lineages established in the Kamakura period, the school of Nichiren emerged from Tendai: so the oracle's Tendai affiliation might seem part of a larger pattern of indebtedness. The *Bussho kaisetsu daijiten* lists three versions of the Ganzan oracle: a *Ganzan Daishi hyakusen wage* "transmitted" by a monk named Ningai (fl. ca. 1750?) and printed in 1804; and two "illustrated extracts" (*Ganzan Daishi mikuji eshō*). The first of these is in two volumes (*kan*), the second bears the superscription "enlarged edition" (*zōho*), but no date is given for either of these printings (vol. 2, p. 207d).

Lots and oracles of various kinds are conspicuous at Shintō shrines as well as Buddhist temples. In his account of the Fushimi Inari Shrine south of Kyoto, D. C. Buchanan translates two of the written oracle's responses and publishes their Japanese originals in transcription (Buchanan 1935: 129–32, 146–47). This "Shintō" sequence, too, turns out to be in the Ganzan Daishi oracle. An *editio minor* of some sort appears to be in use at the little shrines dotted on the hillside behind the main Inari complex. Buchanan writes, "One of the most common and popular methods of fortune telling is that noticed by the writer in a number of places on Mount Inari. A brass tube, ten inches long and three inches in diameter, and containing twelve numbered brass sticks, is chained to a frame supporting a placard that tells the fortune of each number. One end of the tube is entirely closed, and the other has a small hole just large enough to permit the passing through it of one stick at a time. The worshipper takes the tube, offers a short prayer, and vigorously shakes until one of the brass sticks is projected. He notices the number, compares it with the number on the placard, and then reads his fortune. This method is so popular that at one place there are ten such tubes, or brass boxes, which are commonly known as 'O-mikuji-bako' ('Honorable-oracle-boxes'). In some cases the sticks do not have any numbers, but only certain dots and lines which are to be interpreted by the shrine authorities. In other cases, there is no placard above, but on application to the priest a folded slip of paper bearing the number of the stick is handed to the inquirer, opening which he may read the message of the deities..." (p. 133). A closer study of those "dots and lines" might prove rewarding in the light of some of the systems of access to written oracles which we shall later examine—though chances are that they simply represent the solid and broken lines of trigrams and hexagrams.

While traveling in Japan, the Reverend Buchanan came upon a mechanized variation on the oracular theme. Like the foregoing, it was under the patronage of the fox-god Inari. In the town of Hikata (Wakayama Prefecture), Buchanan saw a box in the shape of a fox shrine. "In the back of the shrine could be seen Mr. Fox dressed in full ceremonial attire . . . A one *sen* piece is inserted in the slot, and Mr. Fox comes forward to make his bow and greet the worshipper, while out comes the slip of paper bearing the fortune" (Buchanan 1935: 133). Johannes Bolte recorded the presence of a similar contraption on the Eiffel Tower in 1907: "In Paris sah ich 1907 auf dem Eiffelturm ein Glücksorakel in Automatenform; auf den Einwurf eines Zehncentimesstückes drehte sich ein in der Mitte eines doppelten Kreises befindlicher Teufel und wies mit seinem Stabe auf zweimal 12 runde Felder, die je eine Inschrift in französischer Prosa tragen, wie: 'Rothschild möchte Sie gern kennen lernen; geben Sie ihm Ihre Adresse!' Fragen fehlten also" (Bolte 1925, 1: 192). More use will be made of Bolte's studies in Chapter 9, on diffusion. But there is nothing new about mechanized sortilege; cf. note 8 of Chapter 9.

13. Hearn 1894, 1: 37–38.

Chapter 3: Termina Technica

1. Stein 1981: 257.
2. Yang 1961: 211.
3. Pronounced *pue* in Hokkien; cf. Stephan Feuchtwang, "School-Temple and City God," G. W. Skinner 1977: 609, n. 5; Ahern 1981: 45–47. The blocks may be used alone, or to validate the choice of a written oracle text.
4. *Yogen-shū kaisetsu* (Tokyo: Daiichi shobō, 1935), 28–36.
5. Morohashi Tetsuji, *Dai Kanwa jiten*, no. 26099, vol. 8, p. 8928d. This is an extraordinary example of the chasm that gapes between the "learned" tradition and the realities of Chinese daily life. For a work entitled *Ch'ing-lung kao*, known in a Sung printing, cf. note 15 of Chapter 8.
6. Chiang Tzu-wen, who met his death in an untimely and violent manner (third century C.E.), was—after a series of disquieting apparitions—duly enfeoffed as tutelary deity of the capital (Chien-k'ang, the modern Nanking) at North Mountain, alias Bell Mountain. Kan Pao's fourth-century *Sou-shen chi* includes an important group of Chiang Tzu-wen legends (Chapter 5).
7. Nagao 1973, vol. 2: 52–55.
8. Goodrich 1964: 94–97.
9. Yoshimoto 1983: 296–97. Werner Banck's personal collection contains a large number of oracle slips specifically marked "gynaecology" (*fu-k'o*).
10. Doolitle 1872, vol. 2: 504–7 ("Twenty-Eight Temple Oracles or Stanzas") and 507–12 ("Fifty-Six Temple Oracles or Stanzas").

Chapter 4: Modern Studies, Editions, and Translations

1. Eberhard 1965: 11–18; English translation in Eberhard 1970: 191–99.

2. Eberhard 1970: 198.

3. Cf. Eberhard 1966: 148–60; rpt. in Eberhard 1971: 177–89.

4. *Chung-kuo ling-ch'ien yen-chiu, tzu-liao p'ien* (Taipei: Ku-t'ing, 1976).

5. See Banck 1985. For the Fukienese/Japanese Ingen oracle just mentioned, for example, Banck's new materials immediately reveal additional filiations. In this second volume, the oracle and its variants are represented by nos. 5–8, and the data show a greatly extended range of diffusion, as well as a still wider variety of sponsoring deities and saints (pp. 155–58). Banck has elsewhere summarized the results of his analysis of question categories: P'ang Wei 1987: 603–9.

6. T. 2035, vol. 49: 318c13–14. Reproductions of selected images and responses from the T'ien-chu oracle can be found in Fontein 1967, Plate 15a (= stanza 72); Banck 1976, Abbildung I (stanza 78); II, xix–xx (stanzas 75 and 81); Bauer 1973, Abbildung 9 (stanza 83). As Glen Dubridge points out, there were actually three T'ien-chu monasteries. The "Upper" (*shang*) Monastery is presumably meant here; from the twelfth century on, it was one of the chief Kuan-yin cult centers in China. In 1103, P'u-ming, a monk of the Upper T'ien-chu Monastery was divinely inspired to write the *Book of the Deeds of the Bodhisattva Kuan-yin* (*Kuan-yi p'u-sa pen-hsing ching*, which may lie behind a later work of great importance, the *Hsiang-shan pao-chüan*; cf. Dudbridge 1978: 45. On visiting the sites in 1973, Professor Dudbridge "found only odd bits of stone at the Lower and Middle positions, but the Upper, now converted into some sort of school, still has at least a main hall standing" (letter of 20. VIII.83). Werner Banck does not associate the oracle with the monastery, and renders the work's title as "Wirksames Orakel in der indischen [Glaubenslehre]"; Banck 1985: xviii.

7. In Banck's first volume, it is no. 23; in the second, no. 83 (pp. 200–201). The entire subject of illustrations in divination manuals is of great interest. It is also of potential importance in studying the genre's diffusion. Wolfgang Bauer's monograph, *Das Bild in der Weissage-Literatur Chinas*, provides a valuable survey of a wide range of Chinese texts, with many extraordinary reproductions (Bauer 1973).

8. Kleinman 1976: 210–21. Jin Hsü's associate and collaborator, Wen-Hsing Tseng, has also written on temple oracles as psychotherapy in terms indistinguishable from Hsü's: Tseng 1976: 164–78; Tseng 1978: 311–28 (esp. 314–15).

9. Kleinman 1980: 254. The section on temple oracles occupies pp. 243–58. Kleinman observes that the interpreters "are middle-aged or elderly men. Most are literate members of the lower class who have retired from work or now only work part time and who have family or friendship ties to the owner of the temple." Some receive a small stipend from the temple, others are said to be altruistically motivated. Though not regarded with awe and fear, they are often "appreciated as men of experience who possess both a wide practical knowledge

of the everyday world" and an understanding of religious matters (ibid., p. 246). The anthropologist Emily Martin Ahern applies Kleinman's material and analysis in her chapter on divination, which she classifies under "codes": "formal features of Chinese ritual, which include constitutive rules and restricted codes." She argues that "divination involving interpersonal communication works by means of prearranged codes based on constitutive rules"; Ahern 1981: 4, 47–49, 60–63. Kleinman's initial work on oracle consultation forms part of his study, "Comparisons of Patient–Practitioner Transactions in Taiwan: The Cultural Construction of Clinical Reality" (Kleinman 1978).

10. Morgan 1987b: 163–191. Morgan's complete translation of this sequence and its commentary appeared as *Les fiches divinatoires de Huang Daxian* (Morgan 1987a). One may also mention in passing Jean-Michel de Kermadec, *Les sapèques d'or: jeux divinatoires inspirés du Yijing* (de Kermadec 1984), which includes "les 32 pentagrammes, ou la divination par les 5 sapèques d'or" (pp. 13–50)—employing coins rather than sticks: cf. Banck's sequence II: 6, and Morgan 1987b: 169—followed by 64 oracle slips with images.

In the heyday of Chinese export wares, at least one game based on Chinese temple oracles was created and sold for domestic use in the English-speaking world. My student Louise Paige kindly gave me the battered remains of a game that was played until recently by members of her family in Santa Cruz, California. It consists of a crumbling booklet containing 78 responses and a torn and fractured cardboard cylinder holding 78 bamboo sticks, 15 cm × 0.6 cm (or 6″ × 1/4″). Each stick has a number roughly penned at one end. The cylinder (7 cm, or 2 3/4″, in diameter) was covered all around with glossy yellow paper, with writing and an image in now sadly faded red: a drawing of a well-groomed Western male shaking the cylinder "with a snappy downward motion" (as the text beneath directs). To the left of this is the game's title: *CHI CHI Chinese Fortune Teller*. Still further to the left stand the Chinese characters *Kuan-ti ling-ch'ien* (*Transcendent Oracles of Monarch Kuan*). The booklet's title page is unfortunately missing. The "Preface" reads: "While touring China, the author of this book had his fortune told in a Chinese Joss House. The method used was by shaking a box full of bamboo sticks numbered from 1 to 78 in such a manner that just one number would mysteriously jump out of the box. This number would then be your fortune and an interpreter would read it to you from his book. Why this one stick will jump out from the rest and determine your fate we do not attempt to explain. We only know this method of fortune telling has been used by that mysterious and ancient race, the Chinese, for centuries. It appealed to us as such a novelty and their philosophy so true and quaint, that we secured after considerable time and expense a translation of their fortune telling book. We then imported their native bamboo sticks and after protecting the idea for the United States, by patent and copyright, we now offer it to the public. A native son of China never thinks of entering business for the day without first having his fortune told from these mysterious sticks. He gets first his luck for the day, believing in it and acting on the advice implicitly. (If the number is shaken out after sundown, the fortune refers to the following day.) He then gets his future and important events that will occur as well as lucky gambling numbers. It is all told him from this ancient book of fortunes which is in poetry, hence the author has tried to observe the same method as nearly as possible in the translation which is here offered as the oldest and best known method of fortune telling in the world." The first two responses will serve as a sample of "their philosophy so true and quaint":

> 1. Your luck for today—
>   Your fortune for today is "One,"
>   No business matters should be done.
>   Your fortune—
>   Not liked at heart by many friends
>   Your never ought to roam,
>   But stick to close relations
>   Where your work is best, at home.
>   Expect soon a letter of great importance.
>   *You will not get your wish.*
>
> 2. Your luck for today—
>   Your number for today is "Two,"
>   The best of luck it means for you.
>   Your fortune—
>   Be careful in your actions,
>   Your love affairs seem wrong;
>   If you do not use discretion
>   You'll ruin them all ere long.
>   A long journey soon from which you will benefit.
>   *You will get your wish.*

None of the 78 responses exhibit any specific Chinese cultural traits, and Werner Banck's inventory contains no sequence of 78 verses; the closest is 79 (vol. 2, no. 126), and there is another with 76 (ibid., no. 111). I should hazard a guess that *CHI CHI Chinese Fortune Teller* dates from the 1920s or 1930s—the Silver Age of chinoiserie.

11. "Le quatrain perd sa force oraculaire. Il se borne souvent à la description d"un paysage, d'un sentiment, d'une réunion d'amis, etc., dont il serait impossible de tirer un présage sans l'adjonction d'un autre élément."

12. Morgan 1987b: 169–70. Morgan illustrates this by the oracle's seventh response. The poem is a conventional autumn landscape:

> C'est l'automne. Les oies sauvages s'envolent vers le sud.
> Une à une, les feuilles rouges tombent en voltigeant.
> Des remparts, on entend le bruit du linge qu'on bat au lavoir;
> Tandis que le reflet des érables cerne de feu la jetée.

This tranquil scene is titled "Jen-kui returns home": and so the hitherto commonplace geese take on new meaning. General Hsüeh Jen-kui is the hero of several vernacular novels and appears often in popular prints. After eighteen years of victorious campaigns, he is on his way home when he notices a boy shooting wild geese with amazing skill. The envious general is preparing to kill the boy when a tiger, sent by the boy's foster father, a Taoist adept, intervenes. In one version, it then turns out that the boy is Hsüeh's own son. The evaluation of this verse is "moderately auspicious" (*chung-chi*), and prudence is conselled. The itemized list of applications runs:

> Departures: better wait than depart.
> Travelers: return is blocked.
> Engagements and marriages: will not take place.
> House and family: prudence.
> Ailments: pray.
> Births: pray.
> Projects and ambitions: outlook poor.
> Lost objects: hard to find.
> Personal matters: be careful in autumn.

By such means, General Hsüeh's situation is made occultly one's own (Morgan 1987a: 28–29; Morgan 1987b: 170). Morgan has also discovered that there are two different versions of the oracular brochure in circulation. Though the two seem identical at first glance, some forty titles vary, and often involve a completely different story, or vignette. The vagueness of the mantic verses allows the publisher or printer considerable flexibility, should he decide to modify the import of particular responses (Morgan 1987b: 180–83).

13. Morgan 1987b: 183–85. Morgan also translates five specimen slips, one from each division of the medical series (pp. 189–91).

14. Morgan 1987b: 185–87, including a good photograph of a portion of Diviner's Lane. The Tung Wah Hospitals Group has also shown its benevolent interest in temple oracles through the publication of a sequence from the Man Mo Temple on Hollywood Road, Hong Kong, in English translation: S. T. Cheung, compiler and translator, *Fortune Stick Predictions, Man Mo Temple* (Hong Kong: The Tung Wah Group of Hospitals, 1982). Almost as if Carole Morgan had divined it, in this book the original oracle verses have vanished entirely. What remains is simply the historico-anecdotal title and a doggerel interpretation, or "opinion of the Sage" (*sheng-i*). The Man Mo Temple is possibly the oldest in Hong Kong, and has been under the Tung Wah Group's management since 1908: it is the all-important Temple of the City God (Ch'eng-huang), and the book includes a number of color photographs.

15. Morgan 1987b: 189.

16. Pas, "Temple Oracles in a Chinese City; A Study about the Use of Temple Oracles in Taichung, Central Taiwan." I am grateful to Julian Pas for sending me the typescript of this article, in October 1984. It has since been published in

the *Journal of the Royal Asiatic Society, Hong Kong Branch* 24 (Pas 1988). Pas proposes the creation of a Chinese Christian oracle sequence, based on biblical stories. Possible opposition from the Church, he suggests, could be countered by presenting the oracle as a method of prayer, rather than divination (pp. 31–32). History repeats itself; cf. notes 6 of Chapter 7 and 67 of Chapter 9.

Chapter 5: New Evidence: A Clutch of Taoist Oracles

1. Cf. Schipper 1975; Weng 1966.

2. To be published by the University of Chicago Press. This pan-European project was carried out under the auspices of the European Science Foundation.

3. See Kalinowski (forthcoming).

4. I have been greatly aided by copies of his articles, in preliminary draft, kindly provided by Marc Kalinowski. A comprehensive study by the same author, "La Littérature divinatoire dans le Daozang," has appeared in *Cahiers d"Extrême-Asie* (Kalinowski 1989).

5. For manifestations of I-sheng, third of the quartet, who watched over the Sung's founding in 960, cf. Boltz 1987: 83–86. Boltz has also analyzed the documents on Chen-wu (or Hsüan-wu), the Perfect (or Dark) Warrior (pp. 86–91). Icons of the four are mentioned by Hung Mai; Ho Cho, ed., *I-chien chih* (4 vols., Peking: Chung-hua, 1981), pp. 329, 799, 837. Among the extant images are the early fourteenth-century wall paintings from the Taoist Yung-lo kung (Shanhsi), cf. *Yung-lo kung* (Peking: Jen-min mei-shu, 1964), pl. 101–2; *The Yongle Palace Murals* (Peking: Foreign Languages Press, 1985), pl. 37, 45. The martial quartets are elegantly grouped in a hanging scroll belonging to the great liturgical series used in the Water and Land Ritual, *shui-lu chai*. This is the last of the great Tantric rituals to survive in China. In it the Buddhist and Taoist pantheons are fully fused with all of Chinese history and every mode of existence. Cf. the fine fifteenth-century set reproduced in *Pao-ning ssu Ming-tai shui-lu hua* (Peking: Wen-wu, 1985), pl. 78; for this and other sets of Shui-lu paintings, see Gyss-Vermande 1988 (two sets in the Musée Guimet, Paris); and Gyss-Vermande's reviews of the book on the Pao-ning ssu paintings, and of the publication of still another set, wall paintings from the Pi-lu ssu in Hopeh; *Arts Asiatiques* 1987, 42: 123–25.

6. The origins and development of Wen-ch'ang's cult are fully described by Terry Kleeman: "Wenchang and the Viper: The Creation of a Chinese National Gods" (1988; Ph.D. thesis). This work contains valuable materials on, inter alia, the deity's prophetic role in the expanding system of civil-service examinations, and automatic writing. By the end of the twelfth century, Wen-ch'ang's responses were regularly being issued by means of spirit-writing. Kleeman translates a contemporary description of the practice as carried out in his chief temple (pp. 52–53). Wen-ch'ang's *Book of Transformations* (*Hua-shu*) was revealed by

that means, starting in 1181; Kleeman provides a complete translation (pp. 147–453). Werner Banck has entered the god's 365-response oracle in his second volume's inventory (no. 133). Possibly China's biggest oracle, it boasts more answers than any other sequence in his collection.

7. On the principal authors of the Southern School (or Southern [ritual] Clan), cf. Boltz 1987: 173–90. The outstanding figure in this group is the early thirteenth-century Po Yü-ch'an, whose life and dates, however, are enigmatic almost beyond belief (ibid., pp. 176–79, and p. 318, n. 456).

8. On the cult and literature of the Brothers Hsü, cf. Boltz 1987: 52–53, 195–97; and L. Davis 1985: 1–56.

9. This work, entered by Banck as no. 81 in his second volume's inventory, appears to be singularly lacking in indications of provenance or association.

10. The term *chou-tz'u*, "oracular verses," is drawn from the *I-lin* of the first century C.E. On this oracle composed or transcribed by Fu Yeh, cf. Boltz 1987: 249.

11. For an arresting example, cf. Banck 1985: xxii–xxiii—the dream-revelation of the Hearth-god's oracle in 1862 to a certain Ch'eng Ying-hsing, who was later able to confirm the sequence's authenticity when he discovered it in a battered volume, in an out-of-the-way schoolhouse where he chanced to be taking refuge from a storm. Such is the origin of the Hearth-god's 50-stanza oracle, no. 153 in Banck's inventory.

12. The same sequence was also used at the now fossilized "Joss House" in Weaverville, Trinity County, Calif.

13. In the 1920s and 1930s; Graham quotes three examples in substandard translation; Graham 1961: 136–38.

14. Banck 1985, no. 124 (pp. 226–31). The Japanese *Sokkō hyakusen* is illustrated in Banck's Abbildung no. 21; for the Mongolian version, see his Abbildung no. 29, and his notes among the Addenda, p. 393.

15. On the role of the Southeast in what I have called the Taoist Renaissance of the Twelfth Century, cf. Strickmann 1978b: 331–54.

16. Boltz's *Survey of Taoist Literature* is filled with examples of direct scriptural revelation throughout the Sung, Yüan, and Ming dynasties. They were all following, to some degree, the precedent set at fourth-century Mao Shan. See also Strickmann 1981.

17. Boltz 1987: 94–96. On the Taoist cult of holy fools, usually temple menials, cf. Strickmann 1994.

18. Van der Loon 1984: 284, n. 192. Not having found these "twelve lords" elsewhere in Taoist works, I wonder if there might possibly be a connection between this title and the *Sortes apostolorum*, of which Turkish and Sogdian fragments have been found at Turfan and Tun-huang (notes 69, 70, and 72 of Chapter 9). But this is sheer speculation; there are other significant groups of twelve, chiefly astrological.

19. Banck 1976: vii.

20. This curious book has been the subject of several detailed Japanese studies. Now one may fortunately turn to the lucid work of Christine Mollier (Mollier 1986). On the life and works of Tu Kuang-t'ing, see Verellen 1989.

21. This example was kindly brought to my attention by Ursula-Angelika Cedzich, on October 20, 1983 (Berlin).

22. Cf. Strickmann 1981; and Strickmann 1977: 1–64.

23. Cf. above. Apart from prophetic texts and works related to *I-ching* and *T'ai-hsüan ching* procedures, the Taoist Canon also includes other mantic matter, like the instructions for lamp-divination given in HY 220, 24.4b–5b: *Great Rites of the Jade Hall (Yü-t'ang ta-fa)*, compiled in 1158.

Chapter 6: New Evidence: The Oldest Buddhist Sequence

1. Banck 1976: vii–viii; Banck 1985: xi–xv. See also below.

2. Cf. Strickmann 1990.

3. Ibid.; also, Strickmann 1982a, esp. pp. 57–58.

4. Stein 1322, a "very good early 7th century MS," according to L. Giles, and Peking *san* 112.

5. T. 1331, XXI: 528c12–19. The stipulation that one may consult the oracle up to three times in succession until a satisfactory answer is obtained seems common wherever oracles are found. Marc Kalinowski observes that only the *Ling-ch'i ching* explicitly forbids multiple drawings; Kalinowski 1994. For the *Ling-ch'i ching*, cf. infra.

6. The formal structure of this chapter is identical to that of Chapter 7. There it is Śakra, King of the Gods, who presents an exorcistic procedure, using a wooden seal inscribed with names of power. Here, Brahmā offers a written verse oracle. In each case, a "secular" god sponsors the Buddhist adaptation of a Chinese practice. For Chapter 7 and "ensigillation," cf. Strickmann 2002, Chap. 4.

7. See Mollier 1986; and Strickmann 2002, chap. 3: "The Literature of Spells."

8. In Buddhism, monks and nuns were officially directed to view the Buddha as the Great Physician and Enlightenment as his universal panacea; cf. Paul Demiéville, "Byō," *Hōbōgirin* 3 (1937), pp. 224–65; Mark Tatz, trans., *Buddhism and Healing: Demiéville's Article 'Byō' from Hōbōgirin* (Lanham, Md.: University Press of America, 1985). Or they were instructed to employ in their doctoring only medicaments excreted by their own bodies; cf. May 1967. In early Taoism, the faithful were taught that ailments derived from transgressions committed either by themselves or their ancestors. Conventional medicines were therefore useless, and only ritual might prevail; cf. Strickmann 2002, chap. 1, "Disease and Taoist Law."

9. Christopher Marlowe, *The Tragicall Historie of Doctor Faustus*, 1982: 312.

10. Cf. Welch 1967: 358–62.

11. Chap. 3, 501c–3b. Among Buddhist scriptures that correlate the Three Refuges and Five Precepts with Chinese numerical categories are the

Ching-tu san-mei ching and the *Book of Trapuṣa and Bhallika* (*T'i-wei po-li ching*); cf. Makita 1976: 148–211, 247–71.

12. On animal sacrifice as a characteristic of "profane" cults outside the sanctified context of Taoism and Buddhism (and hence a "demonic" trait), see Stein, 1979: 53–81; and Strickmann 1981: 132.

13. On the various types of demonic agents abroad in early medieval China, cf. Strickmann 2002, chaps. 2 ("Demonology and Epidemiology") and 3 ("The Literature of Spells").

14. The *Declarations of the Perfected* (*Chen-kao*) contains several descriptions of such tests, as does much medieval Taoist and Buddhist hagiography, not to mention "secular" literature. Many anecdotes turn upon the need for distinguishing authentically divine visitors from diabolic impersonators, and some Taoist texts even furnish lists of identifying traits: square pupils in the eyes, for example, are an infallible sign of a genuine immortal.

15. On *cheng*, straight, true, and *hsieh*, false, twisted, cf. Strickmann 1980: 225. On the same dichotomy in medicine, see Unschuld 1985: 67, 83.

16. Cf. Strickmann 1988: 25–46.

17. Among the official in charge of the dead, medieval Taoist most feared the Water Officer (*shui-kuan*) and his department, the Water Bureau (*shui-fu*). The Water Officer was the third of the Three Officers (*san-kuan*) who served as inquisitors of the newly dead, and he seems to have assumed the functions and fearsomeness of the ancient Lord of the River.

18. Cf. Yang 1961: 263.

Chapter 7: *La Trahison Des Cléromanes: Divination in a Buddhist Setting*

1. For one example, see this work's instructions for driving out disease-demons by using an inscribed seal with those given in a Taoist text: Strickmann 2002, chap. 4.

2. HY 179, *Records of the Perfect Ones on Prohibitions for Immortals* (*Hsien-chi chen-chi*), p. 3a; ca. C.E. 365.

3. Esnoul 1968: 119–21. For the text, see Rhys Davids 1956: 15–26. We do indeed find the *Samantapāsādikā* declaring that "The Buddha is like a divination-expert who knows the specialities of a proper site [for a building]." The technical term here is *vathuvijjācariya*, which the Chinese version renders as *chih hsiang-ti shih*: a master skilled in topographical scrutiny, a *feng-shui* expert. It is evidently the Buddha's clear perception of circumstances and conditions that are alluded to, rather than any use of particular mantic systems or devices. Like an expert topographer, the Buddha can assess an aspirant's situation and prescribe the appropriate object for meditation. Cf. Bapat and Hirakawa 1970: 295–96.

4. T. 1484, XXIV: 1007a24–26, b16–19; cf. De Groot 1893: 61–62.

5. T. 1471, XXIV: 927a6–10. On *ku* magic (a mystico-material poisoning), see Feng and Shryock 1935: 1–35; Unschuld 1985: 46–50.

6. Hargrave 1930: 161–62. Another closely comparable Christian specimen, a fifteenth-century German Book of Fate, has been published by Eckerhard Simon; see below.

7. Lévi and Chavannes 1916: 5–304, esp. 215 ff.; Strong 1979: 50–88. The Chinese text credited to Hui-chien is T. 1698, XXXII: 784b–c.

8. On the legends of Mu-lien and their place in Chinese ritual culture, see Teiser 1988. The "Wheel of Existences" (*saṃsāramaṇḍala*) was explicitly intended to supplant Maudgalyāyana's eyewitness accounts of posthumous rewards and punishments for good and bad deeds. Conflated with the Wheel of the Law (*dharmacakra*), it became the *bhavacakra*. This object of meditation depicts, inter alia, the five modes of birth (hell-beings, animals, pretas, gods, and men), with Love, Hate, and Error in the middle, represented by a dove, a snake, and a pig, respectively. As so often, the creation of Buddhist iconic and mantic expedients is presented as an historical (or eschatological) necessity: the Buddha puts his disciples on notice that once Maudgalyāyana has left the world, rare indeed will be the bhikṣus capable of visiting the hells or other worlds to obtain firsthand information about rebirths. Cf. de la Vallée Poussin 1898, chap. 3, "Le yoga bouddhique," Appendix B, "Le *Bhavacakra*," pp. 98–100.

A vast portion of Buddhist literature is taken up with the question of good and bad actions and their consequences, in this life and lives past and future. For a straightforward specimen, see Lévi 1932, which represents an enlarged version of a sūtra in the *Madhyamāgama*. Among other mantic methods that Buddhism in time adopted and disseminated, we may mention incubation (sleeping in a temple, in the god's presence, to obtain a prophetic dream), casting a tooth-cleaning stick into which one has bitten, to determine by the direction of its fall whether or not one is qualified to enter the maṇḍala for consecration (*abhiṣeka*) as Tantric master—for these practices, see Strickmann 1988: 25–46; and Strickmann 1996, chap. 6 ("Les rêves et la divination"). There is also induced possession of various types, with a wide range of vehicles; see Strickmann 2002, chaps. 5 ("The Genealogy of Spirit Possession") and 6 ("Tantrists, Foxes, and Shamans"). Finally, there is an abundant literature on Buddhist astrology, splendidly studied in Morita 1941.

9. T. 839, XVII: 902b16–23.

10. See Lai 1990: 175–206; the tops and the system of calculation are described, pp. 178–82. Predictably, in this scripture designed for the Last Age of the Law, the mechanical divining device was an eschatological expedient. It is presented in a context of intense penitence appropriate to the times. In Whalen Lai's words, "Not fatalism, not magical manipulation, but, ultimately, confession and purgation are what ensures the success of the divination, which is only the beginning of a long spiritual journey" (p. 182). On this text, see also Chie 1977: 571–79, and Kuo 1994. An Indian royal prototype was at one time preserved in Thai usage: "Top-spinning was performed in the seventh lunar month (Jyaiṣṭha), and attracted large crowds of people who were eager to learn the fortunes of the realm as foretold by the Brahmans on this occasion. Three tops

'as large as pumpkins' and made of the nine metals which correspond to the nine planets, symbolized the three gods of the Hindu triad, and were carried out in procession from the temple of Śiva. They were spun on a board by means of a silken string of five colors, ten cubits long. Omens were drawn from the length of spin and the kind of noise emitted from the tops"; Wales 1931: 298. Tops and teetotums once had a place in Christian churches, as well. It is said that during the rite called "Burial of the Alleluia," performed before the octaves of Easter, "a choir boy used to whip a top, marked with *Alleluia*, written in golden letters, from one end of the choir to the other"; Hone 1826, 1: 199a. These spinnings recall medieval wheels of fortune, which are certainly related to oracle books in the Islamic world and the West; see Patch 1927: 155, n. 4; Pickering 1970: 168–222 ("Fortune"); Nelson 1980: 227–33, pl. 28–29.

11. See Waley 1932, vol. 2: 552; also, *Nāgārjuna's Treatise on the Five Sciences* (*Lung-shu wu-ming lun*, T. 1420, XXI: 956b–968c)—a wild array of extravagant magic. It has been studied by Osabe Kazuo (Osabe 1982: 234–47); cf. Strickmann 2002, chap. 4.

12. E.g. in the cases of "filial piety," assumed to be a virtual Chinese monopoly; but now see Schopen 1984.

13. For an excellent presentation of the *I-ching* in the context of the alternative book and system devised by Yang Hsiung (53 B.C.E. to 18 C.E.), the *T'ai-hsüan ching*, see Nylan and Sivin 1988: 41–99.

14. See Fahd 1966: 183.

15. Herodotus, *Histories*, IV.67: "They [the Scythians] have amongst them a great number who practice the art of divination; for this purpose they use a number of willow twigs, in this manner: They bring large bundles of these together, and having untied them, dispose them one by one on the ground, each bundle at a distance from the rest. This done, they pretend to foretell the future, during which they take up the bundles separately, and tie them again together" (trans. William Beloe, London, 1825). No mention of writing here; it sounds almost like the preliminary operations for obtaining an *I-ching* response. Of the Germans, Tacitus wrote, "To divination and the lot they pay as much attention as anyone: the method of drawing lots is uniform. A bough is cut from a nut-bearing tree and divided into slips: these are distinguished by certain runes and spread casually and at random over white cloth: afterwards, should the inquiry be official the priest of the state, if private the father of the family in person, after prayers to the gods and with eyes turned to heaven, takes up one slip at a time until he has done this on three separate occasions, and after taking the three interprets them according to the runes which have already been stamped on them: if the message be a prohibition, no inquiry on the same matter is made during the same day; if the message be permissive, further confirmation is required by means of divination"; *Germania*, 10; trans. Maurice Hutton, Loeb Library (1920), pp. 277–79. In describing the slips as being distinguished "by certain runes" (*notis quibusdam*) the translator was acquiescing in the widely held view that the marks on the slips were runic characters; see Elliott 1959: 65–66. Thus

did Ammianus Marcellinus describe the Halani: "They have a remarkable way of divining the future; for they gather very straight twigs of osier and sort them out at an appointed time with certain secret incantations, and thus clearly learn what impends" (XXXI.240; trans. John C. Rolfe, Loeb Library 91952), vol. 3, p. 395.

16. *Hou Han shu* 38.1a. A rather more striking example from later times is found in a civil rather than a military context. According to a manual for magistrates published in 1699, newly appointed provincial magistrates would draw lots to determine their posting. The ceremony took place at the Board of Civil Office, to the east of the Gate of Heavenly Peace, in Peking. There were two tubular receptacles, one containing the names of the candidates, the other the names of the posts. An official would draw one of the candidate's names, the man in question would then step forward and draw the name of his destined post from the other container. When in time the new appointee reached his post, he was to fast and spend the night in the temple of the City God. There he took his oath of office, received the official seals, and composed a series of odes in honor of the City God, the Hearth God, and the gods of the Yamen gates. See Huang Liu-hung, *Fu-hui ch'üan-shu*, 1.3b ff.; Djang Chu 1984: 94–98. The term for "drawing lots" is *ch'e ch'ien*. Once again, "elite" meets "popular"—elite *is* popular. Glen Dubridge has contributed another interesting occurrence, found repeated in several medieval sources. The Lord of Lin (Lin-chün), legendary progenitor of a Szechuan royal line, apparently casted lots of some kind to divine for the site of his city. At a spot along the I River where a part of the bank had collapsed, he found a large flat rock. There he stopped, and he seems either to have cast his divining sticks and made the calculations; and every time it came up "rock"—i.e., "build on a rock"; or perhaps he simply threw a stick or sticks that invariably landed on, or perhaps even got stuck in, the rock. (In favor of this latter interpretation is the story's opening; it begins with Lin-chün throwing a sword into a cave. What later attracted him to the riverside site was its resemblance, from afar, to a cave. He explicitly draws the parallel: "As I have just come out of a cave, so shall I enter this one.") However, the passage is to be understood, the omen was favorable, and he founded his city beside the rock (*Chin-shu chiao-chu* 120:1b–2b; Glen Dudbridge, letter of August 31, 1983; see *T'ai-p'ing kuang-chi* 481.39b3–4; and Verellen 1989: 172. Another shift of scene: among the street-vendors of old Peking was one who sold sugar figurines of men and animals. His client drew a bamboo stick from a set of 32, proffered in a bamboo cylinder. Each lot was inscribed with domino-points, and the sugar figurine bore corresponding dot patterns; see *Pei-ching min-chien feng-su po-t'u* (Peking: Shu-mu wen-hsien ch'u-pan she, 1983: pl. 45).

17. On divination texts recovered by archeology in recent years, see the outstanding study by Marc Kalinowski, "Les traités de Shuihudi et l'hémérologie chinoise à la fin des Royaumes-Combattants" (Kalinowski 1986a).

18. For illustrations of the game, cf. Finsterbusch 1971, figures 715 and 993; Hayashi 1976, figures 8–10, 8–11, and text, pp. 386–88. On the literary sources, see Montell 1949: 70–83.

19. Needham 1962: 328.

20. Rudolph 1978: 279–81.

21. Harper 1986: 69–89. The great historian of Chinese literature, art, and theater, Aoki Masaru (1887–1964), published several entertaining and instructive studies of Chinese drinking-lore and custom. See Aoki 1962; and his anthology of Chinese poems on drinking, *Chūka inshu shisen* (Aoki 1964). Aoki was long fascinated by a set of 48 woodblock prints, the *Wine-Cards of the Immortals* (*Lieh-hsien chiu-p'ai*), created by the brilliant figure-painter Jen Hsiung (Jen Wei-ch'ang), who seems to have died before reaching the age of forty, ca. 1856. Aoki notes that the work has survived in booklet form, and that examples of the original edition are scarce (Aoki 1962: 64–66). Mine, purchased in Kyoto, 1972, bears the seals of Jen Wei-ch'ang. A separate page is devoted to the image of each immortal, accompanied by a poem (evidently to be read aloud) and directions for drinking, quite in the old T'ang manner (figure 340). Aoki first described this work in a 1927 article, later included in his volume of essays, *Kōnan shun* (Aoki 1941: 211–18). See also *Jen Wei-ch'ang mu-k'o jen-wu* (Shanghai: Shang-hai jen-min mei-shu ch'u-pan she, 1980).

22. Culin 1895; Reprint as *Games of the Orient: Korea, China, Japan* (Rutland/Tokyo: Tuttle, 1958), xix ff.

23. Needham 1962: 328. Needham himself has there provided a remarkable "Chart to show the genetic relationships of games and divination-techniques in relation to the development of the magnetic compass": see ibid., 331, Table 53.

24. Caquot 1968: 86.

25. J. D. Bate, "The Oracle of Hubal." *Indian Antiquary* 1883, 12: p. 4—an agreeably quaint article that cites older European literature on the subject.

26. Fahd 1958.

27. Fahd 1966: 524. Arrow-divination is still in use among Tibetans; cf. Radha 1981: 14. In the West, the patron saint of arrow-divination might well be the Hyperborean Abaris, who "went round the world carrying his arrow (or flying on his magic arrow through the air), prophesied, and delivered Sparta from a plague"; Cornford 1952: 89. Cf. Bolto 1962: 157–58; Dodds 1951: 141.

28. Fahd 1966: 139–40, 184.

29. Harper 1986: 77–78. For scripture-burial and the receptacles employed, see Sekine 1968. These time-capsules were usually prepared for storage until the coming of the future Buddha, Maitreya. Then they would be discovered and the merit, amassed long before by the copyist, would be fully credited to his karmic account. R. C. Bell illustrates and describes a Chinese ivory dicing cup, apparently made in the second half of the eighteenth century. It closely resembles the oracle-stick containers, and depicts the Eight Immortals. A verse inscription runs, "The Immortals at dice in their Celestial Heaven,/ Have turned dry river into flooding stream;/ But I have wandered for years in the desert/ Alone with the stones, and the wind's wild scream." Cf. Bell 1969, pl. 25 and Appendix A, pp. 144–46.

30. For a broad perspective on all this, see Needham 1959: 68–80 ("Mechanical Aids to Calculation"), and the chapter on "Tally Sticks" in Menninger 1969: 223–48. Also, Marc Kalinowski, "La divination par les nombres dans les manuscrits de Dunhuang" (Kalinowski 1994), drawn on for divination systems attested at Tun-huang, below.

31. Yang 1961: 208, 212–15. For texts on monastic lotteries, see Mujaku Dōchū (1653–1745), *Zenrin Shōkisen*; Mujaku 1963: 479–80; on auction of deceased monks' effects, ibid., 570–72.

32. See Durt 1979: 431–56.

33. T. 1804, XL: 116c–117a; Gernet 1973: 81–85.

34. See Durt 1979: 437 ff.; see also Durt 1974. Pilgrims to Upagupta's shrine near Mathurā could marvel at a cave or cell entirely filled with counting sticks left by those who had attained arhatship through Upagupta's teaching. They were seen by the seventh-century Chinese monk Hsüan-chuang; cf. Watters 1904, vol. 1: 307; Strong 1985: 877, n. 63.

Chapter 8: Writing and Chinese Ritual

1. Plutarch, *De defectu oraculorum*; Dodds 1965: 55 f.

2. Thompson 1978: 19–42.

3. Chadwick 1942: 1–3.

4. Michaux 1933: 145.

5. Finnegan 1970: 194.

6. Chadwick and Chadwick, 1932–40, vol. 3: 645.

7. Finnegan 1970: 187.

8. *Ssu-ku t'i-yao pien-cheng*, Peking, 1937; rpt. Taipei: I-wen, 1957: 733–39.

9. Yü Chia-hsi, Suzuki 1963; revised, expanded edition, 1974: 431–593. Suzuki provides a partial edition and Japanese translation, pp. 657–736.

10. Ibid., p. 489.

11. *Wen I-to ch'üan-chi* (Peking: San-lien, 1982), vol. 4: 138–52.

12. The largest collection of these intriguing, portentous snippets—prophetic ditties from the mouths of babes—is the massive *Ku yao-yen*, assembled by Tu Wen-lan (1815–81). It includes the full context of each enigmatic example (Peking: Chung-hua, 1958; rpt. 1984).

13. Suzuki Yoshijirō, *Kan'eki kenkyū*, 1963: 438, n. 3.

14. Dudbridge 1970: 115.

15. Needham 1962: 326. Cf. Yü Chia-hsi, *Ssu-k'u t'i-yao pien-cheng*, pp. 730–33, and the studies by Marc Kalinowski and Carole Morgan cited later. Werner Banck reproduces specimen pages from an illustrated Sung manual of divination using divining blocks. Below each image the throw is depicted, and the oracular poems are variously in verses of four, five, or seven syllables (cf. Figure 24). The work's title is *Ch'ing-lung kao*, or "Divining-Blocks of the Blue Dragon [Temple?]," and it is included in a larger Sung collection of mantic texts, the *Yen-ch'in san-shih hsiang-fa*. This has been reproduced in Japan as

Sō-kanpon Enkin sanzezō (Tokyo, n.d.). There is also a Taiwanese facsimile edition of the *Hsiang-t'u yen-ch'in san-shih hsiang-fa*: the *Ching-k'ao Yen-ch'in san-shih hsiang-fa* (Taichung 1969); Banck 1976: vii–viii, pl. 2; Banck 1985, pl. 2. This short, undated Sung text should prove useful in a more thorough study of the illustrated Books of Fate, and may be compared with a number of the various Eurasian dice-oracles described in our next chapter on diffusion.

16. Goody 1968, 1977, 1987.

17. Goody 1987: 130.

18. Ibid., p. 303, n. 5.

19. See Vandermeersch 1974: 29–51. Vandermeersch has suggested that the origins of the parallelism that so strongly marks prose and poetry in literary Chinese are anchored in the most ancient mantic texts; see also Vandermeersch 1989.

20. The initial, path-breaking study of Taoist liturgy by Kristofer Schipper, "Taoism; the Liturgical Tradition" (1968), has never been published, but has been given full and proper credit by (among others) Joseph Needham, in Needham 1974: 128 ff. Cf. also Welch 1969–70; and Schipper 1974: 309–24.

21. Cf. "Le culte tantrique du feu," in Strickmann 1996.

22. See the striking illustration of this in Billeter 1989: 15. A kneeling woman offers incense and candles before a great, looming, red Chinese character for "Buddha" (*Fo*) graven in a rock behind the Nan P'u-t'o ssu (or "Southern Poṭalaka Temple"), in Amoy. As Billeter observes, the written sign takes the place of the deity's image. On the special role of calligraphy in medieval Taoism, cf. Ledderose 1984: 246–78. There is copious information on paper money, burnt for the gods as well as the dead, in Hou 1975; and Osgood, 1975, vol. 2: 627–68. For paper items, inscribed or not, burnt for the benefit of the dead, see Watson and Rawski 1988, *passim*.

23. Cf. Strickmann 1981: 14–17.

24. I am grateful to Léon Vandermeersch and Jao Tsong-yi for thorough discussion of this point at the Centenary Conference on Ritual sponsored by the Fifth Section of the École Pratique des Hautes Études, September 22–25, 1986. It is certainly significant that early in the fourteenth century we find a Taoist author maintaining that it was the Taoists who had most faithfully preserved the authentic ceremonial (*li*) of ancient times (HY 1221, *Tao-shu yüan-shen ch'i*, preface dated 1305). The great fourth- and fifth-century elaboration of Taoist liturgy came to pass in a milieu long reputed for its scholastic tradition with respect to the books of ceremonial, as well as the *Book of Changes* (Strickmann 1981: 98–116). It is my impression that the Taoists simply attempted to encompass all this within their comprehensive cosmic and social vision of "Law," i.e., ritual.

25. Cf. Shizutani 1974: 43–46, *et passim*.

26. HY 421, *Teng-chen yin-chüeh*, 3.5b5; Cedzich 1987: 107.

27. Schipper 1985: 21–57.

28. Even Taoist priests make this distinction nowadays, between their own "Tao" and the "*fa*" used by other, lesser practitioners—that is, between

meditation and magic or trance; cf. Strickmann 1980: 226. The pragmatic differences between *tao-shih* and *fa-shih* in southern Taiwan actually involve a clear complementarity, delineated by Kristofer Schipper; Schipper 1985: 35, *et passim*.

29. See Strickmann 2002, chap. 6: "Tantrists, Foxes, and Shamans."

30. Elliot 1955: 56–58; Berthier 1987: 86–100.

31. There is now a comprehensive study of this phenomenon and the supporting social groups: Jordan and Overmyer 1986. Still valuable is the study of historical records of spirit-writing by Hsü Ti-shan, *Fu-chi mi-hsin te yen-chiu* (Hsü 1941).

Chapter 9: Visions of Diffusion: Central Asia and the West

1. Macdonald 1967: 26: "One did not simply adapt Indian tales to a Tibetan milieu. One amalgamated Indian narratives with indigenous narratives and with other narratives that were probably not indigenous, but foreign to Tibet while being well known there. The *ro-sgruṅ* ["Tales of the *vetāla*"] are indeed a good example of that syncretism commonly called 'Lamaism,' which is not merely constituted by factors indigenous to Tibet."

2. Sotzmann, "Die Loosbücher des Mittelalters," *Serapeum* 4, 5, and 6 (1850): 49–62, 65–80, and 81–9, respectively. The second part of his study appeared in *Serapeum* 20, 21, and 22 (1851): 305–16, 321–33, and 337—42, respectively. On Fanti's *Trionfo di Fortuna*, see Thorndike 1923–58, vol. 6: 469–72.

3. Sotzmann 1851: 307–9, 314. On German Losbücher generally, we may quote the description penned in 1456 by an outspoken witness, Dr Johann Hartlieb:

> Es ist ain gemain püch, das haisst man ain loss püch. etlichs würft man mit würffeln, etlichs treibt man vmb bis vff ain zal, nach der zal sücht man dann die fräg, warumb der mensch gefrägtt hatt, es sey von weiben, vich, eer oder ampt zu erwerben oder sunst gar manigerlay; ob der siech sterb oder genes, ob der ellend pald chom, oder der mensch jn disen oder jn den sachen gelück oder vngelück haben sol. die posshait ist so weit vssgetailt mit jren fragen, das kain ding jn der welt ist, man vind es jn disen frägen. nach dem chomt man an ainen alten, der weisst dann zu ainem richter, der legt uss die selbigen frag. das ist alls ain vngelaub vnd vast wider got, wann es hat kainen grund weder gaistlich noch natürlich vnd ist vast verpotten von der hailigen kirchen jn decretis. die losspücher sol dein gnad vnd ain yeglicher cristenmensch meiden und fliehen.

["There is a well-known book which is called the Book of Lots. One throws dice, until one reaches a number; in accordance with that number, one looks for the question, which someone has asked—be it for a wife, for cattle, for honor, for office or whatever else; whether the ill person will die or recover, whether the banned will return, whether a person will have good or bad luck in these and other matters. This evil is so widespread with its question, that there is nothing one will not find in these questions. Afterwards one gets to an old man who points the way to a judge, who will explain the self-same questions. This is all a singular disbelief and it stands in sharp opposition to [the will of] God, for it has neither a spiritual or natural basis and is thus prohibited by the Holy Church in its decrees. You and every Christian should avoid these Books of Lots and flee from them."] Cf. Ulm 1914: 31. (Translated with the help of Charlotte Fonrobert.)

4. Zingerle 1858: 55–84, "Ein altes Loosbuch."

5. The manuscript had been discovered ca. 1860 in the wall of a demolished house at Cordes (Tarn); Dusan 1866–67; also Chabaneau 1880–81, noting another previous edition by Napoléon Peyrat in his *Histoire des Albigeois* (1872). Chabaneau's article appeared as a separate brochure in Montpellier in 1881. Meanwhile, Félix Rocquain had published "Les sorts des saints et des apôtres" in *Bibliothèque de l'École des Chartes* (Rocquain 1880), in which he sets both the Provençal text and its Latin prototype in the larger context of medieval Christian divination. Rocquain's and Chabaneau's studies and editions were reviewed by Paul Meyer in *Romania* 10 (1881): 296.

Bruno Dusan's translation was reprinted by the folklorist Pierre Saintyves (i.e., Émile Nourry, 1870–1935) in his book, *En marge de la Légende Dorée* (Saintyves 1987: 792–95). In a section on "Survivances," Saintyves includes an entire chapter on "Les sorts des saints et leurs modèles païens" (ibid., 765–803). He describes Greek and Roman rhabdomancy (or rather, rhabdiomancy), the *Sortes Homericae*, and *Sortes Vergilianae* as background to "La bibliomancie chez les chrétiens et les *Sorts des Saints*," tracing the history of Christian bibliomancy from the fifth to the fourteenth century and beyond (ibid., 771–90). He discusses the *sortes apostolorum* separately (ibid., 790–800), following the distinction made by Richard Ganszyniec. Ganszyniec maintained that scholars all too often confused the *Sortes sanctorum* (which made use of Holy Writ, especially the Psalms and Prophets) with those independent oracles specifically composed for mantic use, which stood under the Apostles' patronage; see Ganszyniec 1928.

Louis Brandin dominated the subsequent publication of Romance-language oracle texts: "Le *Livre de preuve*" (Brandy 1927); "Un livre de bonne aventure anglo-français en vers" (Brandy 1928); "Les Prognostica du ms. Ashmole 304 de la Bodléienne" (Brandy 1932). For other medieval examples, we have the excellent study by T. C. Skeat, "An Early Medieval 'Book of Fate': The *Sortes XII Patriarchum*. With a Note on 'Books of Fate' in general" (Skeat 1954). Skeat's chief exhibit is an oracle first found in twelfth-century manuscripts, which is notably free from Arabic influence. It opens with ritual instructions resembling those in the medieval Latin text published by Pierre Pithou: three days' preliminary prayer and fasting, a vigil with two candles on the eve of consultation, then a Mass and the aspersion of holy water. Nor is the querent to omit the "Pater" or "Credo," and he must not forget to cross himself. Skeat cites earlier publications of this manuscript material by A. Boutemy, J. H. Mozley, R. H. Hunt, and Francis Wormald.

6. *Codex canonum vetus Ecclesiae romanae a Francisco Pithoeo ad veteres manuscriptos codices restitutis et notis illustratus* ... (Paris: e typographia regia, 1687), 370–73.

7. Du Cange 1710, vol. 3, columns 999–1004, *sors* s.v.; Thiers 1741, vol. 1: 229–42; or Didot edition (Paris, 1846), vol. 6: pp. 304–5. Other early studies, listed by Saintyves, are: Jean-Baptiste Thiers, *Traité des superstitions* (third edition, Paris, 1712), vol. 1: 229–42 ("De la divination qui se fait par le sort"); Abbé du Resnel, "Recherches historiques sur les Sorts appelés communément par les Payens: Sortes Homericae, Sortes Virgilianae, etc., et sur ceux qui parmi les chrétiens on été connus sous le nom de Sortes Sanctorum" (du Resnel 1744: 287–310); Johan Friedrich Cotta, *De Sortibus Sanctorum* (Tübingen 1758); R. P. Pierre Le Brun, *Histoire critique des pratiques superstitieuses* (Paris, 1750–51), vol. 2: 134–43 ("De la coutume de consulter les livres saints pour deviner l'avenir"); Louis de Jaucourt, "Sorts des Saints," in *Encyclopédie, ou dictionnaire raisonné* ... (of Diderot et d'Alembert, Paris, 1875), vol. 15: 379–80; Dom Augustin Calmet, "Dissertation sur les élections par le sort," in *Sainte Bible, édition de Vence* (Paris, 1822), vol. 21: 376–85; Nicias Gaillard, "Les sorts des saints," *Mémoires de la Société des Antiquaires de l'Ouest*, I (1835), 59–74; Ludovic Lalanne, *Curiosités des traditions, des moeurs et des légendes* (Paris, 1847), pp. 13–22 ("Les sorts des saints"); Auguste François Lecanu, "Sorts des saints," *Dictionnaire des prophéties et des miracles* (Paris: J. P. Migne, 1854), vol. 2: 1052–59.

8. Bouché-Leclerc 1963, vol. 1: 189–97. For the *kleroterion*, a mechanical device used in Athenian jury-selection, see Dow 1939: 1–34; Brumbaugh 1966: 65–67.

The Renaissance re-discovery of ancient mechanical arts (notably in the works of Heron of Alexandria) eventually generated material relevant to our theme. We find it among the fascinating automata that have been studied with such skill and acumen by Alfred Chapuis and his collaborators: Chapuis 1947; Chapuis and Gelis 1984; A. Chapuis and Droz 1949. For example, in the 1949 volume by Chapuis and Droz, one section deals with eighteenth-century figures of "devins, escamoteurs et acrobates" (pp. 251–70). Eighteenth-century treatises describe the construction of little temples for automated soothsayers or magicians. They furnish very general answers to a series of numbered questions, selected by means of a dial in the upper part of the structure. Some of this mantic chinoiserie reached China. Chapuis and Droz note that in 1795 a Dutch embassy took two such devices, manufactured in Switzerland, to present to the Emperor in Peking; one broke en route (p. 253). Two "magiciens de Maillardet," made by Jean-David Maillardet at Fontaines in the Val de Ruz, Switzerland, are preserved at the Musée d'horlogerie at La Chaux-de-Fonds. "Le grand magicien" (Chapuis and Droz, figures 295, 296, and pp. 252–56) has a long curly beard and wears a cloak and a tall peaked cap. He holds a book in his left hand, a wand in his right. The oracular questions are inscribed on twelve elliptical brass plates. When one of these is placed in a drawer and the drawer pushed in, the magician stirs, stands up, rolls his eyes, and waves his wand toward a little oval window above his head. The window's two flaps open and the answer appears. According to Chapuis and Droz, the action of this extraordinary device is remarkably smooth. Sample questions and answers: "What is the noblest reward of science?" "To illustrate ignorance." "How should one consider morality?" "As the hygiene of the soul." Eighteenth-century wisdom indeed. Chapuis and Droz describe another complicated specimen, in a snuff-box (*tabatière*). It contains an automated magician who emerges from a grotto, goes to an enchanted tree, waves his wand; and lo! a branch swings up and reveals the answer to the question that has been inserted in a drawer. The seven questions and answers: 1. A rare thing? A friend. 2. What does one give too easily? Advice. 3. What gives illusory happiness? Money. 4. The greatest treasure? Wisdom. 5. The desire of a fifteen-year-old girl? To be sixteen. 6. The confidant of the bride? A mirror. 7. The fortunate error? Hope. While the question is being asked and answered, the magical snuff-box also plays one of two musical airs. If the drawer is pushed in empty, a death's head appears (pp. 256–58).

9. Bouché-Leclerc 1963, vol. 4 (1882: 145–59; on the possible significance of the statues' reported movements, cf. p. 154. A curious oracular verse-fragment, possibly from one of the celebrated Italic shrines, was published by Franz Buecheler as no. 331 in his *Carmina latina epigraphica* (Buecheler 1895; *Anthologia Latina, pars posterior*), vol. 1, pp. 159–61. It is significant that each of the 17 loosely-constructed hexameter verse begins with a fresh letter of the alphabet, from C through Q.

10. Bouché-Leclerc 1963, vol. 1: 196.

11. Hirschfeld, *Monatsberichte der Berliner Akademie*, 1875, p. 716; Kaibel, 1876; Kaibel 1878, no. 1038, p. 454.

12. Heinevetter 1912. Cf. Ch. Naour 1980.

13. Pausanias VII.25.10; Frazer 1913, vol. 1: 368. "Having descended from Bura in the direction of the sea, we come to a river named Buraicus and to a small image of Hercules in a grotto. This image is also surnamed Buraicus, and there is a mode of divination by means of dice and a tablet. The person who inquires of the god prays before the image, and after paying he takes four dice and throws them on the table. There are plenty of dice lying beside the image. Each die has a certain figure marked on it, and the meaning of each figure is explained on the tablet." In his note on this passage, Frazer translates four specimen responses from inscriptions found in Asia Minor, and even refers to Chinese examples: the use of our temple oracles on shipboard, to divine the prospects for sailing. Frazer considered this mode of divination especially worthy of comparison with the Greek practice (vol. 4, pp. 172–74; his information on the Chinese and Cochin-Chinese was derived from the German ethnographer A. Bastian). Heinevetter translates the phrase on dice-casting rather more precisely: "Zu jedem Wurf der Astragalen bietet das auf der Tafel Geschriebene eine genaue

Erklärung des Wurfes" ["The script on the tablet offers a detailed explanation for each throw of the knucklebones"]; Heinevetter 1912: 32. Thus, the dice are thrown on a table; but the various throws are written out on a "table" of quite another sort. Confusion regarding tables marked into sectors for gaming on and separate lists or tables of throws dogged the interpreters of ancient Indian dicing and dice-oracles, as well.

14. Heinevetter 1912: 33–52. On letter-oracles, see now Zevi 1982.

15. Bean 1968: 125–26: "That this dreadful rubbish should have had so wide a vogue speaks poorly for the common sense of the ancients."

16. Ibid., pp. 172–73.

17. Turner 1968: 29.

18. Already in the fifth century B.C.E., Aristophanes had parodied the χρησμολόγος or soothsayer who went about with a little book filled with the oracles of Bakis and lived off credulous clients; cf. Aune 1983: 43–44. (Aune's book is a very comprehensive survey of every form of prophecy.) "Bakis" is mentioned in other ancient sources, and Goethe took the name for his own verse oracle; cf. note 45 below. Among the papyrus finds was a Homeric verse oracle, using three six-sided dice inscribed from 1 to 6. It was published in Preisendanz 1973–74, 7: 1–148; English translation in Betz 1986: 112–19.

The most recent account of all these oracle-types as a background to early Christianity is in Robin Lane Fox's superb book, *Pagans and Christians* (Lane Fox 1986, chap. 5), "Language of the Gods," esp. pp. 208–15. As Lane Fox points out, the frequency of oracle questions concerning prospects in love and business, travel and public service, "distinguish their clients from contemporary tribal societies whose diviners are more concerned to analyze the past than to choose between options for the future" (p. 215). Such ancient oracle sequences were not only written on papyrus and graven on stone. A similar Losbuch fragment has been found inscribed in cuneiform on a clay tablet in the British Museum (no. 33333B). It dates from the 135th year of the Seleucid Era: 177/176 B.C.E., and like many other Losbücher, this Mesopotamian specimen brings together mantic birds, dice, and constellations. Five birds were listed: swallow, raven, eagle, and an unidentified bird, and a fifth whose name has not been preserved. The birds are correlated with the throws of the dice or astragaloi and reappear in the oracular responses, which the veteran Assyriologist Ernst Weidner found to be full of uncertain readings and most difficult to understand. On the other side of the tablet is a chart of the twelve signs of the zodiac. Weidner surmised that the querent's astrological sign was somehow combined with the numerical result of his dice-throw and the related bird of fate, to determine the oracle's answer. Weidner found remarkable similarities between this text and the Arabic *Königslose* published and studied by Gotthold Weil (note 53 below). Considering its comparatively late date, Weidner doubted whether the cuneiform Losbuch represented an autochthonous Babylonian form of divination. Since there were no earlier examples, indigenous origin seemed very improbable. The oracle was almost certainly a creation of the Hellenistic period; Weidner 1956, esp. pp. 179–80.

Strangely, the same issue of the journal *Syria*, the Charles Virolleaud Festschrift, contains an article by Jean Bottéro, "Deux curiosités assyriologiques" (Bottéro 1956). The first of these "curiosities" proved to be a fragment from a very similar text, in Neo-Babylonian. Bottéro ventured a translation of the oracular answers, pp. 20–21, and speculated that this unusual tablet might either represent some sort of graphic game, or else a talisman (pp. 24–25). The fated coincidence of Weidner's and Bottéro's articles led to comparison and the writing of supplementary notes by both scholars. In view of the early date assigned by Bottéro to his text, Weidner was inclined to modify his own initial view of a necessary Greek origin (pp. 182–83). For his part, Bottéro entered fully into Weidner's Losbuch suggestion. He also noted that in many cases the oracle's response was directly derived from the character of the related zodiacal sin. For example: "Gemini; you will have a companion. Leo; you will be as strong as a lion. Libra; you will be like one who weighs money. Capricorn; you will be like the leader of a flock" (p. 32; cf. pp. 30–35). Both Widner and Bottéro now recognized in the oracle the presence of the Star-Decans, who were later to exercise so great an influence on astrology and iconography; cf. Gundel 1969; Seznec 1940: 36 ff.; English trans., 1953: 38 ff. Returning to these texts eighteen years later, Bottéro dated both examples to the Seleucid period. He described the zodiacal diagram as a kind of "draughts-board" and, drawing on B. Landsberger's observation that it bore the title "Game of Princes," concluded that it had served for entertainment: it was more a game of chance than oracle: Bottéro 1974: 122. For Walter Burkert's survey of mantic and ritual contracts between Mesopotamia and Greece, cf. note 115 below.

19. Rostovtzeff 1926: 427–28; cf. Lewis 1983: 98–99 and 219–220, n. 17.

20. Cf. note 5 of Chapter 4.

21. Björck 1939: 86–98.

22. *Metamorphoses* IX.8; the quotation and translation are taken from the Loeb edition: S. Gaselee, ed., *Apuleius, The Golden Ass* (London: William Heinemann, 1915), pp. 412–13.

23. R. Helm, ed., *Apuleius I; Metamorphoseon libri XI* (Leipzig: Teubner, 1931; rpt. 1968), p. 208; Björck 1939: 90–91.

24. Björck 1939: 94–98. Cf. Turner 1968: 149 and 188, n. 59. Rudolf Hercher produced the editio princeps of the *Sortes Astrampsychi: Oraculorum decades CIII Rudolphus Hercher ex codicibus Italicis nunc primum edidit*, in *Jahresbericht über das Königliche Joachimsthalsche Gymnasium* (Berlin: Gebrüder Unger, 1863). The Greek text was reprinted (without its prologue) by J. Rendel Harris in his book, *The Annotators of the Codex Bezae, with some notes on Sortes sanctorum* (Harris 1901), Appendix C, "The Sortes of Astrampsychus" (pp. 128–60). In these latter days, this exceedingly prosaic work has benefitted from the devoted attentions of Gerald M. Browne. He first analyzed its mode of construction and method of operation in Browne 1970: 95–100. He then published a critical edition and translation of what he had determined to be the original oracle and a subsequent revised version, probably made by the original

author: *The Papyri of the Sortes Astrampsychi* (Browne 1974). Here he points out, inter alia, Christian alterations in later, medieval manuscripts of the oracle (pp. 24–25; p. 60, n. 21; p. 61 n. 28). In "The Origin and the Date of the *Sortes Astrampsychi*" (Browne 1976), Browne argued that the work was written in the third century c.e. See also "A New Papyrus Codex of the *Sortes Astrampsychi*" (Browne 1979). For additional references to work on Graeco-Egyptian oracle texts, see Henrichs 1973: 115–19.

The Latin *Sortes sangallenses* were first published by Hermann Winnefelds: *Sortes Sangallenses, adjecta sunt alearum oracula ex codice Monacensi primum edita* (Winnefelds 1887), on the basis of the unique sixth- (or, more plausibly, seventh-) century palimpsest. Winnefeld's edition was revised by Paul Meyer in *Romania* XVIII (1888): 156–157. The text was reprinted by J. Rendel Harris, who (Skeat found) convincingly demonstrated its dependence on the system of the *Sortes Astrampsychi*: cf. Harris 1901, Appendices D ("The *Sortes Sangallenses*," pp. 161–79) and E ("The Munich Sortes alearum," pp. 180–84). The most recent edition appears to be that by Alban Dold, who suggested that the work was probably composed in Southern Gaul during the later fourth century c.e.: *Die Orakelsprüche in St. Galler Palimpsestcodex 908 (die sogenannten "Sortes Sangallenses")* (Dold 1948). Cf. Meister 1951. T. C. Skeat (in whose learned article "An early medieval 'Book of Fate' " I found many of these references) notes that a good facsimile of a page of this manuscript is printed in Aemilius [Émile Louis Marie] Chatelain, *Vncialis scriptvra codicvm latinorvm novis exemplis illvstrata* (Paris: H. Welter, 1901, plate XXXI).

The use of a meticulously crafted table of responses linked to a numerical key for selecting the right answer (as demonstrated for the Astrampsychos oracle by G. M. Browne) suggests an analogy with a system observed in nineteenth-century Egypt by E. W. Lane. It employed a table attributed to Idris (or Enoch) composed of a hundred little squares, each containing an Arabic letter. After thrice reciting the opening chapter and the 59th verse of the 6th *su'ura* of the Koran ("With Him are the keys of the secret things: none knoweth them but He: and He knoweth whatever is on the land and in the sea, and there falleth not a leaf but He knoweth it, nor a grain in the dark parts of the earth, nor a moist thing nor a dry thing but it is noted in a distinct writing"), the querent places his finger at random on a letter, without looking at it. He next looks at it, writes it down, and then writes down each fourth letter, until he returns to the starting point. The letters are so arranged as to yield only five answers, no matter where the inquirer begins. In Lane's deft English transposition, they are: "Do it without fear of ill," "Who does it will do wrong," "Abstain and enjoy peace," "Wait and attain thy wish," and "Who waiteth succeedeth." Lane observes that the table's author, familiar with human nature, gives only one affirmative answer and four negative (Lane 1895: 269–70).

For an example of the Late Antique use of dice in fate-calculation *without* an oracle book, see the following instructions from a Greek magical papyrus: "A means to learn from a die whether a man is alive or has died, for example: Make the inquirer throw this die in the above bowl. Let him fill this with water. Add to the cast of the die 612, which is the numerical value of the name of the god, i.e. 'Zeus,' and subtract from the sum 353, which is the numerical value of 'Hermes.' If then the number remaining be found divisible by two, he lives; if not, death has him"; Betz 1986: 293. For dicing as a life-or-death matter in Tibet, cf. note 98 below. A classic account of Greek and Roman dice and games with dice is found in Becq de Fouquières 1869: "Des jeux de dés" (pp. 302–24), and "Des jeux des osselets" (pp. 325–56); also, "Le jeu des douze lignes" (pp. 357–83), with important observations on dicing cups and gaming boards.

25. Björck 1939: 92–94.

26. Bolte 1903, Anhang: "Zur geschichte der Losbücher," pp. 276–48. Bolte published addenda in the *Bibliothek des literarischen Vereins in Stuttgart* 241 (1906), 349–50. For Chinese oracles, he used the same source as James Frazer: Bastian 1867, vol. 3: 125; cf. note 12 of Chapter 1 and note 13 above.

27. Bolte 1903: 280–84.

28. Bolte 1903: 284–87. Cf. Weber 1859: 158–80; rpt. in Weber, *Indische Streifen* (Berlin: Nicolaische Verlagsbuchhandlung, 1868), vol. 1: 274–307; J. E. Schröter, *Pāśakakēvalī* (dissertation, Leipzig, 1900), which has not been accessible to me.

29. Weber 1868: 276, 282–83.

30. Hoernle 1893–1912. Cf. Filliozat 1985: 157.

31. Hoernle 1893–1912, pt 4: 197–202, and pt 5: 209–21, for the translations.

32. Cf. for example the *Mātaṅgi-sūtra* series, early Chinese adaptations of Hellenistic astrology in Indian Buddhist guise, T. 551, 552, 1300, and 1201; the complex questions of dating and attribution have been studied by Hayashiya Tomojirō (Hayashiya 1945: 524–43). But Hoernle's "Mātaṅga woman" is more likely to have been the sign of an elephant (*mātaṅga*) placed on one of the three dice as a distinguishing mark.

33. Hoernle 1893–1912: 210.

34. Hoernle 1893–1912: 211: "And this shall be for a token to thee: thou hast held sexual intercourse, but that rival wife of thine is disappointed and ready for marking." Hoernle observes (n. 17) that "*lakshita*, 'marking' or 'marked,' is a euphemism for cohabitation or *effusio seminis*."

35. Weber 1868: 292, 306.

36. Lüders 1907.

37. Lüders 1907: 17.

38. Lüders 1907:17–19; on medicinal uses, cf. Perry 1980: 80. Lüders also studies literary references to cowry-shells used as dice, and compares the counting sticks (*śalākā*); Lüders 1907: 19–20. On the Buddhist use of counting sticks, cf. notes 32 and 34 of Chapter 7.

39. Lüders 1907: 22–23; cf. Hoernle 1893–1912: xciii, "Introduction."

40. Lüders 1907: 5, 8 ("Die Apsaras und das Würfelspiel"), and 8–9 ("Die Frauen und das Würfelspiel"). Lüders refers to another Jātaka-tale (the *Aṇḍabhūta-Jātaka*) where the same spell or gaming-song is chanted by a king

before play. It makes him invincible. His household priest and gaming-partner, fearing impoverishment, contrives to bring up a girl in perfect chastity. Not until she has reached womanhood does he play at dice again with the king, and then he takes care to recite "except my wife" after the king's spell. The king loses every game. Only by discovering what has happened and hiring an enterprising young scoundrel to seduce the priest's wife is the monarch able to regain the mastery; Lüders 1907: 9. The *Aṇḍabhūta-Jātaka* (no. 62) is translated in Cowell 1895–1907; rpt. London 1957, vol. 1: 151–55. The *Vidhurapaṇḍita-Jātaka* (no. 545) is found in vol. 6: 126–56. Its great gaming scene, between the king and the Yakkha (Yakṣa) Puṇṇaka, is on pp. 136–38; the names of the throws and references to dicing technique in this text inspired Lüder's study. Unfortunately, the English translators omitted the "song of play" about winding rivers and wayward women, since it is found only in one Burmese manuscript of the tale. Like games of chance, hunting was associated with (and of course, compared to) love. See Haraprasad Shastri, trans., and Mohan Chand, ed., *Śyainika śāstram: The Art of Hunting in Ancient India* (Delhi: Eastern Book Linkers, 1982), a sixteenth-century treatise that draws frequent parallels between love and hunting and gives a decidely erotic glow to the sport, for example p. 81 (vv. 11, 12, 14), pp. 128–29 (vv. 53–56), etc.

41. Lüders 1907: 17, n. 7.

42. Esnoul 1968, vol. 1: 137–38. The folklorist William Crooke described another version: "A favorite method of the Sikhs is by the Dhal, a little wooden hexagon, on each face of which are engraved certain letters of the Gurmukhi alphabet. This is thrown twice, and the letters which come uppermost are compared with a little book, called the Paintís Akhari, containing a series of lines each beginning with one of the thirty-five letters of the same alphabet. This is done before undertaking a journey or enterprise, and the verses thus selected give an omen which foretells whether the result will be lucky or unlucky"; Crooke 1906: 141.

43. Donalson 1938: 194.

44. Cf. Filliozat 1953: 353–67; Pingree 1978; Delatte 1932. Needless to say, Alexander's expedition simply marked the opening of a long period of cultural and commercial interchange.

45. Flügel 1861.

46. Flügel 1861: 42. For *al-Fihrist*, see Dodge 1970.

47. Goethe, "Weissagungen des Bakis," *Goethe's Sämtliche Werke* (Stuttgart u. Tübingen: J.G. Cotta'scher Verlag, 1840), vol. 1, pp. 295–302; thirty-two quatrains, with the epigraph: "Seltsam ist Propheten Lied;/ Doppelt seltsam, was geschieht." Cf. Jantz 1966. See also Goethe's remarks on "Buch-Orakel" in the *West-östlicher Divan, Sämtliche Werke*, vol. 4: 240–41. Playful, or in earnest? In Goethe's day, "oracles" also circulated as parlor games. They were often printed in the form of cards for drawing or other manipulations, and oracular iconography was sometimes expressed in rebus ("non verbis sed rebus") form. One example: *Präciosa's Orakelsprüche in sechsunddreissig Rätselbildern* (Leipzig:

Magazin für Industrie und Literatur, 1830–32; rpt. as a set of cards, Leipzig: Verlag Edition, 1974; as a booklet, Frankfurt am Main: Insel Verlag, 1987). I owe my copy of this attractive and challenging oracle to Renate Voit, Munich.

48. Flügel 1861: 42–44.

49. Flügel 1861: 45–46. For a clear example of correlative thinking regarding letters and numbers, cf. Nasr 1964: 209–12. Certain Greek sources also indicate that a "mystical" association was made among objects of different species whose names began with the same letter; cf. Waegeman 1987. See too Fahd 1966: 216–21.

50. See note 35 above. Ja'far ibn Muḥammad al-Ṣādiq was the 6th Shī'ite Imām, renowned for his learning. He died in 765 (or possibly a bit later). His son Mūsa succeeded him as seventh of the twelve visible Imāms. His eldest son, Ismā'īl (who had predeceased his father by some five years), had been Ja'far's original choice as a successor, but he had changed his mind owing to Ismā'īl's intemperance. Yet Ismā'īl had loyal following, for whom an Imām's innate perfection could not be compromised by a love of wine. For these Ismā'īlites, Ja'far's eldest son is still the Hidden Mahdi; cf. Hitti 1969: 442. Of Ja'far, d'Herbelot wrote, " ... il est reconnu pour le sixième Imán, & il a une telle autorité parmi les Musulmans pour sa doctrine, qu'ils tiennent pour une tradition authentique ce qu'il avoit coutume de leur dire: 'Interrogez-moi souvent pendant que je suis avec vous; car il ne viendra personne après moi qui vous puisse instruire comme moi' ". No wonder he became their oracle; "On lui attribue aussi un Livre de sorts, ou *Ketab Corráat*, qui se trouve dans la Bibliothèque du Roi, no. 1007"; B. d'Herbelot (1625–95), *Bibliothèque orientale ou dictionnaire universel* ... (Paris, 1697; revised edition, 1783), vol. 3: 13, 15.

51. Flügel 1861: 59–74.

52. Flügel 1861: 53.

53. Weil 1929; originally published in *Mitteilungen des Seminars für Orientalische Sprachen* 31, 2. Abteilung 1928, 1–69.

54. Weil 1929: 9–10. Toufic Fahd gives additional information on this most arbitrary mode of divination that comes under the general heading of *fa'l*, omens, and omen-lore. He provides examples of what he terms "*fa'l* onomantique" and discusses its principles, including "antiphrases et euphemiss," "clédonisme," and "*fa'l* intrinsèque et *fa'l* extrinsèque"; *La divination arabe*, 450–61. On portentous "dream words" recited (often unconsciously) while falling asleep, and the significant words uttered by those at the point of death, cf. Rosenthal 1967: 83–85.

55. Weil 1929: 13; cf. Fahd 1966: 214, n. 2.

56. Weil 1929: 213; cf. *al-Fihrist* VIII.3 (in a section devoted to "The Books Composed about Freckles, Twitching, Moles, and Shoulders, and the Books Composed about [Good] Omen, Augury, Conjectural Prediction, and Similar Things, [by] Persian, Indians, Greeks, and Arabs"): "Of *Pythagoras* on the drawing of lots, by which one can decide by lot for every need; The Drawing of Lots of the Two Horned [*Alexander* the Great]; The Drawing of Lots, as

composed by Christians; The Drawing of Lots, related to *Daniel*; The Drawing of Lots with Arrows, related to Alexander"; Dodge 1970, vol. 2: 737.

57. Weil 1929: 13–14; a book of this sort, attributed to Daniel, was already recorded by al-Nadīm. Bess Allen Donaldson noted that Daniel was the patron of a system of *raml* that rivaled and even surpassed the one credited to the Imām Ja'far. It was carried out with four brass dice strung upon a wire and used in conjunction with an astrolabe, to gain access to the Prophet's oracular book. Apparently "it was used to such an extent in gambling, that about the year 1925 the [Persian] government forbade its practice"; Donaldson 1938: 194. In medieval Europe, Daniel was the great patron of oneiromancy; cf. Fischer 1982.

58. Weil 1929: 14–15.

59. Weil 1929: 15–16.

60. Weil 1929: 16–17.

61. Weil 1929: 17–19.

62. Bolte 1925: 185–214; the sentence quoted is on p. 190.

63. Tannery, *Le Rabolion (oeuvre posthume); traités de géomancie arabes, grecs et latins*, in J.-L. Heiberg, ed., *Mémoires scientifiques de Paul Tannery*, vol. 4: *Sciences exactes chez les byzantins, 1884–1919* (Toulouse: Edouard Privat, Paris: Gauthier-Villars, 1920), 295–411. This includes an essay on "La géomancie chez les arabes" by Baron Carra de Vaux, 299–317.

64. Savorelli 1959. See Thorndike 1923–58, vol. 2: 110–23.

65. S. Skinner 1980. The same author earlier published a substantial manual of applied geomancy, *The Oracle of Geomancy; Divination by Earth* (Skinner 1977; rpt. 1986). Geomancy (or *al-raml*, or *ars notoria*, or *Punktierkunst*) "may be briefly defined as a method of divination in which, by marking down a number of points at random and then connecting or canceling them by lines, a number or figure is obtained, which is used as a key to sets of tables or to astrological constellations"; Thorndike 1923–58, vol. 2: 110. The tradition taken over from the Arabs in the Middle Ages has survived on the continent into our own time. Cf. Freudenberg 1919: 50–57, "Geomantie *speziell* Punktierkunst," quoting Agrippa von Nettesheim (1486–1536), a major latter-day source; *Encyclopédie de la divination* (Paris: Editions Tchou, 1965; rpt. Henri Veyrier, 1982), 393–459, "Géomancie," a well-illustrated account. Belonging to this tradition is a popular work, *The Book of Fate formerly in the possession of and used by Napoleon, rendered into the English Language by H. Kirchenhoffer from a German translation of an Ancient Egyptian Manuscript found in the Year 1801 by M. Sonnini in One of the Royal Tombs near Mount Libycus in Upper Egypt*. Kirchenhoffer's preface is dated London, June 1, 1822. The work ("Napoleon's Book of Fate") has been often reprinted: Scranton, Penn.: Personal Arts, 1923; London: W. Foulsham, 1958, etc. As Skeat points out, this work seems to be known only in the English-speaking world. See Skeat 1954: 53.

66. This had of course been recognized long before by folklorists such as Bolte, specialists in medieval scientific transmission like Moritz Steinschneider (writing in 1877, in *Zeitschrift der Deutschen Morgen ländischen Gesellscheft* (ZDMG) 31, pp. 762–65), and others. Skinner's *Terrestrial Astrology* includes an extensive classified bibliography of sources and scholarship.

67. "Losbücher," in Bachtold-Stäubli 1927–42, vol. 5, columns 1386–1401; also, "Los, losen," columns 1351–86. Since this was the last great survey of the entire field, we may briefly summarize post-war German Losbuch research. Earlier, Alfred Götze had studied a sixteenth-century German dice-oracle, which he published in facsimile (Götze 1918); Ernst Vouillème reprinted a humorous fifteenth-century specimen, *Losbuch: Ein scherzhaftes Wahrsagebuch gedruckt von Martin Flach in Basel um 1485* (Vouillème 1923). In 1956, the great specialist in medieval Fachprosa, Gerhard Eis, edited a German geomantic oracle, based on a Latin prototype: *Die Sandkunst der sechzehn Richter*; in Eis 1956: 7–13, 29–48. The Codex Vindobonensis, series nova, no. 2652, which had occupied Sotzmann and Bolte, was the focus of Abraham 1968. Abraham returned to this manuscript in a second study (Abraham 1971). (See also his Introduction to the facsimile edition of this codex, Graz: Akademische Druck- und Verlagsanstalt, 1976; Codices Selecti, 38.) He makes excellent use of prior studies and other printed and manuscript materials in elucidating the elements of his chosen oracle. Karin Schneider published a sumptuous facsimile of an illustrated fifteenth-century manuscript: *Ein Losbuch Konrad Bollstatters, aus CGM 312 der Bayerischen Staatsbibliothek München* (Schneider 1972–76). Schneider later brought out a pocket-sized version, with the oracle put into modern German: *Ein mittelalterliches Wahrsagespiel; Konrad Bollstatters Losbuch in CGM 312 der Bayerischen Stattsbibliothek* (Schneider 1978). Meanwhile, Eckehard Simon had edited "An unpublished fifteenth-century 'Losbuch' from the Houghton Codex MS GER 74" (Simon 1975). I quote Simon's concise description:

> "Our 'Losbuch' contains fifty-six statements in irregular
> rhymed couplets corresponding to the maximum number of combinations
> attainable with three dice... The prophetic 'Sprüche' are assigned to: Christ,
> Joseph (called on twice), Mary, the guardian angel, four archangels, eight
> worthies of the Old Testament (with Jeremiah speaking twice), nine apostles
> (with Matthew and John invoked twice) and twenty-seven saints, both male
> and female. Attached to each name is a three-dice pattern beginning with
> three sixes (for Christ) and ending with three ones (for Saint Werenher)....
>
> It was apparently the object of a game involving players each of whom
> would throw three dice and then look up and read aloud the statement affixed
> to the dice pattern indicated by the throw. The statements vary rather widely in
> their content: some promise heavenly rewards for good conduct and dispense
> advice as to how to avoid impending dangers, others speaking critically of
> the person's present way of life, issue prophecies of good fortune and counsel
> acceptance of one's lot. In every case, however, they are morally upright
> in tone and enjoin the reader to lead a stalwart Christian life" (pp. 98–99).

As we have seen, in late Medieval Europe Losbücher were very widespread in manuscript, and they were among the first works to be printed. Though the intention of many of these oracles may have been in part entertainment, they nonetheless encountered stern opposition from the ecclesiastical authorities, as well as from right-thinking laymen like Johann Hartlieb. This seems to have led to regular, if perfunctory, disavowal of any serious purport by the works' own authors, scribes, and printers. But it also promoted other developments, like the oracle studied by Simon. Here we have the proper Christian response to this "gin of the Devil." Craftier by far than those who fulminate against the insidious booklets, the author of this little work has adapted the Enemy's weapons to a Christian cause, thus bringing the neo-pagan oracles back into the tradition of the *Sortes sanctorum.* It was Simon's study of this pious text, so similar to the Chinese Buddhist sequence in the *Book of Consecration* a thousand years earlier, that first aroused my interest in European Losbücher and their literature. Elaine Tennant provided me with a copy of Simon's work, for which I am most grateful. For a new project to Christianize pagan oracles, this time in Chinese, cf. note 16 of Chapter 4. In English, the only recent survey of the field seems to be Skeat 1954.

68. Cf. the German title of Albert von le Coq's report on the second and third German Turfan Expeditions: Auf Hellas Spuren in Osttürkistan (von Le Coq 1926). Between 1902 and 1914, von Le Coq led a total of four expeditions to the Turfan region, and sent back quantities of booty to Berlin; Cf. Hartel 1982.

69. Thomsen 1912; the oracle booklet is published, translated, and studied, pp. 190–214.

70. Cf. Thomsen's note on the word *uzuntonlu* in this stanza: " 'a long-coat,' i.e., one who bears long coat; as it appears, a particularly, though not exclusively Manichaean expression;... As the fact is specially emphasized that they are provided with a food-bowl, a drinking-vessel,... and, here, a bell, they thereby appear to be characterized as mendicant friars or ecclesiastics, not Manichaeans in general. In the translation I use the term 'monk' " (Thomsen 1912: 212). Response no. 42 opens, "a monk departed leaving his cup and bowl." When discussing the manuscript's date, Thomsen adds, "Nor can it be definitely settled whether the book is of Buddhist or Manichaean origin; but most outer and inner criteria speak in favour of the latter" (p. 196). Jean-Paul Roux views these long-robed personages in quite a different light. In addition to the "hommes à la longue tunique," there is also "une vieille femme divine." She appears in the 13th response, which Thomsen translates: "A pious [*tanrilig*] old woman stayed at home. By licking the edges of a greasy spoon she lived and escaped death." Roux terms this trio (the two long-robes of nos. 22 and 42, and the saintly crone of no. 13) "trois personnages assez embarrassants qui peuvent être des chamans ou on ne sait quoi d'autre." Instead of dropping a a bell into the lake, Roux has the long-tunic dropping a mirror—though Thomsen specifically noted that *küzünü,* "a little bell," was to be distinguished from *közünü,* "a mirror" (p. 212). In the enigmatic old woman Roux sees a possible indication of "la prééminence absolue du sexe faible dans le chamanisme ancien." Perhaps where the early twentieth century was inclined to see Manichaeans, the late twentieth century is happier with shamans; cf. Roux 1984: 69. The Chinese references alone make this text an unlikely vehicle for pristine shamanism, and the colophon seems to confirm that it issued from some academy of studies in Chinese territory—if not

a Manichaean, then a Buddhist establishment (Thomsen 1912: 209, 214). The images, of course, may have been carried over from a very different context.

71. von Le Coq 1908; the text, transcription, and translation of the Christian oracle-fragment are on pp. 1205–8.

72. Bang 1926: 40–75. The oracle-fragment is transcribed, translated, and discussed, pp. 53–55; philological observations follow.

73. Bang and von Gabain 1929: 241.

74. Sims-Williams 1976. This fragment no. 18 is transcribed, translated, and analyzed, pp. 63–65. It was generously brought to my attention by Martin Schwartz (April 25, 1989), who wonders if the *Sortes apostolorum* might not be the origin of the widely diffused children's game "Simon Says."

75. Bang and von Gabain 1929: 241–68.

76. Bang and von Gabain 1929: 243. This is by no means certain in view of all the possible alternatives, as we see even among those Chinese Tun-huang texts studied by Marc Kalinowski that vaunt their relationship to the *I-ching* (v. *infra*).

77. ". . . bist du geworden. Der Dienst aller Länder ist hoch gekommen. Vor dir haben sich das göttliche Glück und der Sieg von selbst niedergelassen. In deiner Zeit ist der Sonne Glanz aufgegangen und erstrahlte. Das Antlitz der braunen Erde wurde grün und schön. Eine weisse Wolke stieg auf und es regnete. Der Staub legte sich. Im Osten und Westen sind die Länder nach deinem Wunsch. Im Süden und Norden sind die Städte und Reiche nach deinem Herzen. Deinen nierdrigen Namen hast du verbessert; deinen kleinen Namen hast du erhöht. Wer wird ein dir nicht Folgender sein? Deine [Waren-]Bundel sind unterwegs. Deine . . . Befehle wurden ausgeführt. Wenn du seit langem ein Kind wünschst, so bekommst und erhältst du es sogleich. Die Krankheit ist gewichen . . . . . . Mache dein Herz froh. Erde und Himmel bringen Freude dar!"[77]

78. [*Kua* 44] "Wenn dieses "Zusammentreffen" genannte Zeiche her-auskommt, so sagt es durch sein Wort folgendermassen: Grimmige, strenge, heftige Worte sind in einer Gegenwart hochgekommen. Wind auf Wind wehte brausend [unaufhörlich] bei deinem Haus. Wenn du zur Krankheitszeit [bei Gelegenheit der Krankheit] . . . siehst . . . . durchstach dich, um dich zu verwun-den. Krankheit verfolgte dich, um deinen Körper zu qualen. In den Oberarm trat Krankheit; [nun] sind [dort] Schmerzen; man muss [ihn] pflegen. In das Herz trat Feuer [d.h. Sorge] ein; [nun] ist [dort] Kummer; man muss [sich] davon befreien. Aus dieser Gefahr [Wiederwärtigkeit] dich zu erretten, zeigt sich kein Weg. [Oder: Aus dieser Gefahr muss man sich befreien. Keine Möglichkeit zeigt sich für dich.] Ruhe und Freude für dich finden sich nicht. Der Sonnengott trat in die Erde ein [d.h. er ging unter]; sein Leuchten wurde gehindert. Die am blauen Himmel fliegenden Vögel konnten nicht weiter fliegen. Der Fürst wird gequält, ohne ein Unternehmen zu finden [?]. Ärklig-Qans Befehle *arqulayu turur* in deinem Hause. Betrügerische Leute betrügen dich in deiner Gegenwart. Der Sonne und des Mondes Glanz zu behinder bemühen sie sich. Guter Menschen Weg abzuschneiden bestrengen sie sich. Fünf Dämone bekämpfen sich. Drei

Geister schlagen sich. Alle Unternehmungen lass! Verdienstvolle gute Werke tue! Die Widerwärtigkeiten werden vergehen, Gutes wird kommen."[78]

79. "If you have desired a child for a long time, you will receive it right away. If you desire goods and chattels, you will receive them right away. [The] sickness has disappeared."

80. "The enemies that surround you have grown numerous. Your advantage and your honor have diminished. Your property diminished. Suffering and agony are plentiful. Danger surrounds your body. A path promising you advantages does not become evident."

81. On divination generally among the Turks of Central Asia, see Roux 1984: 83–94. We have already mentioned Roux's views, dramatically different from Thomsen's, on the oracle text in Turkish runic script (note 70 above). See also, Roux and Boratav 1968.

82. Francke 1924a: 5–20; Francke 1924b: 110–18.

83. Francke 1924a: 7–12.

84. I. 1. Die Kamele gingen zum Wassertrinken, und der Tag wurde heiss...

2. Der Mond ging auf. Dann wurde es Nacht. Dann ging die Sonne auf...

3. Beim Zusammentreffen mit...freute sich das Herz. Auch du, O Mensch...

4. es wird [deinen] Gedanken gemäss geschehen. Gib den freudlosen Sinn auf!

o o o

II. 1. Aus dem Mund der Zeichendeuter: Du Mensch [wirst] ein grosser Glorreicher...

2. demgemäss wird es kommen, es wird erfullt werden...

o o o

III. 1. Der Rākṣasa sprach: Nicht reich werdend [oder ein reicher Mann] Reichtümer...

2. ......auch nicht durch das Tamburin eingeladen......

85. IX. 1. ...hoch sind....wenn auch der Götterberg verspottet wird, [bleibt er doch] ein hoher Berg.

2. ....Ruhm [?] verbreitet sich nicht, fest seiend... denkend...

3. ...Sehnsucht nach dem Götterberg, oben entfalten Sonne und Mond [ihren Glanz].

4. ......kalter Wind im offenen Feld, grüsst keinen hellen Tag.

o o o

IX. 1. Auch, wenn der Pfeilkönig lahm ist, wissen sich die

2. wilden Vögel nicht zu retten und wissen nicht zu

3. fliegen. Obgleich dem sanften Hirsch die Hörner auf dem Kopf zum Vorteil wären, zeigt er sienicht, wenn er aufgestört wird."

86. Francke 1924a: 11–12.

87. Francke 1924b: 113; cf. Snellgrove 1967: 34, 1. 26: *phya g'yaṅ dpal gyi lha brgyad mchod*; "Worship the eight gods of Prediction and Good Fortune." See also Hoffmann 1950: 192–96: on the *phya*-spirits and Bön divination (pp. 192–93) and specifically on Francke's oracle-fragments (p. 196).

88. Francke 1924b: 113; "Die Silbe *'adre* wird mit *piśāca* ubersetzt; phoṅ, vielleicht *phoṅs*, scheint 'arm' zu bedeuten; und *srin* heisst rākṣasa. Wenn wir den Ausdruck mit 'arme Seele' übersetzen, kommen wir der Grundbedeutung vielleicht nahe."

89. Francke 1924b: 110–11. Cf. R. A. Stein on the microcosm of the human body: "On the shoulders live the 'warrior god' (*dgra-lha*) and the 'man's god' (*pho-lha*)." With other members of this protective cohort, they appear in domestic architecure, as well: "On the roof of the house, two altars of heaped-up stones represent the man's god (*pho-lha*) and the woman's god (*mo-lha*). A flag set up beside them is the warrior god (*dgra-lha*; Stein 1972: 222; Stein 1959: 312, n. 117).

90. M. Aurel Stein, *Ancient Khotan* (Stein 1909; rpt. 1975), Pl. LXXIV, N.xv.004, and pp. 374 and 411: "Ivory die, oblong, square ends. On rectangular sides are the spots, marked each by a circle and dot in center, as though engraved with a two-pointed instrument, the mark being the dot of one point which acts as a pivot round which the other point revolves to describe the circle. Order of dots is 3 opposite 1 and 4 opposite 2. Length 7/8″, width 3/8″ nearly." This was found at Niya. Another die was discovered at Endere: Pl. LII, E.001.b. It was of bone instead of ivory, and cube-shaped rather than rectangular; pp. 374 and 442: "Cubical bone die with spots shown by circles with center dots. The sum of the spots on any two opposite sides is 7. Length of edges 1/2″." Or again, "a cubical die of bone with the incised spots arranged exactly as in classical dice, the sum of any two opposite sides being seven" (p. 438). Cf. Francke 1924b: 114, and Róna Tas 1956: 179, for other dice found at Central Asian sites.

91. Weber 1868: 276; Francke 1924b: 116–17. On other Tibetan kleromantic systems, cf. Waddell 1894, *Lamaism in Sikhim* (originally "Lamaism in Sikkim," in *The Gazetteer of Sikkim*, Calcutta, vol. 1, 1894: pp. 241–391; rpt. Delhi: Oriental Publishers, 1973), pp. 90–94, "Divination by Lots"; also, pp. 94–98, "Divination by Dice." Waddell noted the use of a solitary die, for divination by the manual of Mañjuśrī. It had six faces, on each a syllable of Mañjuśrī's spell, A RA PA CA NA. The accompanying oracle was arranged according to nine question-categories: House, Favours, Life, Medical, Enemy, Visitors, Business, Travel, Lost Property (pp. 95–96). The Arapacana syllabary leads to a Buddhist science of alphabet-magic or letter-mysticism. It is already outlined in the Khotanese *Book of Zambasta* (fifth or sixth century?); cf. Emmerick 1968: 120–21, 454–55. After Arapacana dice, Waddell went on to describe several other dicing procedures. The following year, all this was incorporated into his classic book, *The Buddhism of Tibet, or Lamaism* (1895; rpt. 1959, 1972), in a

comprehensive chapter on "Astrology and Divination" (pp. 450–74). Relevant data are also found elsewhere in that work. For example, in the course of a funeral service, "some Lamas find,... consulting their lottery-books, that the spirit has been sent to hell, and the exact compartment in hell is specified. Then must be done a most costly service by a very large number of Lamas" (p. 493). During the scapegoat ceremony held at Lhasa on the 29th and 30th days of the second month, a debate between the black-and-white-garbed scapegoat (the "ghost-king") and his antagonist, a lama, was resolved by casting dice. But they were loaded: the lama's die had six on all sides, whilst the scapegoat's die had all ones (p. 512). As Waddell earlier explained, such dicing determined the caster's next mode of rebirth (pp. 471–73, though the numerical associations appear to be different there). For other desultory notes on Tibetan dicing and the political use of lots, cf. Brauen 1974: 70, 129–30. According to David Macdonald, "On the fifteenth day of the fifth month every oracle in the country publishes his forecast of the ensuing months. The gods controlling the oracles are believed to assemble that day at the monastery of Samye, where they gamble with dice for the souls of men"; Macdonald 1929: 211.

92. "va-dava"

> Frager merke dies!
> Du wirst diese deine Ziele so gut wie wirklich erreichen!
> Wozu denn dem Gesunden Medizin geben?
> Bring dein Herz zur Ruhe! Es ist genug des Hassens!
> Die Ziele werden in schöner Weise wohl erreicht werden.
> Die Feinde draussen werden zurückgestossen! Wozu den
> Friedensschluss fürchten?
> Deshalb bringe deinen Göttern gehörig [Preis] dar!
> Weil du das getan hast, wirst du dein Ziel erreichen und
> keine Feinde haben!
> Auch werden die Feinde verletzt davon gehen.
> Dadurch wirst du für dein Werk Vorteil finden und wirst du
> dein Ziel wirklich erreichen.

93. Francke 1924b: 117–18. R. A. Stein's studies of other *fée-* and fauna-filled Tibetan fragments from Tun-huang provide a substantial body of similar material; cf. Stein 1971. After half a century, Stein 1939 remains the most complete analysis of any Tibetan oracle sequence. This sequence, of uncertain date and provenance but possibly written by a Ladhaki, has the advantage of being fully illustrated; Stein's article thus represents an important contribution to mantic iconography, as well. Tibetan Tun-huang texts were also published and translated by Thomas 1957, chap. 6, "Mo-Divination" (pp. 113–57); an introductory section describes the texts in relation to the older studies by Weber, Hoernle, Francke, Luders, Waddell, and Thomsen (pp. 113–18). I am grateful to Kenneth Eastman for a copy of Thomas's chapter.

94. Thomas 1957: 113–57.

95. Róna Tas 1956. Cf. Laufer 1911. We should remember that Waddell observed a Tibetan system of dice-divination predictive of rebirth in which the dice were cast without reference to oracular responses; the numbers themselves had prophetic significance.

96. Róna Tas, 1956: 168. Cf. Tucci 1949, vol. 2: 616–17.

97. For example, in the fine set of late eighteenth-century scrolls presented by Joan and Neal Donnely to the National Museum of Natural History, Smithsonian Institution, Washington.

98. Drège 1981a; Drège 1981b; Hou 1979; Jao 1979.

99. See Morgan 1981: 51–60 and pl. 39–40; Morgan 1984: 255–61 and pl. 41; Morgan 1987c: 55–76, which may be read in conjunction with Berthold Laufer's classic study, "Bird Divination Among the Tibetans" (Laufer 1914), based on the Tun-huang MS Pelliot 3530. Among Marc Kalinowski's many studies of Chinese divination and computations are "Les instruments astro-calendriques des Han et la méthode *liu ren*" (Kalinowski 1983); "La transmission du dispositif des neuf palais sous les Six-Dynasties" (Kalinowski 1985); "Les traités de Shuihudi et l'hémérologie chinoise à la fin des Royaumes-Combattants" (Kalinowski 1986a); "L'astronomie des populations Yi du Sud-Ouest de la Chine" (Kalinowski 1986b); "La littérature divinatoire dans le *Daozang*" (Kalinowski 1989–90); "Introduction;" "Hémérologie"; "Cléromancie" (in Kalinowski 2003).

100. Morgan 1993. Carole Morgan has very kindly given me a copy of this paper before its publication.

101. HY 1035, *Ling-ch'i pen-chang chen-ching*, preface, 6b–7a. For the passage on Phytolacca, cf. *Ch'ung-hsiu Cheng-ho ching-shih cheng-lei pei-yung pen-ts'ao* (rpt. Taipei: Southern Materials Center, 1976), chap. 11: 263c3–5. This herbal offering to the spirits is in keeping with the oracle's overall Taoist tone, as noted by Morgan. Minakata Kumagusu (1867–1941) studied Phytolacca as an East Asian counterpart of the Mandrake. Its anthropomorphism suggests that the offering was intended to stand in lieu of a human sacrifice. Cf. Minakata 1971–73.

102. HY 1035, preface, 7a–8b, for the spells and seasonal offerings and interdictions. This is followed by a separate table of *kua*-names, listed with the corresponding throws. Next come the responses themselves, comprising the body of the book. Each stanza is followed by one set of remarks attributed to Yen Yu-ming (fourth century), another set credited to Ho Ch'eng-t'ien (fifth century), and an additional passage of "explanation" (*chieh*).

103. Ōfuchi 1979: 740–45; cf. Ōfuchi's descriptions of the mss. in Ōfuchi 1978: 335.

104. Kalinowski 1994 [esp. "Méthode des pions transcendants *Lingqi bufa*"].

105. T. 1277, *Āveśa* [possession] *Ritual of Instant Efficacy, Expounded by Maheśvara* (*Shu-chi li-yen Mo-hai-shou-lo-t'ien shuo a-wei-she fa*); cf. *Hōbōgirin* 1 (1929), 7: "Abisha"; Macdolnald 1975: 113–28, esp. p. 117; Strickmann 2002,

chap. 6 ("Tantrists, Foxes, Shamans"). On Śiva/Maheśvara in Buddhism, cf. Iyanaga 1983: 713–65 and pl. 45; and Iyanaga 1985.

106. Kalinowski 1994; cf. *Tun-huang i-shu tsung-mu so-yin* (1962; rpt. Chung-hua, 1983), p. 224a.

107. Ibid., p. 36.

108. Ibid., pp. 16–17.

109. Ibid., pp. 22–23. This appears to be related to what Gotthold Weil termed the "Caliph Ma'mūn" type of oracle in Weil 1969. Such texts sired a considerable progeny among the later European Losbücher, and may also be connected with the Tibetan Arapacana dice-oracle discussed by Waddell (note 91 above).

110. Ibid., 23–24; *Sui-shu* 78.16b–17a (Palace edition), 1778 (Chung-hua edition: *K'ung-tzu ma-t'ou i-shu,* 1 *chüan*). For Confucius as a patron of divination (among Tibetans as well as Chinese), cf. Stein 1981.

111. Ibid., pp. 20–22. For the life and legends of Kuan Lo, cf. *San-kuo chih chi-chieh,* 29.19b–43a (Palace edition). Kalinowski's work on these varied mantic systems clarifies the great importance of counting sticks and their intimate relationship with lots and lot-drawing. In this connection, we should recall Hubert Durt's study of "The Counting-Stick [*śalākā*] and the Majority/Minority Rule in the Buddhist Community" (Durt 1974), as well as Karl Menninger's chapter on "Tally Sticks" in Menninger 1969, and the study of "Mechanical Aids to Calculation" by Joseph Needham (Needham 1959: 68–80).

112. And such prosperity or its portents would in turn directly benefit the religious institutions that created and promoted oracles. Cf. Strickmann 1982: pp. 58–59, and Bareau 1959: 303–9.

113. While evoking the universality of divination, we should also remember its obsessive–compulsive character, and the early age at which such patterns are inculcated. A friend (Angharad Pimpaneau) recalls the ubiquity of various rudimentary forms of divination during her childhood in Anglesey (North Wales) in the 1940s. It was a constant feature of life, and included spinning a knife at table (to decide which of the children was to do some task), counting-out procedures (using plum-stones or comparable counters) for a similar end, controlled movements of the "step on a crack" variety, as well as scrying from tea leaves and coffee grounds. She notes that such forms of compulsive behavior were variously directional, numerological, formal, and aesthetic. We should not forget the widespread flower oracles of Europe and America, in which petals of a flower are removed, one by one, while a phrase or set of rhyming verses is recited, relating to the matter in question. When the petals come to an end, the corresponding word represents the answer; cf. Newell 1903; rpt. 1963: 105–7. These and other examples will be found in Opie and Opie 1959: 274–75, 328–42, as well as all the standard folklore repertories. Cf. also Piaget and Inhelder 1951; English trans. 1975.

114. Dummett 1980. In passing, the author of this magisterial work discusses several European Losbücher and quotes additional German scholarship to which

I have not referred (pp. 94–95). From Dummett's research it is clear that playing cards only came to be used in European divination many years after their introduction. Here we may recall the views of T. F. Carter, who saw playing cards as a vital component in the movement of printing to the West. He believed that the transition from dice to cards took place at about the same time as the change from manuscript rolls to paged books (Carter 1955: 183–92). Regarding the complex interrelationship of Chinese oracles and boardgames, hypotheses and suggestions have been put forward by Yang Lien-sheng: "A Note on the So-Called TLV Mirrors and the Game *Liu-po*," and "An Additional Note on the Ancient Game *Liu-po*," in Yang 1969: 138–65; Needham 1953; Morgan 1993; and Kalinowski 1994.

115. A short study by Walter Burkert could well serve as a model: "Itinerant Diviners and Magicians: A Neglected Element in Cultural Contacts" (Burkert 1983). He finds remarkable similarities in purification rituals from Assyrian incantation texts and those performed in Athens during the fifth century B.C.E. Between Mesopotamia and Etruria in the seventh century B.C.E., the liver models with their technical terminology confirm definite contact. Foundation deposits, as at the temple on the acropolis of Gortyn, in Crete (eighth century B.C.E.), establish parallels with Hittite practice in Cilicia—homeland of the seer Mopsus. "It seems that at the time when a Syrian goldsmith had established his workshop at Knossos, craftsmen and seers of similar origin found employment at Gortyn" (p. 118). Three Babylonian votive figurines, representing a prying man followed by a big dog (belonging to the cult of the Sumero-Babylonian healing goddess Gula, "the great physician"), were found at the temple of Hera in Samos (first half of the seventh century B.C.E.). Burkert notes the importance of the dog in the cult of the primary Greek healing god, Asclepius, and there are like indications for the cult of Apollo, father of Asclepius and himself a god of healing. There is suggestive evidence from proper names, as well, but Burkert judiciously leaves this aside, to focus on ritual practice (both in prescriptive and descriptive texts) and archeological remains. He finds strong evidence for Eastern influence on Greek prophecy and healing, appearing toward the end of the eighth and during the seventh century B.C.E. in Greece's so-called "orientalizing period." "It is important at the same time to realize that seers and similar charismatic persons naturally take to an itinerant life"—and that they are organized on the model of a family, and this "would make both local mobility and a certain diachronic stability of lore possible." Burkert illustrates the kind of transformation regularly produced by adoption through cultural contact. In Babylonia, the purification ritual with suckling pig as surrogate victim was employed only against disease, not against murder. In Greece, it was used for protection against diseases inflicted as a consequence of murder. Burkert points out that in Babylonia, murder had been the object of set judicial procedures regulated by a written code for more than a millennium. In early Archaic Greece, neither the law code nor the procedure existed. Hence the same ritual assumed different functions in each society: in Mesopotamia, a treatment for private ailments, in Greece,

"a larger, communal function... where it had to fill a void. Thus this difference... constitutes a model of transformation of adopted forms within a new system" (p. 19). The study of cross-cultural diffusion requires not only a careful choice of subject matter. Context and function are vital—and valuable deductions can be made from the putative transmitter's way of life. (On a cuneiform Losbuch-fragment with possible Greek connections, cf. note 18 above.) Taking India as an important axis for transmission of this sort, two representative works come to mind. Willibald Kirfel's monograph on the rosary documents its Indian origin and subsequent diffusion to both ends of Eurasia (Kirfel 1949). More recently, Victor Mair has published *Painting and Performance; Chinese Picture Recitation and its Indian Genesis* (Mair 1988). Like the rosary, the paintings used in connection with storytelling and preaching were embedded in a ritual matrix. They were more than mere artifacts; their dissemination and metamorphoses imply the transmission of an entire corpus of behavior, itself subject to constant change and reinterpretation. Mair has presented a remarkable tableau of worldwide diffusion for what may be "the first picture-show."

116. Kalinowski 1994: n. 65.
117. Chambers 1869: 284b.
118. Thomas 1971: 289.

BIBLIOGRAPHY

Works by Michel Strickmann

1975. "Sōdai no raigi: Shinsō undō to Dōka nanshū ni tsuite no ryakusetsu." *Tōhō shūkyō* 46: 15–28.

1977. "The Mao Shan Revelations: Taoism and the Aristocracy." *T'oung Pao* 64: 1–64.

1978a. "A Taoist Confirmation of Liang Wu Ti's Suppression of Taoism." *Journal of the American Oriental Society* 98: 467–75.

1978b. "The Longest Taoist Scripture." *History of Religions* 17: 331–54.

1979. "On the Alchemy of T'ao Hung-ching." In Anna K. Seidel and Holmes H. Welch, eds., *Facets of Taoism: Essays on Chinese Religion*, 123–92. New Haven: Yale University Press.

1980. "History, Anthropology, and Chinese Religion." *Harvard Journal of Asiatic Studies* 40, 1: 201–48.

1981. *Le taoïsme du Mao Chan: Chronique d'une révélation*. Paris: Presses Universitaires de France.

1982a. "India in the Chinese Looking-Glass." In D. Klimburg-Salter, ed., *The Silk Route and the Diamond Path: Esoteric Buddhist Art on the Trans-Himalayan Trade Routes*, 52–63. Los Angeles: UCLA Art Council.

1982b. "The Tao Among the Yao: Taoism and the Sinification of South China." In Sakai Tadao sensei koki shukuga kinen no kai, ed., *Rekishi ni okeru minshū to bunka*, 23–30. Tokyo: Kokusho kankōkai.

1983a. "Homa in East Asia." In Frits Staal, ed., *Agni: The Vedic Ritual of the Fire Altar*, vol. 2: 418–55. Berkeley: Asian Humanities Press.

1983b. Ed., *Tantric and Taoist Studies in Honour of R. A. Stein*. 3 vols. Brussels: Institut Belge des Hautes Études Chinoises.

1985. "Therapeutische Rituale und das Problem des Bösen in frühen Taoismus." In Gert Naundorf, Karl-Heinz Pohl, and Hans-Hermann Schmidt, eds., *Religion und Philosophie in Ostasien: Festschrift für Hans Steininger zum 65. Geburtstag*, 185–200. Würzburg: Königshausen und Neumann.

1988. "Dreamwork of Psycho-Sinologists: Doctors, Taoists, Monks." In Carolyn T. Brown, ed., *Psycho-Sinology: The Universe of Dreams in Chinese Culture*, 25–46. Lanham, Md.: University Press of America.

1990. "The *Consecration Sūtra*: A Buddhist Book of Spells." In Robert E. Buswell, Jr., ed., *Chinese Buddhist Apocrypha*, 75–118. Honolulu: University of Hawai'i Press.

1990–91. "Buddhas In and Out of Bodies." *Discours Social/Social Discourse* 3, 3–4: 107–20.

1993. "The Seal of the Law: A Ritual Implement and the Origins of Printing." *Asia Major*, third series 6, 2: 1–83.

1994. "Saintly Fools and Chinese Masters (Holy Fools)." *Asia Major*, third series 7, 1: 35–57.

1995. "The Seal of the Jungle Woman." *Asia Major*, third series 8, 2: 147–53.

1996. *Mantras et Mandarins: Le bouddhisme tantrique en Chine*. Paris: Gallimard.

2002. *Chinese Magical Medicine*. Ed. Bernard Faure. Stanford: Stanford University Press.

East Asian Sources

A-cha-p'o-chü kuei-shen ta-chiang shang fo t'o-lo-ni shen-chou ching (Book of Spells of Āṭavaka, King of Demons). T. 1238, vol. XXI.

A-cha-p'o-chü yüan-shuai ta-chiang shang fo t'o-lo-ni ching hsiu-hsing i-kuei. T. 1239, vol. XXI.

Book of Spirit-Spells. See *T'ien-ti pa-yang shen-chou ching*.

Brahmajāla-sūtra (Fan-wang ching), in *Dīrghāgama (Dīrghanikāya, Ch'ang a-han ching)*. T. 1, vol. I.

Chan-ch'a ching. See *Chan-ch'a shan-e yeh pao-ching*.

Chan-ch'a shan-e yeh-pao ching (Book on Divining the Requital of Good and Evil). T. 839, vol. XVII.

Chen-kao (Declarations of the Perfected Ones), by T'ao Hung-ching (456–536). HY 1010 (CT 1016, TT 637–40).

Ch'ing Pin-t'ou-lu fa (The Rite of Inviting Piṇḍola). T. 1689, vol. XXXII.

Chin shu (History of the Chin). Peking: Chung-hua shu-chü, 1974.

Chin shu chiao-chu. Taipei: Hsin-weng-fen ch'u-pan kung-ssu, 1975.

Chiu-t'ien yü-shu pao-ching (Precious Book of the Jade Pivot of the Nine Heavens). HY 16 (CT 16, TT 25).

Fan-wang ching. Apocryphon. T. 1484, vol. XXIV.

Fo-shuo kuan-ting Fan-t'ien shen-ts'e ching (Book of Consecration Expounded by the Buddha Concerning Brahmā's Spirit-Tablets). Ms. Stein 1322.

Fu-hui ch'üan-shu, by Huang Liu-hung [manual for magistrates published in 1699] [Djang Chu 1984].

Fu-t'ien kuang-sheng ju-i ling-ch'ien (Wish-Fulfilling Oracles That Uphold Heaven and Enhance the Sages). HY 1293 (CT 1303, TT 1012).

History of the Sui Dynasty. See *Sui shu*.

Hou Han shu (History of the Later Han). 12 vols. Peking: Chung-hua shu-chü, 1963.

Hou Han shu hsi-chieh. Taipei: Hsin-wen-feng ch'u-pan kung-ssu, 1975.

Hsien-chi chen-chi (Records of the Perfected Ones on Prohibitions for Immortals). HY 179 (CT 179, TT 77).

Hsüan-t'ien shang-ti po-tzu sheng-hao (Sage Appellation in One Hundred Characters of the Supreme Monarch of Heaven Sublime). HY 1471 (CT 1482, TT 1108).

Hu-kuo chia-chi Chiang-tung Wang ling-ch'ien (Oracles of the King of Chiang-tung, Guardian of the State and Transcendent Succour). HY 1294 (CT 1305, TT 1012).

Hung-en ling-chi chen-chün ling-ch'ien (Oracles of the Perfect Lords of Transcendent Succour and Vast Benignity). HY 1291 (CT 1301, TT 1011).

I-chien chih (Record of the Listener), by Hung Mai (1123–1202). Revised by Ho Chuo. 4 vols. Peking: Chung-hua shu-chü, 1981.

I-ching (Book of Changes). Text in *A Concordance to the Yi Ching*, Harvard-Yenching Institute, Sinoligigal Indexes Series, Peking, 1935.

I-lin, traditionally attributed to Chiao Yen-shou (first century B.C.E.), but more probably composed ca. 25 C.E. by Ts'ui Chuan. *Ssu-ku t'i-yao pien-ch'eng*, Peking, 1937. Reprint, Taipei: I-wen, 1957.

I-lin ch'iung-chih, by Wen I-to. In *Wen I-to ch'üan-chi*, vol. 4. Peking: San-lien, 1982.

Kan-chou Sheng-chi miao ling-chi li (On the Transcendent Manifestation at the Temple of Sagely Succour in Kan-chou). CT 1304, TT 1012.

Kuan-ting ching (Book of Consecration). T. 1331, vol. XXI.

Ling-chi chen-chün chu-sheng T'ang ling-ch'ien (Transcendent Oracles from the Hall of Infusing Life of the Perfect Lords of Transcendent Succour). HY 1292.

Ling-ch'i ching. See *Ling-chi pen-chang cheng-ching.*

Ling-ch'i pen-chang chen-ching (Book of the Empowered Draughtsmen). HY 1035 (CT 1041, TT 719).

Ling-pao tu-jen ching. See *Ling-pao wu-liang tu-jen shang-p'in miao-ching.*

Ling-pao wu-liang tu-jen shang-p'in miao-ching (Book of Salvation). HY 1 (TT 1–13).

Lung-shu wu-ming lun (Nāgārjuna's Treatise on the Five Sciences). T. 1420, vol. XXI.

Madhyamāgama. Translated by Gautama Saṅghadeva. T. 26, vol. I.

Mo-hai-shou-lo pu-fa (Maheśvara's Method of Divination). Ms. Stein 5614.

Oracles of the King of Chiang-tung. See *Hu-kuo chia-chi Chiang-tung Wang ling-ch'ien.*

Po-chang ch'ing-kuei (complete title: *Ch'ih-hsiu Po-chang ch'ing-kuei*), compiled by Te-hui. T. 2025, vol. XLVIII.

Samantapāsādikā. See *Shan-chien-lü p'i-p'o-sha.*

San-kuo chih chi-chieh. In *Erh-shih-wu shih.* Taipei: Hsin-wen-feng ch'u-pan kung ssu, 1975.

Sha-mi shih-chieh fa ping wei-i (Ten Precepts for Novices, Together with Their Deportment). T. 1471, vol. XXIV.

Shan-chien-lü p'i-p'o-sha, by Saṅghabhadra. T. 1462, vol. XXIV. English translation by P. V. Bapat and Hirakawa Akira, *Shan-Chien-P'i-P'-o-Sha.* Poona: Bhandarkar Oriental Research Institute, 1970.

Shou-shen chi (In Search of the Supernatural), by Kan Pao (fl. 317–50). Peking: Chung-hua shu-chü, 1979.

Shu-chi li-yen Mo-hai-shou-lo-t'ien shuo a-wei-she fa (Āveśa Ritual of Instant Efficacy, Expounded by Maheśvara). Trans. Amoghavajra (705–74). T. 1277, vol. XXI.

Ssu-sheng chen-chün ling-ch'ien (Transcendent Oracles of the Four Sages). HY 1288 (CT 1298, TT 1010).

Sui shu (History of the Sui Dynasty, 636), by Wei Cheng (580–643) et al. Peking: Chung-hua shu-chü, 1973; Taipei: Hung-yeh shu-chü, 1974.

T'ai-hsüan ching (Book of the Great Mystery), by Yang Hsiung (53 B.C.E. to 18 C.E.). Ed. Ssu-pu pei-yao. Shanghai: Chung-hua shu-chü.

T'ai-p'ing kuang-chi (978), compiled by Li Fang (925–66) et al. Peking: Jen-min wen-hsüeh ch'u-pan-she, 1959; Chung-hua shu-chü, 1981; Taipei: Ku-hsin shu-chü, 1980.

Tao-shu yüan-shen ch'i, preface dated 1305. HY 1221 (CT 1231, TT 988).

Ta-tz'u hao-sheng chiu-t'ien wei-fang sheng-mu yüan-chün ling-ying pao-ch'ien (Precious Oracles of the Transcendent Response of the Sage Mother, Primal Sovran, Guardian of the Alcove of the Nine Heavens, Most Kindly Fosteress of Life). HY 1290.

Teng-chen yin-chüeh (Secret Instructions for the Ascent to Perfection), by T'ao Hung-ching (456–536). HY 421 (CT 421, TT 193).

T'ien-ti pa-yang shen-chou ching (Book of the Spirit-Spells of the Eightfold Yang of Heaven and Earth). T. 2987, vol. LXXXV.

T'i-wei p'o-li ching (Book of Trapuṣa and Bhallika). S. 2051, P. 3732. Edited in Makita Tairyō, *Gikyō kenkyū*, Kyoto: Kyōto daigaku jinbun kagaku kenkyūjo, 1976: 184–209.

Tung-yüan shen-chou ching (The Book of Spirit-Spells of the Abyss). HY 335 (TT 170–73).

Wu-shih erh-ping fang (Fifty-Two Medical Prescriptions). Anonymous (second century B.C.E.). Peking: Wen-wu ch'u-pan-she, 1979.

Yü-t'ang ta-fa (Great Rites of the Jade Hall), compiled ca. 1158 by Lu Shih-chung. (Complete title: *Wu-shang hsüan-yüan san-t'ien yü-t'ang ta-fa*). HY 220 (CT 220, TT 100–4).

Secondary Literature

Abraham, Werner. 1968. "Studien zu einem Wahrsagetext des späten Mittelalters." *Hessische Blätter fur Volkskunde* 59: 9–29.

Abraham, Werner. 1971. "Gereimtes Losbuch; Codex Vindobonensis Series Nova 2652." *Zeitschrift fur deutsche Philologie* 90: 70–82.

Adler, Alfred, and Andras Zempléni. 1972. *Le Bâton de l'aveugle; divination, maladie et pouvoir chez les Moundang du Tchad*. Collection Savoir. Paris: Hermann.

Ahern, Emily Martin. 1981. *Chinese Ritual and Politics*. Cambridge Studies in Social Anthropology, 34. Cambridge: Cambridge University Press.

———. 1982. "Rules in Oracles and Games." *Man* (n.s.) 17, 2: 302–12.

Aoki Masaru. 1941. *Kōnan shun.* Tokyo: Kōbundō.

———. 1962. *Shuchu shū.* Tokyo: Chikuma shobō.

———. 1964. *Chūka inshu shisen.* Chikuma soho, 32. Tokyo: Chikuma shobō.

Apuleius. 1915. *The Golden Ass.* London: William Heinemann.

———. 1931. *Metamorphoseon libri XI.* Ed. R. Helm. Leipzig: Teubner. Reprint, 1968.

Aston, W. G. 1908. "A Japanese Book on Divination." *Man* 8: 116–20.

Astrampsychus, and Randall O. Stewart. 2001. *Sortes Astrampsychi, vol. 2: Ecdosis altera.* Bibliotheca scriptorum Graecorum et Romanorum Teubneriana. Ann Arbor: University of Michigan Press.

Aune, David E. 1983. *Prophecy in Early Christianity and the Ancient Mediterranean World.* Grand Rapids: Eerdmas.

Bachtold-Stäubli, Hans, ed. 1927–42. *Handwörterbuch des deutschen Aberglaubens,* vol. 5. Berlin/Leipzig: Walter de Gruyter & Co.

Banck, Werner. 1976. *Das chinesische Tempelorakel.* Chung-kuo ling-ch'ien yen-chiu, Tsu-liao p'ien. Taipei: Ku-t'ing.

———. 1985. *Das chinesische Tempelorakel, Teil II.* Asiatische Forschungen, 90. Wiesbaden: Otto Harrassowitz.

Bang, Willy. 1926. "Türkische Bruchstücke einer nestorianischen Georgspassion." *Le Muséon* 39: 40–75.

Bang, Willy, and A. von Gabain. 1929. "Turkische Turfan-Texte, I. Bruchstücke eines Wahrsagebuches." *Sitzungsberichte der Preussischen Akademie der Wissenschaften, Philosophisch-Historische Klasse,* 241–68.

Bapat, P. V., and A. Hirakawa, trans. 1970. *Shan-Chien-P'i-P'-o-Sha: A Chinese Version by Saṅghabhadra of Samantapāsādikā.* Bhandarkar Oriental Series, 10. Poona: Bhandarkar Oriental Research Institute.

Bareau, André. 1959. "Constellations et divinités protectrices des marchands dans le bouddhisme ancien." *Journal Asiatique* 247: 303–9.

Bastian, Adolf. 1867. *Die Völker des östlichen Asien, vol. 3: Reisen in Siam im Jahre 1863.* Jena: Hermann Costenoble.

Bate, J. D. 1883. "The Oracle of Hubal." *Indian Antiquary* 12: 4.

Bauer, Wolfgang. 1973. *Das Bild in der Weissage-Literatur Chinas.* Munich: Heinz Moos Verlag.

Bean, George E. 1968. *Turkey's Southern Shore: An Archaelogical Guide.* London: Ernest Benn.

Becq de Fouquières, L. 1869. *Les jeux des anciens; leur description, leur origine, leurs rapports avec la religion, l'histoire, les arts et les moeurs.* Paris: C. Reinwalt.

Bell, R. C. 1969. *Board and Table Games from Many Civilizations,* vol. 2. London: Oxford University Press.

Berthier, Brigitte. 1987. "Enfant de divination, voyageur du destin." *L'Homme* 101: 86–100.

Betz, Hans Dieter, ed. 1986. *The Greek Magical Papyri in Translation, Including the Demotic Spells, vol. 1: Texts.* Trans. Morton Smith. Chicago: University of Chicago Press.

Billeter, Jean-François. 1989. *L'Art chinois de l'écriture*. Geneva: Skira.

Björck, Gudmund. 1939. "Heidnische und christliche Orakel mit fertigen Antworten." *Symbolae Osloenses* 19: 86–98.

Blondeau, Anne-Marie. 1976. "Les religions du Tibet." In *Histoire des Religions*, vol. 3: 233–329. Encyclopédie de la Pléiade. Paris: Gallimard.

Bolte, Johannes, ed. 1903. *George Wickrams Werke*, vol. 4. Tübingen: Literarischen Vereins in Stuttgart.

Bolte, Johannes. 1925. "Zur Geschichte der Punktier-und Losbücher." In Wilhelm Fraenger, ed., *Die Volkskunde und ihre Grenzgebiete*, 185–214. Jahrbuch für Historische Volkskunde, 1. Berlin: Herbert Stubenrauch.

Bolto, J. D. P. 1962. *Aristeas of Proconnesus*. Oxford: Clarendon Press.

Boltz, Judith M. 1987. *A Survey of Taoist Literature, Tenth to Seventeeth Centuries*. China Research Monograph, 32. Berkeley: Institute of East Asian Studies, University of California.

Bottéro, Jean. 1956. "Deux curiosités assyriologiques." *Syria* 33: 16–35.

Bottéro, Jean. 1974. "Symptomes, signes, écritures en Mésopotamie ancienne." In Jean-Pierre Vernant et al., eds., *Divination et rationalité*, 70–197. Paris: Seuil.

Bouché-Leclerc, A. 1963 (1879–82). *Histoire de la divination dans l'antiquité*. Brussels: Culture et Civilisation.

Brandin, Louis. 1913. "Le *Livre de preuve*." *Romania* 42: 204–54.

———. 1927. "Un livre de bonne aventure anglo-français." In *Mélanges de philologie et d'"histoire offerts à M. Antoine Thomas par ses élèves et amis*, 51–60. Paris: H. Champion.

———. 1928. "Un livre de bonne aventure anglo-français en vers." In *Mélanges de linguistique et de littérature offerts à M. Alfred Jeanroy par ses élèves et ses amis*, 639–55. Paris: E. Droz.

———. 1932. "Les Prognostica du ms. Ashmole 304 de la Bodléienne." In Mary Williams and James A. de Rothschild, eds., *A Miscellany of Studies in Romance Languages and Literatures presented to Leon E. Kastner*, 57–67. Cambridge: W. Heffer and Sons.

Brauen, Martin. 1974. *Heinrich Harrers Impressionen aus Tibet: Gerettete Schätze*. Innsbruck: Penguin.

Browne, Gerald M. 1970. "The Composition of the *Sortes Astrampsychi*." *University of London Institute of Classical Studies Bulletin (BICS)* 17: 95–100.

———. 1974. *The Papyri of the Sortes Astrampsychi*. Beiträge zur klassischen Philologie, 58. Meisenheim am Glan: Verlag Anton Hain.

———. 1976. "The Origin and the Date of the *Sortes Astrampsychi*." *Illinois Classical Studies* 1: 53–58.

———. 1979. "A New Papyrus Codex of the *Sortes Astrampsychi*." In G. W. Bowersock, ed., *Arktouros: Hellenic Studies Presented to Bernard M. W. Knox on the Occasion of his 65th Birthday*, 434–39. Berlin/New York: Walter de Gruyter & Co.

———. 1983. *Sortes Astrampsychi I: ecdosis prior*. Bibliotheca Teubneriana. Leipzig: Teubner.

———. 1987. "The *Sortes Astrampsychi* and the Egyptian Oracle." In Juergen Dummer et al., eds., *Texte und Textkritik: eine Aufsatzsammlung,* 67–71. Berlin: Akademie Verlag.

Brumbaugh, Robert S. 1966. *Ancient Greek Gadgets and Machines.* New York: Thomas Y. Crowell.

Buchanan, Daniel C. 1935. "Inari: Its Origin, Development, and Nature." *Transactions of the Asiatic Society of Japan,* 2nd series, vol. 12.

———. 1939. "Some Mikuji of Fushimi Inari Jinja." *Monumenta Nipponica* 2, 2: 518–35.

Buecheler, Franz. 1895. *Carmina latina epigraphica.* Leipzig: Teubner.

Burkert, Walter. 1983. "Itinerant Diviners and Magicians: A Neglected Element in Cultural Contacts." *Skrifter utgivna av Svenska Institutet i Athen 30 (Stockholm),* 115–20.

Buswell, Robert E., Jr., ed. 1990. *Chinese Buddhist Apocrypha.* Honolulu: University of Hawai'i Press.

Caillois, Roger. 1958. *Art poétique.* Paris: Gallimard.

Caquot, André. 1968. "La divination dans l'ancien Israël." In André Caquot and Marcel Leibovici, eds., *La divination,* vol. 1. Paris: Presses Universitaires de France.

Caquot, André, and Marcel Leibovici, eds. 1968. *La divination.* 2 vols. Paris: Presses Universitaires de France.

Carter, Thomas F. 1955 (1925). *The Invention of Printing in China and its Spread Westward.* New York: Ronald Press.

Cedzich, Ursula-Angelika. 1987. "Das Ritual der Himmelsmeister im Spiegel früher Quellen." Ph.D. dissertation, Würzburg.

Chabaneau, C. 1880–81. "Les sorts des apôtres: texte provençal du XIIIe siècle." *Revue des Langues Romanes,* 3e série, 4: 157–78; 5: 63–64.

Chadwick, H. M., and Nora K. Chadwick. 1932–40. *The Growth of Literature.* 3 vols. Cambridge: Cambridge University Press.

Chadwick, Nora K. 1942. *Poetry and Prophecy.* Cambridge: Cambridge University Press.

Chambers, Robert. 1869. *The Book of Days; A Miscellany of Popular Antiquities in Connection with the Calender.* London and Edimburgh: W. & R. Chambers.

Chapuis, Alfred. 1947. *Les automates dans les oeuvres d'imagination.* Neuchâtel: Éditions du Griffon.

Chapuis, Alfred. 1984 (1928). *Le monde des automates: Étude historique et technique.* Geneva: Éditions Slatkine.

Chapuis, Alfred, and Edmond Droz. 1949. *Les automates, figures artificielles d'hommes et d'animaux: histoire et technique.* Neuchâtel: Éditions du Griffon. English translation by Alec Reid, *Automata: A Historical and Technological Study.* Neuchâtel: Éditions du Griffon/London: B. T. Batsford, Ltd., 1958.

Chapuis, Alfred, and Édouard Gelis. 1984 (1928). *Le monde des automates: étude historique et technique.* Geneva: Éditions Slatkine.

Chemla, Karine, Donald Harper, and Marc Kalinowski, eds. 1999. "Divination et rationalité en Chine ancienne." *Extrême-Orient, Extrême-Occident* 21. Paris: Presses Universitaires de Vincennes.

Chie Tek-su. 1977. *Shiragi bukkyō kairitsu shisō kenkyū.* Tokyo: Kokusho kankōkai.

Ch'ung-hsiu Cheng-ho ching-shih cheng-lei pei-yung pen-ts'o. Reprint, Taipei: Southern Materials Center, 1976.

Cornford, F. M. 1952. *Principium Sapientiae: The Origins of Greek Philosophical Thought.* Cambridge: Cambridge University Press.

Courant, Maurice. 1894–96. *Bibliographie coréenne.* Paris: Publications de l'École des Langues Orientales Vivantes. Reprint, New York: Burt Franklin, n.d.

Cowell, E. B., ed. 1895–1907. *The Jātaka or Stories of the Buddha's Former Births.* Cambridge: Cambridge University Press. Reprint, London: Luzac & Co., 1957.

Crooke, William. 1906. *Things Indian, being Discursive Notes on Various Subjects Connected with India.* London: John Murray.

Culin, Stewart. 1895. *Korean Games.* Philadelphia. Reprinted as *Games of the Orient: Korea, China, Japan.* Rutland (Vt.) and Tokyo: Charles E. Tuttle, 1958.

Davis, Edward L. 1985. "Arms and the Tao: Hero Cult and Empire in Traditional China." In *Sōdai no shakai to shūkyō,* 1–56. Sōdai-shi kenkyūkai kenkyū hōkoku, 2. Tokyo: Kyuko sho'in.

De Groot, J. J. M. 1893. *Le code du Mahāyāna en Chine.* Amsterdam. Reprint, Wiesbaden: Martin Sandig, 1967.

de Gubernatis, A. 1878. *La mythologie des plantes, ou les légendes du règne végétal,* vol 1. Paris.

de Kermadec, Jean-Michel. 1984. *Les sapèques d'or: jeux divinatoires inspirés du Yijing.* Paris: L'Asiathèque.

Delatte, Armand. 1932. *La catoptromancie grecque et ses dérivés.* Bibliothèque de la Faculté de Philosophie et Lettres de l'Université de Liège, 48. Liège/Paris.

de la Vallée Poussin, Louis. 1898. *Bouddhisme: Études et matériaux. Ādikarmapradīpa, Bodhicaryāvatāraṭīkā.* London: Luzac & Co.

Demiéville, Paul. 1937. "Byō." In *Hōbōgirin: dictionnaire encyclopédique du bouddhisme d'après les sources chinoises et japonaises,* vol. 3: 224–65. Paris: Adrien Maisonneuve. English translation by Mark Tatz, *Buddhism and Healing: Demiéville's Article" "Byō" from Hōbōgirin.* Lanham, Md.: University Press of America, 1985.

————. 1953. "Les sources chinoises." In Louis Renou and J. Filliozat, *L'Inde classique, manuel des études indiennes,* vol. 2. Hanoi: Bibliothèque de l'École Française d'Extrême-Orient, 3: 398–463. Reprint in Demiéville, *Choix d'études bouddhiques,* 157–222. Leiden: E. J. Brill, 1973.

————. 1973. *Choix d'études bouddhiques.* Leiden: E. J. Brill.

de Nebesky-Wojkowitz, René. 1975 (1956). *Oracles and Demons of Tibet.* The Hague: Mouton. Reprint, Graz: Akademische Druck- u. Verlagsanstalt.

Diehl, C. G. 1956. *Instrument and Purpose: Studies on Rites and Rituals in South India.* Lund: C.W.K. Gleerup.

Diény, Jean-Pierre. 1986. "Les inscriptions sur os et écaille de l'époque des Zhou." *Journal Asiatique* 274: 455–66.

Djang Chu, trans. and ed. 1984. *A Complete Book Concerning Happiness and Benevolence.* Tucson: University of Arizona Press.

Dodds, E. R. 1951. *The Greeks and the Irrational.* Berkeley: University of California Press.

Dodds, E. R. 1965. *Pagans and Christians in an Age of Anxiety.* Cambridge: Cambridge University Press.

Dodge, Bayard, trans. and ed. 1970. *The Fihrist of al-Nadīm; A Tenth-Century Survey of Muslim Culture.* Records of Civilization: Sources and Studies, 83. New York: Columbia University Press.

Dold, Alban, ed. 1948. *Die Orakelsprüche in St. Galler Palimpsestcodex 908 (die sogenannten "Sortes Sangallenses").* Österreiche Akademie der Wissenschaften, Philosophisch-Historische Klasse. *Sitzungsberichte* 225, 4. Vienna: R. M. Rohrer.

Donalson, Bess Allen. 1938. *The Wild Rue: A Study of Muhammedan Magic and Folk-lore in Iran.* London: Luzac.

Doolittle, Rev. Justus. 1872. *A Vocabulary and Hand-Book of the Chinese Language, Romanized in the Mandarin Dialect.* Foochow: Rosario, Marcal, & Co.

————. 1966 (1865). *Social Life of the Chinese.* Taipei: Ch'eng-wen.

Dow, Sterling. 1939. "An Athenian Lottery Machine." *Harvard Journal of Classical Philology* 50: 1–34.

Drège, Jean-Pierre. 1981a. "Note d'onirologie chinoise." *Bulletin de l'École Française d'Extrême-Orient* 70: 271–89.

————. 1981b. "Clefs des songes de Touen-houang." In Michel Soymié, ed., *Nouvelles contributions aux études de Touen-houang*, 205–49 and pl. 24–38. Hautes Études Orientales, 17. Geneva: Librairie Droz.

Drexler, M. 1994. *Daoistische Schriftmagie, Interpretationen zu den Schriftamuletten fu in Daozang.* Münchener Ostasiatische Studien 68. Stuttgart.

du Cange, Charles du Fresne. 1710 (1678). *Glossarium ad scriptores mediae et infimae latinitatis.* Frankfurt am Main: ex officina Zunneriana.

Dudbridge, Glen. 1970. *The Hsi-yu chi: A Study of Antecedents to the Sixteenth-Century Chinese Novel.* Cambridge Studies in Chinese History, Literature and Institutions, 1. Cambridge: Cambridge University Press.

————. 1978. *The Legend of Miao-shan.* Oxford Oriental Monographs, 1. London: Ithaca Press.

Dummett, Michael. 1980. *The Game of Tarot, From Ferrara to Salt Lake City.* London: Duckworth.

du Resnel, Abbé. 1744. "Recherches historiques sur les Sorts appelés communément par les Payens: Sortes Homericae, Sortes Virgilianae, etc., et sur ceux qui parmi les chrétiens on été connus sous le nom de Sortes Sanctorum." *Mémoires de l'Académie des Inscriptions et Belles-Lettres* 19: 287–310.

Durt, Hubert. 1974. "The Counting-Stick [*Śalākā*] and the Majority/Minority Rule in the Buddhist Community." *Indogaku bukkyōgaku kenkyū* 23, 1: 464–70.

————. 1979. "*Chū.*" In *Hōbōgirin: Dictionnaire encyclopédique du bouddhisme d'après les sources chinoises et japonaises*, vol. 5: 431–56. Paris: Adrien Maisonneuve.

Dusan, Bruno. 1866–67. "Les Sorts des Apôtres, Ms. trouvé à Cordes." *Revue archéologique du Midi de la France* 1: 225–37.

Eberhard, Wolfram. 1965. "Orakel und Theater in China." *Asiatische Studien/ Études Asiatiques* 18/19: 11–18.

――――. 1966. "Fatalism in the Life of the Common Man in Non-Communist China."*Anthropological Quarterly* 39: 148–60. Reprint in W. Eberhard, *Moral and Social Values of the Chinese*. Collected Essays, vol. 3: 177–89. Taipei: Ch'eng-wen, 1971.

――――. 1970. *Studies in Chinese Folklore and Related Essays*. Indiana University Folklore Institute Monograph Series, 23. Bloomington: Indiana University Research Center for the Language Sciences.

――――. 1971. *Moral and Social Values of the Chinese*. Collected Essays, vol. 3. Taipei: Ch'eng-wen.

Eis, Gerhard. 1956. *Wahrsagetexte des Spätmittelalters: Aus Handschriften und Inkunabeln*. Texte des späten Mittelalters, 1. Berlin: Erich Schmidt.

Ekvall, Robert B. 1964. *Religious Observances in Tibet: Patterns and Functions*. Chicago: University of Chicago Press.

Elliot, A. J. A. 1955. *Chinese Spirit-Medium Cults in Singapore*. Monographs on Social Anthropology, 14. London: London School of Economics.

Elliott, Ralph W. V. 1959. *Runes: An Introduction*. Manchester: Manchester University Press.

Emmerick, R. E., trans. 1968. *The Book of Zambasta; A Khotanese Poem on Buddhism*. London Oriental Series, 21. London: Oxford University Press.

Esnoul, Anne-Marie. 1968. "La divination dans l'Inde." In André Caquot and Marcel Leibovici, eds., *La divination*, vol. 1. Paris: Presses Universitaires de France.

Fahd, Toufic. 1958. "Une pratique cléromantique à la Ka'ba préislamique." *Semitica* 8: 54–79.

――――. 1966. *La divination arabe: études religieuses, sociologiques et folkloriques sur le milieu natif de l'Islam*. Strasbourg: Université de Strasbourg, Faculté des Lettres et Sciences Humaines.

Feng, H. Y., and J. R. Shryock. 1935. "The Black Magic in China Known as Ku." *Journal of the American Oriental Society* 55: 1–35.

Feuchtwang, Stephan. 1977. "School-Temple and City God." In G. W. S. Skinner, ed., *The City in Late Imperial China*. Stanford: Stanford University Press.

Filliozat, Jean. 1953. "L'Inde et les échanges scientifiques dans l'antiquité." *Cahiers d'histoire mondiale* 1: 353–67.

――――. 1985 (1953). "Les sciences: la médecine." In Louis Renou and Jean Filliozat, eds., *L'Inde classique: manuel des études indiennes*, vol. 2: 138–66. Bibliothèque de l'École Francaise d'Extrême-Orient, vol. 3. Paris: École Française d'Extrême-Orient.

Finnegan, Ruth. 1970. *Oral Literature in Africa*. Oxford: Clarendon Press.

Finsterbusch, Kate. 1971. *Verzeichnis und Motivindex der Han-Darstellungen*. 2 vols. Wiesbaden: Otto Harrassowitz.

Fischer, Stephen R. 1982. *The Complete Medieval Dreambook. A Multilingual, Alphabetical Somnium Danielis Collation*. Bern: Peter Lang.

Flügel, Gustav. 1861 "Die Loosbücher der Muhammadaner." *Berichte über die Verhandlungen der Königlich Sächsischen Gesellschaft der Wissenschaften zu Leipzig, Philologisch-Historische Classe* 13: 24–74.

Fontein, Jan. 1967. *The Pilgrimage of Sudhana, A Study of Gaṇḍavyūha Illustrations in China, Japan and Java.* The Hague/Paris: Mouton & Co.

Francke, August Hermann H. 1924a. "Tibetische Handschriftenfunde aus Turfan." *Sitzungsberichte der Preussischen Akademie der Wissenschaften, Philosophisch-Historische Klasse,* 5–20.

———. 1924b. "Drei weitere Blätter des tibetischen Losbuches von Turfan." *Sitzungsberichte der Preussischen Akademie der Wissenschaften, Philosophisch-Historische Klasse,* 110–18.

Frazer, G. 1913. *Pausanias's Description of Greece.* London: Macmillan.

Freudenberg, F. 1919. *Die Blick in die Zukunft; Die Wahrsagekunst im Spiegel der Zeit und der Völkergeschichte.* Berlin: Hermann Barsdorf.

Friend, Hilderic. (n.d.) [1883]. *Flowers and Flower Lore,* vol. 1. London: Swan Sonnenschein.

Ganszyniec, R. 1928. "Les sortes sanctorum." In Paul-Louis Couchoud, ed., *Jubilé Alfred Loisy: Congrès d'histoire du christianisme,* vol. 3: 41–51. Annales d'Histoire du Christianisme, 3. Paris: Éditions Rieder.

Gernet, Jacques. 1973 (1956). *Les aspects économiques du bouddhisme dans la société chinoise du Ve au Xe siècle.* Publications de l'École Française d'Extrême-Orient, 39. Paris: École Française d'Extrême-Orient.

Goethe, Johann Wolfgang. 1840. *Goethe's Sämtliche Werke.* Stuttgart u. Tübingen: J. G. Cotta'scher Verlag.

Goodrich, Anne Swann. 1964. *The Peking Temple of the Eastern Peak.* Nagoya: Monumenta Serica.

Goody, Jack, ed. 1968. *Literacy in Traditional Societies.* Cambridge: Cambridge University Press.

———. 1977. *The Domestication of the Savage Mind.* Cambridge: Cambridge University Press.

———. 1987.*The Interface Between the Written and the Oral.* Cambridge: Cambridge University Press.

Götze, Alfred. 1918. *Das Strassburger Würfelbuch von 1529: Facsimiledruck der Erstausgabe.* Strassburg: Karl J. Trübner.

Government-General of Korea, ed. 1972 (1933). *Chōsen enboku to yogen.* Tokyo: Kokusho kankōkai.

Graham, David C. 1961. *Folk Religion in Southwest China.* Smithsonian Miscellaneous Collections, vol. 142, no. 2. Washington, D.C.: Smithsonian Press.

Gundel, Wilhelm. 1969 (1936). *Dekane und Dekansternbilder.* Darmstadt: Wissenschaftliche Buchges. (First published as vol. 19 of *Studien der Bibliothek Warburg.*)

Gyss-Vermande, Caroline. 1988. "Démons et merveilles: vision de la nature dans une peinture liturgique du XVe siècle." *Arts Asiatiques* 43: 106–22.

Hargrave, Catherine Perry. 1930. *A History of Playing Cards.* New York: Houghton Miffli. Reprint, Dover, 1966.

Harper, Donald J. 1982. "The *Wu Shih Erh Ping Fang*: Translation and Prolegomena." Ph.D. dissertation, Berkeley.

————. 1986. "The *Analects* Jade Candle: A Classic of T'ang Drinking Custom." *T'ang Studies* 4: 69–89.

————. 1999. "Physicians and Diviners: The Relation of Divination to the Medicine of the *Huangdi neijing* (Inner Canon of the Yellow Thearch)." In Karine Chemla, Donald Harper, and Marc Kalinowski, eds., "Divination et rationalité en Chine ancienne." *Extrême-Orient, Extrême-Occident* 21: 91–110. Paris: Presses Universitaires de Vincennes.

Harrell, Steven. 1987. "The Concept of Fate in Chinese Folk Ideology." *Modern China* 13, 1: 90–109.

Harris, James Rendel. 1901. *The Annotators of the Codex Bezae, with Some Notes on Sortes Sanctorum*. London: C. J. Clay and Sons.

Hartel, Herbert. 1982. "Introduction." In *Along the Ancient Silk Routes: Central Asian Art from the West Berlin State Museums*, 13–55. New York: The Metropolitan Museum of Art.

Hayashi Minao. 1976. *Kandai no bunbutsu*. Kyoto: Kyōto daigaku jinbun kagaku kenkyūjo.

Hayashiya Tomojirō. 1945. *Iyaku kyōrui no kenkyū*. Tokyo: Tōyō Bunko.

Hearn, Lafcadio. 1894. *Glimpses of Unfamililar Japan*. 2 vols. Boston/New York: Houghton, Mifflin & Co.

Heiberg, Johan Ludvig, and Hieronymus Georg Seuthen, eds. 1884–1919. *Mémoires scientifiques de Paul Tannery, vol. 4: Sciences exactes chez les byzantins*. Toulouse: Édouard Privat, Paris: Gauthier-Villars, 1920.

Heinevetter, Franz. 1912. *Würfel- und Buchstabenorakel in Griechenland und Kleinasien*. Breslau: Grass, Barth & Comp.

Heissig, Walter. 1980. *The Religions of Mongolia*. London: Allen & Unwin.

Henrichs, Albert. 1973. "Zwei Orakelfragen." *Zeitschrift für Papyrus Erforschung* 11/12: 115–19.

Hercher, Rudolf. 1863. *Oraculorum decades CIII*. In R. Hercher, *Jahresbericht über das Königliche Joachimsthalsche Gymnasium*. Berlin: Gebrüder Unger. Most of the text was reprinted by J. Rendel Harris in *The Annotators of the Codex Bezae*, Appendix C, pp. 128–60, Cambridge, 1901.

Herodotus. 1825. *Histories*. Trans. William Beloe. London.

Hitti, Philip K. 1969. *History of the Arabs*. London: Macmillan.

Ho Cho, ed. 1981. *I-chien chih*. 4 vols. Peking: Chung-hua shu-chü.

Hoernle, A. F. Rudolf. 1893–1912. *The Bower Manuscript*. Calcutta: Archaeological Survey of India.

Hoffmann, Helmut. 1950. *Quellen zur Geschichte der tibetischen Bon-Religion*. Akademie der Wissenschaften und der Literatur in Mainz. Wiesbaden: Franz Steiner.

Hone, William. 1826. *The Every-Day Book or Everlasting Calendar of Popular Amusements*. London: Hone.

Hou Chin-lang. 1975. *Monnaies d'offrande et la notion de trésorerie dans la religion chinoise.* Mémoires de l'Institut des Hautes Études Chinoises, 1. Paris: Collège de France.

———. 1979. "Physiognomonie d'après le teint sous la dynastie des T'ang (une étude sur le manuscrit P. 3390)." In Michel Soymié, ed., *Contributions aux études sur Touen-houang,* 55–69 and pl. 18–23. Hautes Études Orientales, 10. Geneva and Paris: Librairie Droz.

Hsü Ti-shan. 1941. *Fu-chi mi-hsin te yen-chiu.* Shanghai: Commercial Press. Reprint, Taipei: Jen-jen wen-k'u, 18, 1966.

Huang Cheng-chien. 2001. *Tun-huang chan-pu wen-shu yü T'ang Wu-tai chan-pu yen-chiu.* Peking: Hsüe-yüan.

Ishizaki Yūzō. 1967. *Kinsei Nihon ni okeru Shina zokugo bungaku shi.* Tokyo: Kiyomizu Kobundō.

Iyanaga Nobumi. 1983. "Daijizaiten." In *Hōbōgirin* 6: 713-765 and pl. 45.

———. 1985. "Récits de la soumission de Maheśvara par Trailokyavijaya, d'après les sources chinoises et japonaises." In M. Strickmann, ed., *Tantric and Taoist Studies in Honour of R. A. Stein,* vol 3: 633–745.

Jantz, Harold. 1966. *The Soothsayings of Bakis: Goethe's Tragi-Comic Observations on Life, Time, and History.* Baltimore: Johns Hopkins Press.

Jao Tsong-yi. 1979. "Les sept planètes et les onze plantes: étude sur un manuel astrologique daté de 974 par K'ang Tsouen: le manuscrit P. 4071." In Michel Soymié, ed., *Contributions aux études sur Touen-houang,* 77–85. Hautes Études Orientales, 10. Geneva and Paris: Librairie Droz.

———. 1983. "Yin-tai I-jua chi yu-kuan chan-pu chu wen-t'i." *Wen-shih* 9.

Johnston, Sarah Iles. 2001. "Charming Children: The Use of the Child in Ancient Divination." *Arethusa* 34, 1: 97–107.

Jordan, David K., and Daniel L. Overmyer. 1986. *The Flying Phoenix; Aspects of Chinese Sectarianism in Taiwan.* Princeton: Princeton University Press.

Kaibel, Georg. 1876. "Ein Wurfelorakel." *Hermes* 10: 193–202.

———, ed. 1878. *Epigrammata Graeca ex lapidibus conlecta.* Berlin: G. Reimer.

Kalinowski, Marc. 1983. "Les instruments astro-calendériques des Han et la méthode *liu ren.*" *Bulletin de l'École Française d'Extrême-Orient* 72: 309–419.

———. 1985. "La transmission du dispositif des neuf palais sous les Six Dynasties." In Michel Strickmann, ed., *Tantric and Taoist Studies in Honour of R. A. Stein,* vol. 3: 773–811. Mélanges chinois et bouddhiques, 22. Brussels: Institut Belge des Hautes Études Chinoises.

———. 1986a. "Les traités de Shuihudi et l'hémérologie chinoise à la fin des Royaumes Combattants." *T'oung Pao* 72: 175–228.

———. 1986b. "L'astronomie des populations Yi du Sud-Ouest de la Chine." *Cahiers d'Extrême-Asie* 2: 253–63.

———. 1989–90. "La Littérature divinatoire dans le *Daozang.*" *Cahiers d'Extrême-Asie* 5: 83–110.

———. 1991. *Cosmologie et divination dans la Chine ancienne: Le Compendium des Cinq Agents (Wuxing dayi, VIe siècle).* Paris: École Française d'Extrême-Orient.

————. 1994. "La divination par les nombres dans les manuscrits de Dunhuang."
In Isabelle Ang and Pierre-Étienne Will, eds., *Nombres, astres, plantes et viscères:
Sept essais sur l'histoire des sciences et des techniques en Asie orientale*, 37–88.
Paris: Institut des Hautes Études Chinoises.

————. 1999. "La rhétorique oraculaire dans les chroniques anciennes de la Chine:
Une étude des discours prédictifs dans le *Zuozhuan*." In Karine Chemla, Donald
Harper, and Marc Kalinowski, eds., "Divination et rationalité en Chine ancienne."
Extrême-Orient, Extrême-Occident 21: 37–65. Paris: Presses Universitaires de
Vincennes.

————, ed. 2003. *Divination et société dans la Chine médiévale: Étude des manuscrits
de Dunhuang de la Bibliothèque Nationale de France et de la British Library*. Paris:
Bibliothèque Nationale de France.

Kirfel, Willibald. 1949. *Der Rosenkranz: Ursprung und Ausbreitung*. Beiträge zur
Sprach-und Kulturgeschichte des Orients, 1. Walldorf-Hessen: Verlag für Orient-
kunde Dr. Hans Vorndran.

Kleeman, Terry F. 1988. "Wenchang and the Viper: The Creation of a Chinese National God." Ph.D. dissertation, Berkeley.

————. 1994. *A God's Own Tale: The Book of Transformations of Wenchang, the
Divine Lord of Zitong*. SUNY Series in Chinese Philosophy and Culture. Albany,
N.Y.: SUNY Press.

————.1996. "The Lives and Teachings of the Divine Lord of Zitong." In Donald
S. Lopez, Jr., ed., *Religions of China in Practice*, 64–73. Princeton: Princeton
University Press.

Kleinman, Arthur. 1978. "Comparisons of Patient–Practitioner Transactions in
Taiwan: The Cultural Construction of Clinical Reality." In Kleinman et al., eds.,
Culture and Healing in Asian Societies, 329–74. Cambridge, Mass.: Schenkman
Publishing.

————. 1976. "Counseling in the Chinese Temple: A Psychological Study of Div-
ination by *Chien* Drawing." In William P. Lebra, ed., *Culture-Bound Syndromes,
Ethnopsychiatry and Alternate Therapies*, 210–21. Mental Health Research in
Asia and the Pacific, 4. Honolulu: University Press of Hawai'i.

————. 1980. *Patients and Healers in the Context of Culture; An Exploration of
the Borderland Between Anthropology, Medicine, and Psychiatry*. Comparative
Studies of Health Systems and Medical Care, 3. Berkeley: University of California
Press.

Kleinman, Arthur, P. Kunstadter, E. Russell Alexander, and J. L. Gates, eds. 1978.
*Culture and Healing in Asian Societies: Anthropological, Psychiatric, and Public
Health Studies*. Cambridge, Mass.: Schenkman Publishing.

Kuo Li-ying, 1994. "Divination, jeux de hasard et purification dans le bouddhisme
chinois: Autour d'un *sūtra* apocryphe. le *Zhanchajing*." In Fukui Fumimasa and
Gérard Fussman, eds., *Bouddhisme et cultures locales: quelques cas de réciproques
adaptations*, 145–167. Paris: École Française d'Extrême-Orient.

Lach, Donald F. 1945. "Leibniz and China." *Journal of the History of Ideas* 6, 4:
436–55.

Lai, Whalen. 1990. "The *Chan-ch'a ching*: Religion and Magic in Medieval China." In Robert E. Buswell, Jr., ed., *Chinese Buddhist Apocrypha*, 175–206. Honolulu: University of Hawai'i Press.

Lane, Edward William. 1895. *Manners and Customs of the Modern Egyptians, Written in Egypt During the Years 1833–1835.* Paisley & London: Alexander Gardner.

Lane Fox, Robin. 1986. *Pagans and Christians.* Harmondsworth: Viking Penguin.

Laufer, Berthold. 1911. *Der Roman einer tibetischen Köningin.* Leipzig: O. Harrassowitz.

——. 1914. "Bird Divination Among the Tibetans." *T'oung Pao* 15: 1–110.

Lebra, William P. 1966. *Okinawan Religion.* Honolulu: University of Hawai'i Press.

Ledderose, Lothar. 1984. "Some Taoist Elements in the Calligraphy of the Six Dynasties." *T'oung Pao* 70: 246–78.

Lenormant, Francois. (n.d.) [1877]. *Chaldean Magic: Its Origin and Development.* London: Samuel Bagster and Sons.

Lévi, Sylvain. 1932. *Mahākarmavibhaṅga: la grande classification des actes.* Paris: Ernest Leroux.

Lévi, Sylvain, and Édouard Chavannes. 1916. "Les seize Arhat protecteurs de la Loi." *Journal Asiatique* 8: 5–48, 189–304.

Lewis, Naphtali. 1983. *Life in Egypt Under Roman Rule.* Oxford: Clarendon Press.

Loewe, Michael. 1988. "The Oracles of the Clouds and the Winds." *Bulletin of the School of Oriental and African Studies* 51, 3: 500–20.

Lüders, Heinrich. 1907. *Das Würfelspiel in alten Indien.* Abhandlungen der Königlichen Gesellschaft der Wissenschaften zu Göttingen, Philologisch-Historische Klasse, New Series, 9.2. Berlin: Weidmannsche Buchhandlung.

Macdonald, Alexander. 1967. *Matériaux pour l'étude de la littérature populaire tibétaine*, vol. 1. Annales du Musée Guimet, Bibliothèque d'Études, 72. Paris: Presses Universitaires de France.

——. 1975. "The Healer in the Nepalese World." In A. Macdonald, ed., *Essays on the Ethnology of Nepal and South Asia*, 113–28. Kathmandu: Ratna Pustak Bhandhar.

Macdonald, David. 1929. *The Land of the Lama: A description of a country of contrasts and of its cheerful, happy-go-lucky people of hardy nature and curious customs; their religion, ways of living, trade and social life.* London: Seeley, Service & Co.

Macdonald, David. 1932. *Twenty Years in Tibet.* London: Seeley, Service & Co.

Mair, Victor. 1988. *Painting and Performance: Chinese Picture Recitation and Its Indian Genesis.* Honolulu: University of Hawai'i Press.

Makita Tairyō. 1976. *Gikyō kenkyū.* Kyoto: Kyōto daigaku jinbun kagaku kenkyūjo.

Marlowe, Christopher. 1631. *The Tragicall Historie of Doctor Faustus.* London: John Wright. Ed. Alec D. Hope, *The Tragical History of Doctor Faustus*, Canberra: Australian National University Press, 1982.

May, Jacques. 1967. "Chinkiyaku." In *Hōbōgirin: Dictionnaire encyclopédique du bouddhisme d'après les sources chinoises et japonaises*, 4: 329–35. Paris: Adrien-Maisonneuve.

Meister, Richard. 1951. *Die Orakelsprüche im St. Galler Palimpsestcodex 908 (die sogenannte "Sortes Gallenses").* Österreichische Akademie der Wissenschaften, Philosophisch-Historische Klasse. *Sitzungsberichte* 225, 5. Vienna: R. M. Rohrer.

Menninger, Karl. 1969. *Number Words and Number Symbols: A Cultural History of Numbers.* Cambridge, Mass.: MIT Press.

Meyer, Marvin, and Paul Mirecki, eds. 1995. *Ancient Magic and Ritual Power.* Leiden and New York: E. J. Brill.

Michaux, Henri. 1933. *Un barbare en Asie.* Paris: Gallimard. English translation by Sylvia Beach, *A Barbarian in Asia.* New York: New Directions, 1949.

Minakata Kumagusu. 1971–73. *Minakata Kumagusu zenshū.* Edited by Iwamura Shinobu. Tokyo: Heibonsha.

Mollier, Christine. 1986. "Messianisme taoïste de la Chine médiévale: Étude du *Dongyuan shenzhou jing.*" Ph.D. dissertation, Université de Paris VII.

Montell, Gosta. 1949. "*T'ou hu*—The Ancient Chinese Pitch-Pot Game." *Ethnos* 5: 70–83.

Morgan, Carole. 1981. "Les 'neuf palais' dans les manuscrits de Touen-houang." In Michel Soymié, ed., *Nouvelles contributions aux études de Touen-houang,* 251–60. Geneva: Librairie Droz.

———. 1984. "L'école des cinq noms dans les manuscrits de Touen-houang." In Michel Soymié, ed., *Contributions aux études de Touen-houang,* vol. 3: 255–61 and pl. 41. Publications de l'École Française d'Extrême-Orient, 135. Paris: École Française d'Extrême-Orient.

———. 1987a. *Les fiches divinatoires de Huang Daxian.* Paris: Guy Tredaniel, Éditions de la Maisnie.

———. 1987b. "A propos des fiches oraculaires de Huang Daxian." *Journal Asiatique* 275: 163–91.

———. 1987c. "Nouvelle étude sur la divination d'après les croassements de corbeaux dans les manuscrits de Touen-houang." *Cahiers d'Extrême-Asie* 3: 55–76.

———. 1993. "An Introduction to the *Lingqi jing.*" *Journal of Chinese Religions* 21: 97–120.

———. 1998. "Old Wine in New Bottles: A New Set of Oracles Slips from China." *Journal of Chinese Religions* 26: 1–20.

Morita Ryūsen. 1941. *Mikkyō sensei hō.* 2 vols. Kōyasan: Kōyasan daigaku. Reprint, Kyoto: Rinsen shoten, 1974.

Mujaku Dōchū. 1963. *Zenrin shōkisen.* Tokyo: Seishin shobō.

Murayama Shūichi. 1976. *Kodai bukkyō no chūseiteki tenkai.* Kyoto: Hōzōkan.

Nagao Ryūzō. 1973 (1940). *Shina minzoku shi.* Tokyo: Kokusho kankōkai.

Naour, Ch. 1980. *Tyriaion en Cabalide: Épigraphie et géographie historique.* Studia amstelodamensia ad epigraphicam, ius antiquum et papyrologicam pertinentia, 20. Zutphen (Holland): Terra Publishing Co.

Nasr, Seyyed Hossein. 1964. *An Introduction to Islamic Cosmological Doctrines.* Cambridge, Mass.: Harvard University Press.

Needham, Joseph. 1959. *Science and Civilization in China,* vol. 3. Cambridge: Cambridge University Press.

———. 1962. *Science and Civilization in China*, vol. 4, part 1. Cambridge: Cambridge University Press.

———. 1974. *Science and Civilization in China*, vol. 5, part 2. Cambridge: Cambridge University Press.

Nelson, Alan H. 1980. "Mechanical Wheels of Fortune, 1100–1547." *Journal of the Warburg and Courtauld Institutes* 43: 227–33.

Nevius, John L. 1869. *China and the Chinese: A General Description of the Country.* New York: Harper & Brothers.

Newell, William Wells. 1903. *Games and Songs of American Children.* New York: Harper & Bros. Reprint, Dover, 1963.

Ngo Van Xuyet. 1976. *Divination, magie et politique dans la Chine ancienne.* Bibliothèque de l'École des Hautes Études, Sciences Religieuses, 78. Paris: Presses Universitaires de France.

Nylan, Michael, and Nathan Sivin. 1988. "The First Neo-Confucianism: An Introduction to Yang Hsiung's 'Canon of Supreme Mystery' (T'ai hsua ching, ca. 4 B.C.E.)." In Charles Le Blanc and Susan Blader, eds., *Chinese Ideas About Nature and Society; Studies in Honor of Derk Bodde*, 41–99. Hong Kong: Hong Kong University Press.

Ōba Osamu. 1967. *Edo jidai ni okeru karabune mochiwataru sho no kenkyū.* Suita.

O'Flaherty, Wendy Doniger. 1981. *The Rig Veda. An Anthology.* Harmondsworth: Penguin Books.

Ōfuchi Ninji. 1978. *Tonkō dōkyō: mokuroku-hen.* Tokyo: Fukutake Shoten.

———.1979. *Tonkō dōkyō: zuroku-hen.* Tokyo: Fukutake shoten.

Opie, Iona, and Peter Opie. 1959. *The Lore and Language of Schoolchildren.* Oxford: Clarendon Press.

Osabe Kazuo. 1982. *Tō Sō mikkyō-shi ronkō.* Kyoto: Nagata bunshodō.

Osgood, Cornelius. 1975. *The Chinese: A Study of a Hong Kong Community.* 2 vols. Tucson, Ariz.: University of Arizona Press.

P'ang Wei [Banck, Werner]. 1987. "Ts'ung ch'ien-shih k'an Chung-kuo ch'uan-t'ung she-hui chia-chih kuan." In Wang Yu-wei, ed., *Chung-kuo ch'uan-t'ung wen-hua te tsai ku-chi*, 603–9. Shanghai: Shang-hai jen-min ch'u-pan she.

Pas, Julian. 1988. "Temple Oracles in a Chinese City; A Study About the Use of Temple Oracles in Taichung, Central Taiwan." *Journal of the Royal Asiatic Society, Hong Kong Branch* 24: 1–45.

Patch, Howard R. 1927. *The Goddess Fortuna in Medieval Literature.* Cambridge, Mass.: Harvard University Press.

Perry, Lily M. 1980. *Medicinal Plants of East and Southeast Asia: Attributed Properties and Uses.* Cambridge, Mass.: MIT Press.

Piaget, Jean, and Barbel Inhelder. 1951. *La genèse de l'idée de hasard chez l'enfant.* Paris: Presses Universitaires de France. Translated as *The Origin of the Idea of Chance in Children.* London: Routledge, 1975.

Pickering, F. P. 1970. *Literature and Art in the Middle Ages.* London: Macmillan.

Pingree, David. 1978. *The Yavanajātaka of Sphujidhvaya.* Harvard Oriental Series, 48. Cambridge, Mass.: Harvard University Press.

Preisendanz, K. 1973–74. *Papyrae graecae magicae, Die griechischen Zauberpapyri*. Stuttgart: Teubner.

Radha, Lama Chime. 1981. "Tibet." In M. Loewe and C. Blacker, eds., *Divination and Oracles*, 3–37. London: Allen & Unwin.

Renou, Louis. 1938. *Hymnes et prières du Veda*. Paris: Adrien Maisonneuve.

Renou, Louis, and Lilian Silburn. 1949. "Sur la notion de Brahman." *Journal Asiatique* 237: 7–46.

Rhys Davids, T. W., trans. 1956 (1899). *Dialogues of the Buddha, Part 1*. Sacred Books of the Buddhists, 2. London: Luzac.

Rocquain, Félix. 1880. "Les sorts des saints et des apôtres." *Bibliothèque de l'École des Chartes* 41: 457–74.

Róna Tas, A. 1956. "Tally-Stick and Divination Dice in the Iconography of Lha-mo," *Acta Orientalia* 6: 163–79.

Rosenthal, Franz, trans. 1967. *Ibn Khaldûn, The Muqaddimah: An Introduction to History*. Bollingen Series. Abridged edition. Princeton: Princeton University Press.

Rostovtzeff, M. 1926. *The Social and Economic History of the Roman Empire*. Oxford: Clarendon Press.

Roux, Jean-Paul. 1984. *La religion des turcs et des mongols*. Paris: Payot.

Roux, J.-P., and P. Boratav. 1968. "La divination chez les turcs." In André Caquot and Marcel Leibovici, eds., *La divination*, vol. 2: 279–329. Paris: Presses Universitaires de France.

Rudolph, Richard C. 1978. "The Enjoyment of Life in the Han Reliefs of Nanyang." In David T. Roy and Tsuenn-hsuin Tsien, eds., *Ancient China: Studies in Early Civilization*. Hong Kong: The Chinese University Press.

Saintyves, Pierre [Émile Nourry]. 1987 (1930). "En marge de la légende dorée: songes, miracles et survivances." In Francis Lacassin, ed., *Les contes de Perrault; En marge de la Légende dorée; Les reliques et les images légendaires*. Collection Bouquins. Paris: Éditions Robert Laffont.

Savorelli, Mirella Brini, ed. 1959. "Un manuale di geomanzia presentato da Bernardo Silvestre da Tours (XII secolo): L'Experimentarius." *Rivista critica di storia della filosofia* 14, 3: 283–342.

Schafer, Edward. 1963. "The Auspices of T'ang." *Journal of the American Oriental Society* 83: 197–225.

——. 1977. *Pacing the Void: T'ang Approaches to the Stars*. Berkeley: University of California Press.

Schipper, Kristofer M. 1974. "The Written Memorial in Taoist Ceremonies." In Arthur P. Wolf, ed., *Religion and Ritual in Chinese Society*, 309–24. Stanford: Stanford University Press.

——. 1975. *Concordance du Tao-tsang; titres des ouvrages*. Publications de l'École Française d'Extrême-Orient, 102. Paris: École Française d'Extrême-Orient.

——. 1985. "Vernacular and Classical Ritual in Taoism." *Journal of Asian Studies* 45: 21–57.

Schipper, Kristofer M., and Wang Hsiu-huei. 1986. "Progressive and Regressive Time Cycles in Taoist Ritual." In J. T. Fraser et al., eds., *Time, Science, and Society in*

China and the West: The Study of Time, 5: 185–205. Amherst, Mass.: University of Massachusetts Press.

Schneider, Karin. 1972–76. *Ein Losbuch Konrad Bollstatters, aus CGM 312 der Bayerischen Staatsbibliothek München*. Wiesbaden: Dr. Ludwig Reichert.

————. 1978. *Ein mittelalterliches Wahrsagespiel; Konrad Bollstatters Losbuch in CGM 312 der Bayerischen Stattsbibliothek*. Wiesbaden: Dr. Ludwig Reichert.

Schopen, Gregory. 1984. "Filial Piety and the Monk in the Practice of Indian Buddhism: A Question of 'Sinicization' Viewed from the Other Side." *T'oung Pao* 70: 110–26.

Sekine Daisen. 1968. *Mainokyō no kenkyū*. Tokyo: Ryūbunkan.

Seznec, Jean. 1940. *La survivance des dieux antiques: Essai sur le rôle de la tradition mythologique dans l'humanisme et dans l'art de la Renaissance*. Studies of the Warburg Institute, 11. London: The Warburg Institute. English translation by Barbara F. Sessions, *The Survival of the Pagan Gods: The Mythological Tradition and Its Place in Renaissance Humanism and Art*, Bollingen Series 38. Princeton: Princeton University Press, 1953.

Shastri, Haraprasad, trans., and Mohan Chand, ed. 1982. *Śyainika śāstram: The Art of Hunting in Ancient India*. Delhi: Eastern Book Linkers.

Shaughnessy, Edward, trans. 1996. *I Ching, The Classic of Changes: The First English Translation of the Newly Discovered Second-Century* B.C. *Mawangdui Texts*. New York: Ballantine Books.

Shina minzoku shi, vol. 2. Tokyo: Shina minzoku shi kankōkai, 1940. Reprint, Tokyo: Kokusho kankōkai, 1973.

Shizutani Masao. 1974. *Shoki daijō bukkyō no seiritsu katei*. Kyoto: Hyakkaen.

Shoolbraid, G. M. H. 1975. *The Oral Epic of Siberia and Central Asia*. Uralic and Altaic Series, 111. Bloomington: Indiana University.

Simon, Eckehard. 1975. "'Losbuch' from the Houghton Codex MS GER 74." *Amsterdamer Beitrage zur alteren Germanistik* 9: 93–117.

Sims-Williams, Nicholas. 1976. "The Sogdian Fragments of the British Library." *Indo-Iranian Journal* 18: 43–82.

Skeat, Theodore C. 1954. "An Early Medieval 'Book of Fate': The *Sortes XII Patriarchum*. With a Note on 'Books of Fate' in General." In Richard Hunt and Raymond Klibansky, eds., *Medieval and Renaissance Studies*, 3: 41–54. London: The Warburg Institute.

Skinner, G. William, ed. 1977. *The City in Late Imperial China*. Stanford: Stanford University Press.

Skinner, Stephen. 1977. *The Oracle of Geomancy: Divination by Earth*. New York: Warner Destiny. Reprint, Bridport, Dorset, and San Leandro, Calif.: Prism Press, 1986.

————. 1980. *Terrestrial Astrology: Divination by Geomancy*. London: Routledge & Kegan Paul.

Smith, Richard. 1991. *Fortune-Tellers and Philosophers: Divination in Traditional Chinese Society*. Boulder: Westview Press.

Snellgrove, David L. 1967. *The Nine Ways of Bon*. London Oriental Series, 180. London: Oxford University Press.

Sotzmann. 1850. "Die Loosbücher des Mittelalters, Part I." *Serapeum* 4: 49–62; 5: 65–80; 6: 81–89.

———. 1851. "Die Loosbucher des Mittelalters, Part II." *Serapeum* 20: 305–16; 21: 321–33; 22: 337–42.

Stein, M. Aurel. 1909. *Ancient Khotan: Detailed Report of Archaeological Explorations in Chinese Turkistan*. Oxford: Clarendon Press. Reprint, New York: Hacker Art Books, 1975.

Stein, Rolf A. 1939. "Trente-trois fiches de divination tibétaine." *Harvard Journal of Asiatic Studies* 4, 3–4: 297–371.

———. 1959. *Recherches sur l'épopée et le barde au Tibet*. Bibliothèque de l'Institut des Hautes Études Chinoises, 13. Paris: Presses Universitaires de France.

———, ed. 1961. *Une chronique ancienne de bSam-yas: sBa-bzed*. Textes et Documents, 1. Paris: Publications de l'Institut des Hautes Études Chinoises.

———. 1971. "Du récit au rituel dans les manuscrits tibétains de Touen-houang." In Ariane Macdonald, ed., *Études tibétaines dédiées à la mémoire de Marcelle Lalou*, 497–547. Paris: Adrien Maisonneuve.

———. 1972. *Tibetan Civilization*. Translated by J. E. Stapleton Driver. Stanford: Stanford University Press.

———. 1979. "Religious Taoism and Popular Religion from the Second to Seventh Centuries." In Holmes Welch and Anna Seidel, eds., *Facets of Taoism*, 53–81. New Haven: Yale University Press.

———. 1981. "Saint et divin, un titre tibétain et chinois des rois tibétains." *Journal Asiatique* 269: 231–75.

Steinmann, Brigitte. 1987. "The Context of Enigmas in the Tamang Buddhist Oral Tradition." Paper to the Csoma de Körsös Symposium, Sopron, Hungary.

Stewart, Randall. 1998. "The Oracles of Astrampsychus." In W. Hansen, ed., *Anthology of Ancient Greek Popular Literature*. Bloomington and Indianapolis: Indiana University Press.

———. 2001. *Sortes Astrampsychi*, vol. 2. Bibliotheca Teubneriana. Munich and Leipzig: K. G. Saur.

Strickmann, Michel. 1978. "The Longest Taoist Scripture."*History of Religions* 17: 331–54.

———. 1979. "On the Alchemy of T'ao Hung-ching." In Holmes Welch and Anna Seidel, eds., *Facets of Taoism; Essays in Chinese Religion*, 123–92. New Haven: Yale University Press.

———. 1980. "History, Anthropology, and Chinese Religion." *Harvard Journal of Asiatic Studies* 40, 1: 203–48.

———. 1981. *Le taoïsme du Mao Chan: Chronique d'une révélation*. Paris: Presses Universitaires de France.

———. 1982. "India in the Chinese Looking-Glass." In D. Klimburg-Salter, ed., *The Silk Route and the Diamond Path: Esoteric Buddhist Art on the Trans-Himalayan Trade Routes*, 52–63. Los Angeles: UCLA Art Council.

———. 1988. "Dreamwork of Psycho-Sinologists: Doctors, Taoists, Monks." In Carolyn T. Brown, ed., *Psycho-Sinology: The Universe of Dreams in Chinese Culture*, 25–46. Woodrow Wilson International Center for Scholars. Lanham, Md.: University Press of America.

———. 1990. "The *Consecration Sūtra*: A Buddhist Book of Spells." In Robert E. Buswell, ed., *Chinese Buddhist Apocrypha*. Honolulu: University of Hawai'i Press.

———. 1994. "Saintly Fools and Chinese Masters (Holy Fools)." *Asia Major*, third series 7, 1: 35–57.

———. 1996. *Mantras et mandarins: le bouddhisme tantrique en Chine*. Paris: Gallimard.

———. 2002. *Chinese Magical Medicine*. Ed. Bernard Faure. Stanford: Stanford University Press.

Strobel, Karl. 1992. "Soziale Wirklichkeit und irrationales Weltverstehen in der Kaiserzeit I: *Sortes Astrampsychi* und *Sortes Sangallenses*." *Laverna* 3: 129–41.

Strong, John. 1979. "The Legend of the Lion Roarer." *Numen* 26: 50–88.

———. 1985. "The Buddhist Avādanists and the Elder Upagupta." In Michel Strickmann, ed., *Tantric and Taoist Studies in Honour of R. A. Stein*, vol. 3: 862–81. Mélanges chinois et bouddhiques 22. Brussels: Institut Belge des Hautes Études Chinoises.

Suzuki Yoshijirō. 1963. *Kan'eki kenkyū*. Tokyo. Revised, expanded edition, 1974.

Tacitus. 1920. *Germania*. Trans. Maurice Hutton. Loeb Library.

Tannery, Paul. 1920. "Le Rabolion (oeuvre posthume): traités de géomancie arabes, grecs et latins." In J.-L. Heiberg, ed., *Mémoires scientifiques de Paul Tannery, vol. 4: Sciences exactes chez les byzantins, 1884–1919*, 295–411. Toulouse: Édouard Privat, Paris: Gauthier-Villars.

Teiser, Stephen F. 1988. *The Ghost Festival in Medieval China*. Princeton: Princeton University Press.

———. 1994. *The Scripture of the Ten Kings and the Making of Purgatory in Medieval Chinese Buddhism*. Kuroda Institute, Studies in East Asian Buddhism 9. Honolulu: University of Hawai'i Press.

Temple, Richard Carnac, ed. 1919. *The Travels of Peter Mundy in Europe and Asia, 1608–1667*, vol 3. Cambridge: The Hakluyt Society.

Thiers, Jean-Baptiste. 1741 (1679). *Traité des superstitions selon l'écriture sainte, les décrêts des conciles et les sentiments des saints pères et des théologiens*. 4th edition. Paris.

Thomas, C. F. W. 1957. *Ancient Folk-Literature from North-Eastern Tibet*. Abhandlungen der Deutschen Akademie in Berlin, Klasse für Sprachen, Literatur und Kunst, Jahrgang 1952, No. 3. Berlin: Akademie Verlag.

Thomas, Keith. 1971. *Religion and the Decline of Magic: Studies in Popular Beliefs in Sixteenth- and Seventeenth-Century England*. London: Weidenfeld and Nicolson.

Thompson, Denys. 1978. *The Uses of Poetry*. Cambridge: Cambridge University Press.

Thomsen, Vilhelm. 1912. "Dr. M. A. Stein's Manuscripts in Turkish 'Runic' Script from Miran and Tun-huang." *Journal of the Royal Asiatic Society* 181–227.

Thorndike, Lynn. 1923–58. *A History of Magic and Experimental Science*. 8 vols. New York: Macmillan.

Tseng Wen-Hsing. 1976. "Folk Psychotherapy in Taiwan." In William P. Lebra, ed., *Culture-Bound Syndromes, Ethnopsychiatry, and Alternative Therapies*, 164–78. Honolulu: University of Hawai'i Press.

——. 1978. "Traditional and Modern Psychiatric Care in Taiwan." In Arthur Kleinman et al., eds., *Culture and Healing in Asian Societies; Anthropological, Psychiatric, and Public Health Studies*, 311–28. Cambridge, Mass.: Schenkman.

Tucci, Giuseppe. 1949. *Tibetan Painted Scrolls*. Rome: Istituto poligrafico dello Stato.

Tun-huang i-shu tsung-mu so-yin. Peking: Shang-wu yin-shu kuan, 1962. Reprint, Chung-hua, 1983.

Turner, E. G. 1968. *Greek Papyri: An Introduction*. Oxford: Clarendon Press.

Ulm, Dora, ed. 1914. *Johann Hartliebs Buch aller verbotenen Kunst*. Halle: Max Niemeyer.

Unschuld, Paul U. 1985. *Chinese Medicine: A History of Ideas*. Berkeley: University of California Press.

Van der Horst, Pieter W. 1998. "*Sortes*: Sacred Books as Instant Oracles in Late Antiquity." In Leonard V. Rutgers, Pieter W. van der Horst, Henriëtte W. Havelaar, and Lieve Teugels, eds., *The Use of Sacred Books in the Ancient World*, 143–74. Louvain: Peeters.

Van der Loon, Piet. 1984. *Taoist Books in the Libraries of the Sung Period: A Critical Study and Index*. Oxford Oriental Institute Monographs, 7. London: Ithaca Press.

Vandermeersch, Léon. 1974. "De la tortue à l'achillée." In Jean-Pierre Vernant et al., eds., *Divination et rationalité*, 29–51. Paris: Seuil.

——. 1989. "Les origines divinatoires de la tradition chinoise du parallélisme littéraire." *Extrême-Orient, Extrême-Occident* 11: 11–33.

Verellen, Franciscus. 1989. *Du Guangting (850–933), taoïste de cour à la fin de la Chine médiévale*. Mémoires de l'Institut des Hautes Études Chinoises. Paris: Collège de France.

Vidyabhushana, S. C. 1913. "*Srid-pa-ho*: A Tibeto-Chinese Tortoise Chart of Divination." *Memoirs of the Asiatic Society of Bengal* 5: 1–11.

von Le Coq, Albert. 1908. "Ein christliches und ein manichäisches Manuskriptfragment in türkischer Sprache aus Turfan (Chinesisch-Turkistan)." *Sitzungsberichte der Berliner Akademie der Wissenschaften* 19: 1202–18.

——. 1926. *Auf Hellas Spuren in Osttürkistan*. Leipzig: J. C. Hinrichs'sche Buchhandlung. English translation: *Buried Treasures of Chinese Turkestan*. London: Longmans, 1929.

von Nettesheim, Agrippa. 1965. *Encyclopédie de la divination*. Paris: Editions Tchou. Reprint, Henri Veyrier, 1982.

Vouillème, Ernst. 1923. *Losbuch: Ein scherz-haftes Wahrsagebuch gedrückt von Martin Falch in Basel um 1485*. Berlin: Reichs-Drückerei.

Waddell, L. Austine. 1894. "Lamaism in Sikkim." In *The Gazeteer of Sikkim*, vol. 1: 241–391. Reprint as *Lamaism in Sikhim*. Delhi: Oriental Publishers, 1973.

———. 1959 (1895). *The Buddhism of Tibet, or Lamaism*. Cambridge: W. Heffer & Son. Reprint, New York: Dover, 1972.

Waegeman, Maryse. 1987. *Amulet and Alphabet; Magical Amulets in the First Book of Cyranides*. Amsterdam: J. C. Gieben.

Wales, H. G. Quaritch. 1931. *Siamese State Ceremonies: Their History and Function*. London: Bernard Quaritch.

Waley, Arthur. 1932. "An Eleventh-Century Correspondence." In *Études d'orientalisme à la mémoire de Raymonde Linossier*, vol. 2: 531–62. Paris: Ernest Leroux.

Watson, James L., and Evelyn S. Rawski, eds. 1988. *Death Ritual in Late Imperial and Early Modern China*. Berkeley: University of California Press.

Watters, Thomas. 1904. *On Yuan Chwang's Travels in India, 629–645* C.E. London: Royal Asiatic Society.

Weber, Albrecht. 1859. "Ueber ein indisches Würfel-Orakel." *Monatsberichte der Königlichen Akademie der Wissenschaften zu Berlin*, 158–80. Reprint in Weber, *Indische Streifen*, vol. 1: 274–307. Berlin: Nicolaische Verlagsbuchhandlung, 1868.

———. 1868. *Indische Streifen*. Berlin: Nicolaische Verlagsbuchhandlung.

Weidner, Ernst. 1956. "Ein Losbuch in Keilschrift aus der Seleukidenzeit." *Syria* 33: 175–83.

Weil, Gotthold. 1929. *Die Königslose: J.G. Wetzsteins freie Nachdichtung eines arabischen Losbuches*. Berlin/Leipzig: Walter de Gruyter & Co.

Welch, Holmes. 1967. *The Practice of Chinese Buddhism, 1900–1950*. Harvard East Asian Studies, 26. Cambridge, Mass.: Harvard University Press.

———. 1969–70. "The Bellagio Conference on Taoist Studies." *History of Religions* 9: 107–36.

Weng Tu-chien. 1966 (1935). *Tao-tsang tzu-mu yin-te: Combined Indices to the Authors and Titles of Books in Two Collections of Taoist Literature*. Harvard-Yenching Institute Sinological Index Series, 25. Taipei: Ch'eng-wen.

Winnefelds, Hermann. 1887. *Sortes Sangallenses, adjecta sunt alearum oracula ex codice Monacensi primum edita*. Bonn: Max Cohen et Filium.

Yamada Etai. 1959. *Ganzan daishi*. Hieizan.

Yang, C. K. 1961. *Religion in Chinese Society*. Berkeley: University of California Press.

Yang Lien-sheng. 1961. "Buddhist Monasteries and Four Money-Raising Institutions in Chinese History." In Yang Lien-sheng, *Studies in Chinese Institutional History*. Harvard-Yenching Institute Studies, 20. Cambridge, Mass.: Harvard University Press.

———. 1969. *Excursions in Sinology*. Harvard-Yenching Institute Studies, 24. Cambridge, Mass.: Harvard University Press.

Yogen-shū kaisetsu. 1935. Tokyo: Dai'ichi shobō.

Yoshimoto Shoji. 1983. "Dōkyō to Chūgoku igaku." In Fukui Kōjun et al., eds., *Dōkyō, vol. 2: Dōkyō no tenkai.* Tokyo: Hirakawa shuppansha.

Zevi, F. 1982. "I oracoli alfabetici: Praeneste." In Maria Letizia Gualandi, ed., *Aparchai: nuove ricerche e studi sulla Magna Grecia e la Sicilia antica in onore di Paolo Enrico Arias.* Biblioteca di studi antichi, 35. Pisa: Giardini.

Zingerle, Ignaz, ed. 1858. *Barbara Pachlerin die Sarnthaler Hexe, und Mathias Perger der Lautefresser: Zwei Hexenprozesse.* Innsbrück: Wagnerische Buchhandlung.

INDEX

A YA VA DA syllables, 113, 117, 133
Abhavapraśna, 117
Abjad, 117; *see also* Indian dice oracles
Africa, West, mantic poetry from, 88
Alexander the Great, 122, 174n56
al-Fihrist, 118, 122, 173n56
al-Kur'a al-ma'mūnija, 122
Al-Nadīm, 118
al-raml, xxiv–xxv, xxviii, 93, 117, 118, 125, 140, 174n57, 174n65
Analects, Confucian, 83
"*Analects* Jade Candle" (*Lun-yü yü-chu*), 83
anuttarasamyaksambodhi (supreme and perfect Enlightenment), 69
Aoki Masaru, 161n21
Apuleius, 110
Arrow-divination, 7, 161n27
Arrows, casting, throwing, or drawing, 83–84
Ars notoria, 93
astragaloi, 122
Astrampsychos, 111, 121, 123, 124, 139
Atharva-veda, 116
Auspicious oracles, 10–26; Ganzan Daishi, 18, 20, 23, 24; Ingen Daishi, 10; Nichiren, 26; *see also* Inauspicious oracles
Automata, 166n8

Bamboo sticks, 7
Banck, Werner, 35, 52, 88, 155n6; *see also* Eberhard, Wolfram
Banck's collection, 37, 88
Banck's oracle sequences, 36–40
Bang, Willy, 128, 129
Bastian, Adolf, 4
Bcun-mo bka'i thaṅ-yig, 136
Bean, George E., 108–109
Belomancy, 83, 84; *see also* Kleromancy
Bhavacakra, 158n8
Björck, Gudmund, 110, 111
Bodhisattva precepts (*P'u-sa chieh*), 78
Boehme, Fritz, 125, 126
Bok Kai Temple, 52
Bolte, Johannes, 111, 124, 147n14
Book of Changes, 2, 28, 82, 124, 129, 139, 140, 141; *see also* I-ching
Book of Consecration expounded by the Buddha concerning Brahmā's Spirit-Tablets (*Fo-shuo kuan-ting Fan-'ien shen-ts'e ching*), 58, 59, 61, 71, 72, 76, 79, 81, 113, 139, 142, 176n67; *see also* Kuan-ting ching
Book of Salvation (*Ling-pao tu-jen ching*), 54
Book of Spirit-Spells of the Abyss (*Tung-yüan shen-chou ching*), 54, 55
Book of the Empowered Draughtsmen, 91, 137; *see also* Ling-ch'i ching